George Washington and
the Final British Campaign
for the Hudson River, 1779

ALSO BY MICHAEL SCHELLHAMMER

*The 83rd Pennsylvania Volunteers in the
Civil War* (McFarland, 2003; softcover 2009)

George Washington and the Final British Campaign for the Hudson River, 1779

Michael Schellhammer

McFarland & Company, Inc., Publishers
Jefferson, North Carolina, and London

LIBRARY OF CONGRESS CATALOGUING-IN-PUBLICATION DATA

Schellhammer, Michael.
    George Washington and the final British campaign for the Hudson River, 1779 / Michael Schellhammer.
        p.   cm.
    Includes bibliographical references and index.

    ISBN 978-0-7864-6807-2
    softcover : acid free paper ∞

    1. New York (State) — History — Revolution, 1775–1783 — Campaigns. 2. United States — History — Revolution, 1775–1783 — Campaigns. 3. Hudson River Valley (N.Y. and N.J.) — History, Military — 18th century. 4. Washington, George, 1732–1799 — Military leadership. I. Title.
    E230.5.N4S28 2012
    973.3—dc23   2012017597

BRITISH LIBRARY CATALOGUING DATA ARE AVAILABLE

© 2012 Michael Schellhammer. All rights reserved

No part of this book may be reproduced or transmitted in any form or by any means, electronic or mechanical, including photocopying or recording, or by any information storage and retrieval system, without permission in writing from the publisher.

Front cover image: George Washington as general and commander-in-chief of the Continental Army, ca. 1787–1790; cover design by David K. Landis (Shake It Loose Graphics)

Manufactured in the United States of America

McFarland & Company, Inc., Publishers
  Box 611, Jefferson, North Carolina 28640
    www.mcfarlandpub.com

For Lisa and Sean

This is no time for slumbering and sleeping; nor to dispute upon trifles, when our Battalions are to fill, supplies to provide, and ruined finances to recover and at a crisis with G. Britain is ready to pour forth her utmost vengeance.

— George Washington to his brother,
John Augustine Washington, May 12, 1779

Table of Contents

Preface	1
Prologue	7
Introduction: Washington's War	11
I. Committee of Conference	19
II. "He Could Fight as Well as Brag"	25
III. The Culper Ring	36
IV. "Chicane Might Draw Him into It"	47
V. "A Very Interesting Crisis"	61
VI. "Men That Will Support the Reputation of His Regiment"	68
VII. Little Gibraltar	77
VIII. "Surrender, You Damned Rebel"	88
IX. "Too Pretty a Place to Burn"	102
X. Desolation Warfare	118
XI. "You'll Hear from Me This Evening"	125
XII. Stand to Arms	135
XIII. The Push of the Bayonet	142

XIV. Colors Flying	156
XV. Veteranship	165
Epilogue: The Ghost of "Mad" Anthony	181
Notes	197
Bibliography	213
Index	219

Preface

George Washington was a good general, but in the early summer of 1779, the British stole a march on him. For the first five months of the year Washington expected the British forces under his opponent, Lieutenant-General Sir Henry Clinton, to launch a summer offensive, as they had every year of the war. The Royal Navy gave Clinton the ability to land almost anywhere along the eastern seaboard and Washington considered several of America's major ports to be possible targets. Washington strained his intelligence system of scouts and spies to find out about British plans, but by late spring he still had very little information to go on.

Then at the end of May, Clinton sent 4,000 soldiers up the Hudson River and seized a crossing site known as King's Ferry, severing Washington's supply line to New England and threatening to give the British control of the lower Hudson River. Washington scrambled to march the Continental Army from its camps in New Jersey to the area around West Point in order to block Clinton's advance. Just over a month later, while the Americans focused on the Hudson, Clinton surprised Washington again with the landing of another 2,500 soldiers at New Haven, Connecticut, which began a series of brutal raids on the coast of Long Island Sound. Both moves were part of a British offensive designed to subdue the American rebellion in New York and New England and draw General George Washington's Continental Army to its destruction. The centerpiece of the campaign, which continually occupied the attention of both commanders, was the Hudson River.

The campaign around the Hudson in 1779 was the last that involved both armies in the northern states as well as Britain's last concerted attempt to gain control of the Hudson, the most strategically important waterway in America at the time. Though it involved all of Washington's main Continental Army and nearly all of the forces around New York City under Clinton's command, the campaign ended without the two armies ever meeting in a massed battle. That does not mean that the summer was without action. American cavalry sparred with their British counterparts in eastern New York; the residents of Connecticut suffered from brutal British raids along their coast that were resisted by thousands of militiamen; most dramatically, Washington stunned the British with daring and brilliantly executed night bayonet attacks on the fortified posts of Stony Point and Paulus Hook.

The results of the campaign influenced the course of the American Revolution. Washington reversed Clinton's offensive and solidified American control of the Hudson, all while husbanding his forces at a time when logistics problems severely limited the capabilities of the Continental Army. The Americans lost barely over 100 Continental soldiers, and gained the time of one vital year for Washington to mature the organization, tactics, and operational methods of the Continental Army and build it into a sophisticated force. For the British, the campaign was their last effort to subdue the rebellion in the north, cost over 1,000 casualties (about the same number the British suffered in the Philadelphia campaign) and heavily influenced Clinton's decision to move the main theater of action to the south, where Britain would eventually lose the war.

Yet this contest between Washington and Clinton has been overshadowed by other periods of the Revolution, almost as if the maneuverings, raids and battles did not justify its being called a "campaign." Today, the United States Army counts sixteen campaign honors from the Revolution, but none of them include Stony Point, Paulus Hook, or anything about the events around New York in 1779, even though both Washington and Clinton often called the events of that summer a "campaign" in their correspondence. In *Almost a Miracle: The American Victory in the War for Independence*, one of the most thorough and comprehensive histories of the war, historian John J. Ferling accurately called the actions of 1779 "the forgotten war."

This book will examine the campaign of 1779 from the strategic planning that began at the beginning of the year to the end of the campaign season the following autumn. It will focus on the strategies that Washington and Clinton pursued, the operational decisions of both generals, and the movements of their armies. From a tactical perspective it will discuss the battles and raids that comprised the campaign and the observations of their participants. In conclusion it will analyze the impact of the campaign and, in the epilogue, summarize what happened to the participants during the remainder of the Revolution and after.

Though there were other actions that influenced the war elsewhere in the same year — a naval battle at Penobscot Bay, the siege of Savannah, a separate campaign on the New York frontier against Native Americans, and political developments — the core of this story is the contest between Washington and Clinton for control of the Hudson River. Therefore I have limited the scope of this book to the military action around New York City. The battle of Stony Point was the pivotal and most dramatic action of the campaign, so I address the action and the forces that fought it in detail. Brigadier-General Anthony Wayne also receives much attention because his planning of the battle of Stony Point and leadership of the Continental Corps of Light Infantry had a profound impact on the battle and the campaign. And to fully understand Washington's and Clinton's moves we also need to understand what the commanders knew or believed at the time, so the book also describes the American and British intelligence systems and the difficulties of spying during the Revolution.

An interest in the professionalism of the Continental and British armies in the Revolution led me to this campaign. Some of the popular myths of the Revolution present American soldiers as clever backwoods riflemen who fought with stealth in the woodlands against rigid formations of Redcoats, and British troops as automatons or haughty fops too inflexible to adapt their European style of fighting in North America. In fact, Washington strove to build the Continental Army into a disciplined, sophisticated force that could employ a combination of European and American tactics to beat the British in conventional battles. British officers were professionals who adapted their tactics to fighting in America, and through experience, came to appreciate the skills of Continental soldiers.

The campaign of 1779 is an excellent case study in these points. During the raids in Connecticut, the American militia fought British forces with classic unconventional tactics. At Stony Point, the Continentals applied their skills in backwoods scouting to the development of a battle plan that combined conventional maneuvers with American innovation, and Major Henry Lee repeated the tactics at the battle of Paulus Hook. Both battles help us understand how one group of professional soldiers succeed over their opponents. Did one side make mistakes? Did other factors such as the strategic situation, intelligence, logistics, or weather impact the battles?

The answers I found to these questions, contained in the following chapters, led me to understand that the two battles were the dramatic high points to an underappreciated campaign that took place around the Hudson River Valley and Connecticut.

Washington and Clinton are the central figures of this book, and thankfully both men left behind a wealth of correspondence with their respective thoughts and outlooks. *The Writings of George Washington*, provided through the University of Virginia, gave me access to all of General Washington's outgoing correspondence, while the George Washington Papers at the Library of Congress offers the general's incoming letters and other relevant documents. Some of the most fascinating letters among the George Washington Papers are those between Washington, his intelligence chief, Major Benjamin Tallmadge, and the "Culper Ring," the network of Continental spies in and around New York. General Clinton's memoirs, *The American Rebellion*, captured the Revolution from his viewpoint. However, since his memoirs were written to justify his generalship, Clinton's letters from the war, available through many printed sources and the Clements Library, are possibly more honest. *The Storming of Stony Point, Midnight, July 15th, 1779*, by Henry P. Johnston contains several battle reports and letters from Clinton's subordinates as well as letters from American officers who fought at Stony Point.

I was unable to locate many other letters from the British participants in the campaign, but the records of the court-martial of Lt. Col. Henry Johnson, Stony Point's commander, contain testimonies about the battle of Stony Point from Johnson and twenty-six of his officers and soldiers. The court-martial records are located at the United Kingdom National Archives, Kew, England. General Wayne's correspondence is available from the Anthony Wayne Papers at the Historical Society of Pennsylvania. The letters of Col. Christian Febiger are found at the Library of Virginia. I wrote much of this book while stationed overseas at an American embassy and obtained many documents and books through online resources. I am thankful to Google Books, Archives.com and Footnote.com for making many excellent resources from the eighteenth and nineteenth centuries available, including the papers of George Washington and memoirs of officers such as Benjamin Tallmadge, William Hull, and George Collier. jstor.com is a fantastic source of scholarly journal articles.

I am not aware of any single book about this topic but other books address portions of the campaign. As mentioned, John J. Ferling's *Almost a Miracle: The American Victory in the War for Independence* is an exceptional history of the entire war, including that of the other activities that occurred in 1779. Readers interested in the battle of Stony Point may want to read *The Storming of Stony Point* by Henry P. Johnston or *The Enterprise in Contemplation: The Midnight Assault of Stony Point* by Don Loprieno, which also includes the full text of Lt. Col. Johnson's court-martial. In *Visible Saints, West Haven, Connecticut, 1648–1798*, Peter J. Malia covers the British raid at New Haven, Connecticut, very thoroughly. My discussion of the American intelligence system is limited to those aspects that influenced the 1779 campaign, but there is much more to the story of intelligence operations and the Culper Ring; readers interested in the full picture should read the fascinating *Washington's Spies: The Story of America's First Spy Ring*, by Alexander Rose.

I was fortunate to receive invaluable assistance with the material for this book from several friendly archivists and historians. My sincere thanks go to Ellen McCallister Clark, Emily Schultz, and Elizabeth Frengel at the Society of the Cincinnati Museum in Washington, D.C., for helping me get the most out of their extensive archives. The same goes for James Campbell at the New Haven Museum and Historical Society. Thanks also to Ray Russell at the Stony Point Historical Museum for showing me around Stony Point. I owe debts of thanks to the folks at the Fairfield, Connecticut, Historical Society, Jessica Jenkins at the Litchfield, Connecticut, Historical Society, and the staff at the Historical Society of Pound Ridge, New York. All of them graciously corresponded with me, made time to discuss the project with me, and helped locate marvelous sources and images. Special thanks to Eleana Nicolaou, Nancy Tessmer Belmont, Lara Dalinsky, and Brandi Phipps for their help with the beautiful maps. All of these experts made this book possible.

Huge thanks also to the family and friends who helped me with research, read my drafts, reread my drafts, consulted with me, and provided invaluable advice. This includes Ken Sanders, who helped with the initial research, and Tina O'Rourke, who was always a great consultant. Thanks to my brother Tom Schellhammer and his better half, Elizabeth Nochlin, for the assistance with researching the New York area, and to my father-in-law, Paul Ramber, for his help in Connecticut. There is absolutely no way in the world that I could have completed this without their kindness, patience, interest, and support.

The most patient, helpful, and understanding of all was my wife, Lisa, who once told me, "You can have all the time you need to write the book." This was a statement that I am sure she came to regret after I spent hours, days, weeks, months and years poring through documents or hunched over a keyboard. Lisa was my best and most dedicated assistant, editor, and consultant on the direction and focus of the book, with advice that was always sound, though I sometimes did not realize it at the time. Her heart, time, and energy also went into this book, so it is as much hers as it is mine.

Prologue

Near midnight on July 15, 1779, Brigadier-General Anthony Wayne led a column of Continental Army soldiers to a hill overlooking a marsh on the west bank of New York's Hudson River. Wayne halted the men and peered into the moonless night. Half a mile ahead of him to the northeast, barely discernable in the darkness, stood Stony Point, a rocky, 150-foot high crag that jutted like a thorn into the waters of the Hudson. Defending the height, though cloaked by the night, were more than 600 veteran British soldiers and American Loyalist troops with sixteen cannon in fortified positions. Two British warships with more guns floated close by. Wayne listened for any indication that the Crown troops were alert and prepared for an attack. If everything went according to his plan, in a few minutes he would lead his men forward and capture Stony Point.

The soldiers who stood behind Wayne comprised one of three columns of American Light Infantry under his command making the attack. Wayne's group, with troops from Pennsylvania, Virginia, and Massachusetts, was the main assault force and approached the hill from the south. A supporting column with North Carolina and Massachusetts troops advanced from the west. A third group of Marylanders and more Pennsylvanians moved in from the north. Together Wayne's three columns formed a trident that would converge on the fort, storm through the fortifications, swarm up the slope of Stony Point, and overwhelm the British by the force of their momentum. To prevent any soldier from giving away the attack by an accidental musket discharge, and to ensure the maximum fury in the assault, Wayne had ordered his men to attack with their muskets unloaded and bayonets fixed. They would take Stony Point with cold steel.

General Wayne looked back at his men. All of them were volunteers from different regiments in the Continental Army, approved for service in the Light Infantry because of their superior military skill and physical strength. General George Washington personally selected many of the officers. Almost all of the troops had served for at least three years, endured the winter at Valley Forge, and fought in the Revolution's most vicious battles. But a corps of experienced men did not guarantee the success of Wayne's attack. The British were sure to defend Stony Point with every soldier, musket and cannon that they had, and a night bayonet attack was an exceptionally difficult operation, even for troops that had trained and fought together for a long time. The Light Infantry had been together for barely a month, Wayne had taken command of the corps only two weeks earlier, and many troops had joined it in the last three days. No attack in the war, even Washington's daring raid at Trenton in 1776, required such a disparate group of soldiers to seize a fortified enemy post with their bayonets only. General Wayne almost certainly wondered how many of his men would live to see the sunrise.

A strong, unseasonably cold wind blew from the north and rippled the waters of the marsh that lay to the northeast, directly between Wayne's column and Stony Point. Due east, over Wayne's right shoulder, the waters of the Hudson lapped at a small beach. To the general's left, where he knew that his supporting columns were also moving in, Wayne saw only the dim shapes of trees shaking in the wind. His men waited with him in silence. The general turned to Colonel Christian Febiger, who was commanding the Virginia troops in the column, and in low tones told him to go back along the ranks and remind the men that musket fire was forbidden and to "place their whole dependence on the bayonet." Then Wayne ordered the line forward.

The Light Infantry moved past him toward the beach along the Hudson. Any noise could alert the British to their presence, and the men stepped carefully. A British obstacle called an "abatis"—a belt of logs sharpened into giant stakes—ran along the base of Stony Point, so Lieutenant George Knox led the column with twenty soldiers armed with hatchets and axes to chop gaps through the barrier. Knox realized that this effort would alert the British and that his men would have no way to fight back or take cover. He, and all of his men, had volunteered for the duty; of all of Wayne's soldiers they stood the least chance of surviving the attacks. In eighteenth-century military terminology, Knox's unit was called a "forlorn hope."

Lieutenant-Colonel Francois-Louis Tesseidre de Fleury, a French army officer serving with the Continentals, followed Knox with 150 troops who had been ordered to rapidly push through the gaps chopped in the abatis and secure a foothold inside the fort. Major William Hull led another 300 soldiers who followed de Fleury's group as the main body of the attacking column. General Wayne expected that the weight of their numbers would provide enough soldiers to swarm through the gaps carved by Knox's men, expand the foothold made by de Fleury, and overwhelm the British defenses.

Wayne walked forward with Lt. Col. de Fleury's group. A musket shot from Stony Point broke the quiet and signaled that an enemy sentry had spotted the American column. From ahead, a British drum beat a long roll. Wayne's men pushed on, still in complete silence, packed into a tight column with their muskets shouldered. The Hudson waters rose to their knees as they waded into the river and followed the bank toward Stony Point. The wind still blew hard from the north, chilling them. Wayne's officers strained to make out Stony Point in the black night. Their soldiers kept their eyes locked on the white cross-belts on the back of the man in front of them. Every soldier anticipated the flashes of muskets. British drums continued to beat but no firing came. It took the Americans about fifteen minutes to wade through the water but it seemed like an eternity at the time as they heard the British troops shouting, the rippling of the water and their own rapidly beating hearts, which, to men going into combat, sounds like thunder.

Knox's men began chopping when they reached the abatis. Suddenly the night lit up as musket fire ripped from Stony Point. Wayne's men surged out of the water, their hearts racing, and scrambled through the gap in the abatis that had been carved by Knox's men. British voices rose in the darkness as their officers shouted orders and organized the defense, and then the American and British lines met head-on. None of Wayne's soldiers spoke or fired a gun. There was still no light, but the night was alive with the sounds of American and British infantrymen in desperate close combat—the clink and thud as bayonets and muskets clashed, swords thrusting, slashing, and parrying, the grisly sound of cold steel sinking into flesh, and the screams of men in pain. The British firing increased, and the blazes illuminated death scenes in brief, macabre flashes.

Though General Wayne was in command, it would be the individual soldiers' bravery, brute strength, and ferocity that decided the outcome of the battle. None of the men, even Wayne, knew that Stony Point was the pivotal battle of the last campaign for control of the Hudson River, a campaign that relied on information obtained from shadowy spy networks, required General Washington to avoid a British trap to destroy the Continental Army, and brought the brutality of war to towns in New York and on the Connecticut shore. The assault of Stony Point was a secret mission, undisclosed to most of the Continental Army, and the success or failure of General Wayne's light infantrymen would affect the course of the American Revolution.

Introduction: Washington's War

In December 1778, in keeping with the military custom of the era, the Continental Army moved into encampments to refit over the winter. The previous summer's campaign had ended with 16,000 British Regulars, Loyalist Americans, and Hessian troops holding New York City; another 3,000 Crown soldiers were at Newport, Rhode Island. To maintain a watch on the British, and enable his own soldiers to subsist off local farms, General George Washington dispersed his army at several camps. Soldiers from Connecticut and New Hampshire were at Reading and Danbury, Connecticut. Massachusetts and New York regiments guarded the highlands of the Hudson River. The cavalry regiments were in Maryland, Pennsylvania, New Jersey, and Connecticut. The largest concentration was a collection of camps around Middlebrook (present-day Somerville and Bound Brook), New Jersey, twelve miles west of Perth Amboy, with 8,000 Virginia, Pennsylvania, North Carolina, New Jersey and Delaware troops. Washington established his headquarters in a rented house at Middlebrook.

While Washington's men moved into their winter camps, the Continental Congress in Philadelphia debated about the best strategy for 1779. Neither Congress nor Washington had clear intelligence about British intentions for the coming year but they perceived several threats. In western Pennsylvania and New York a brutal war of village raids, pillage and murder between American Patriots and Crown Loyalists, along with their allies in the Iroquois Confederacy, threatened the stability of the frontier regions. Offensives by Crown forces at New York and Newport were possibilities, reinforcements from England could land in the Carolinas or Georgia, and since Britain had invaded New York from Canada in 1777 the threat of a similar attempt remained.

Some Congressional delegates advocated direct attacks on British troops at New York and Newport. Others from the southern states wanted the Continental Army in Virginia, the Carolinas, and Georgia. The New Englanders pushed for an invasion of Canada to eliminate the threat from the north. America had launched one expedition to seize Canada in 1775 that failed and made another abortive attempt under the Marquis de Lafayette in early 1778, a move Washington called the "the child of folly."[1] But the New England delegates had their way and in early December 1778, Congress directed Washington to draw up plans for an invasion of Canada in conjunction with French assistance. The request reached Washington while he was moving the Continental Army into winter quarters at Middlebrook, and as soon as the troops were situated the general responded. "I have considered [the plan] in several lights," he said, "and sincerely regret that I should feel myself under any embarrassment to carry it into execution." But to have a full discussion about the next year's strategy with accurate information, Washington suggested that he visit the delegates and "lay before Congress more minutely the State of the Army."[2] Congress accepted the offer, and the gen-

George Washington by James Peale, after Charles Willson Peale, c. 1787–1790. In the early summer of 1779 Washington was concerned about the Continental Army's readiness for a campaign when Gen. Clinton's move up the Hudson River forced him to rapidly reposition the Continental Army from New Jersey to the Hudson Highlands. In this portrait by James Peale, the artist and his brother, Charles Willson Peale, peer over the general's right shoulder; soldiers in the background carry the flag of France (Independence National Historical Park).

eral prepared to depart for Philadelphia about a week before Christmas. He had not left his army in nearly three years.

The war had begun without Washington three years earlier. On April 19, 1775, the British commander at Boston, Lieutenant-General Thomas Gage, sent soldiers to Concord, Massachusetts, to seize colonial weapons and gunpowder, and fighting broke out between Gage's troops and local militia companies on Lexington Green. In what became known as the "Lexington Alarm," militiamen from all over New England gathered along the roads that led from Concord to Boston, and the colonists badly bloodied the Redcoats. An army of 14,000 New England militiamen, commanded by Gen. Artemus Ward of Massachusetts, surrounded Gage's army in Boston.

The British forces were outnumbered and unable to break out of the American encirclement, and on June 17, the Yankees occupied Breed's Hill and Bunker Hill in Charlestown, overlooking Boston. General Lord William Howe led two attacks on the rebel fortifications on Breed's Hill (later misidentified as Bunker Hill) and suffered heavy losses, but a third attack succeeded. In October, London sacked Gen. Gage and appointed Lord Howe as the commander in America, with Sir Henry Clinton as the second-in-command.

The same day as the battle of Breed's Hill, George Washington was in Philadelphia, preparing to leave for Boston. The Continental Congress responded to the Lexington Alarm by authorizing the creation of a "Continental Army" composed of companies from Pennsylvania, Maryland, and Virginia, and named Washington as its commander. After consultations with Congress about the army's structure, regulations, and funding, Washington departed Philadelphia on June 23 and arrived at Cambridge, Massachusetts, on July 2, where he took charge of Gen. Ward's New England troops in his new role as commander of the Continental Army.

Since that time, neither Britain nor America had gained a decisive edge in the war. At Cambridge Washington instilled discipline and organization in the rough militia companies and besieged the British in Boston. Congress authorized an invasion of Canada but the expedition sputtered out at the end of 1775 after it failed to seize the city of Quebec. In March 1776 Washington gave America its first major victory of the war when he emplaced artillery on Dorchester Heights outside Boston and forced the Redcoats to evacuate the city for Nova Scotia. But at the same time, Gen. Sir Henry Clinton led an attempt to seize Charleston, South Carolina, and in May, American forces withdrew from Quebec after the arrival of British reinforcements. In June, Clinton's assault on Charleston failed in the face of a firm American defense. The war took a decisive turn in August, when Gen. Howe returned from Nova Scotia and attacked New York City, one of America's most important seaports. Washington defended the city from Long Island, but Howe outmaneuvered the Americans and seized control of Manhattan. Howe then pushed the Continentals out of New Jersey and forced them onto the defensive in Pennsylvania. In early December Clinton, back with Howe's army after his failed expedition at Charleston, seized the key port of Newport, Rhode Island. At the end of the year Washington struck back with a daring raid at Trenton, New Jersey, that resulted in the capture of the post's Hessian garrison.

In January 1777 Washington opened the new year by defeating the British at the battle of Princeton. Gen. Howe, in turn, went on the offensive that September, landed his army at the head of Chesapeake Bay, beat Washington at the battle of Brandywine Creek, and captured Philadelphia, America's most populous city and the seat of the Continental Congress. Washington struck back again in October at Germantown in an attempt to save Philadelphia, but the attack faltered and ultimately failed. However, that same month Gen. Horatio Gates, commander of the Continental Army's Northern Department, defeated a British invasion force, sent from Canada under Gen. John Burgoyne, at the battles of Freeman's Farm and Bemis Heights in upstate New York. The surrender of Burgoyne's 6,000-man army near the town of Saratoga was a significant blow to the king's cause and a boost for the rebels. At the end of 1777 Gen. Howe made Philadelphia the site for his army's winter quarters, and Washington moved his army to a winter camp at Valley Forge. With 7,500 soldiers, the Continentals were half the size of Howe's force; they were poorly provisioned, demoralized, and on the brink of dissolution. But Washington used the winter pause to shape the Continental Army into a force that would master the era's methods of war, which were complicated and brutal.

Eighteenth century combat centered on maneuvering armies close enough for the soldiers to inflict harm on their opponents with the primary infantry weapon of the time, the smoothbore flintlock musket. The flintlock musket fired a round lead ball, three-quarters of an inch in diameter. (The British "Land Pattern" musket, commonly called the "Brown Bess" and used in American and British forces, fired a 0.71 caliber ball. The French Charleville musket, supplied to the Americans, fired a .069 caliber ball.) It took fifteen separate actions to load a flintlock musket and two more to fire it on command. A soldier's comical axiom of the era said that if God intended men to fire muskets, he would have given them three hands. The ability to repeat the motions while under enemy fire required significant discipline, and a trained soldier could usually shoot two to three rounds a minute during the heat of battle. But without the grooves or "rifling," in the barrel to make the ball spin, the smoothbore musket was rarely accurate at ranges over eighty yards. The only way infantry units could score enough hits on an enemy formation was to form in long lines of battle, two to three ranks deep, and fire their weapons in massed volleys to send balls flying toward an opposing line in great swarms.

With these "linear tactics," battles developed when generals chose to fight on advantageous terrain, such as low hills, or where they could see and control their formations. Armies arrived at the chosen battlefield marching in long column formations and then deployed in the lines that faced their opponent to achieve massed firepower. An army's cavalry corps scouted the enemy for vulnerabilities. Cannon opened fire at long range to cause as many casualties as possible and weaken enemy resolve. The long lines moved toward each other and the troops opened fire at about fifty to eighty yards' range, sometimes less, and often with a single, massive volley to produce maximum casualties and shock. Both sides continued with volley after volley, usually timed to keep up a continuous fire. Within minutes of the opening volley, commanders could barely make out their own troops through the clouds of thick gunpowder smoke that hung close to the ground.

Soldiers wore brightly colored uniforms (the red coat of British troops, scarlet for officers, was world famous) and carried distinctive regimental flags so commanders could identify them in the confusion. The battlefield bordered on the chaotic as the lines fired at each other and maneuvered for advantageous position. A British officer remembered the battle of Brandywine in September 1777: "There was the most infernal fire of cannon and musquetry. Most incessant shouting, 'Incline to the right! Incline to the left! Halt! Charge!' etc. The balls plowing up ground. The trees cracking over one's head. The branches riven by artillery. The leaves falling as in autumn by the grapeshot."[3] When they hit a man, the soft lead musket balls flattened and made gaping holes in flesh, splintered bone, and carried pieces of burned gunpowder, dirt, and the victim's clothing into the wound.

Eventually the casualties mounted enough on one side to cause disorganization. Once morale faltered, the line collapsed as soldiers abandoned their formations and retreated. The opposing side often rushed forward in a charge with their bayonets. Sixteen inches long, triangular shaped, and affixed to the muzzle of a musket, bayonets could cut on all three of their sharpened edges and caused deep stab wounds that were difficult to suture closed. The British army specialized in fast, fierce bayonet charges in which they advanced with a run. Rapid and accurate volleys from an opposing line could break a bayonet charge, but even well-drilled Continental Army troops could barely fire two shots in the time it took for British lines to rush seventy-five yards, which was not enough to halt the momentum of a charging line. British soldiers actually had little training with their bayonets beyond how to "fix" them on their muskets and charge rapidly, but the combined effect of cheering, red-coated soldiers steadily advancing with polished steel bayonets leveled and glittering in the sun could be terrifying to opponents.

To win in battle, commanders had to master linear tactics and position their lines in a series of complex movements that required precise timing. The maneuver for a regiment to wheel to the left or right during battle required six different movements, performed at exactly the right moments to maintain a cohesive formation. Control over the entire scene required staffs with the ability to correctly assess situations, adjust formations, and relay their commanders' instructions. The experiences of 1776 and 1777 showed Washington that the Continental Army lacked more than one of these aspects. Many American regiments fought successfully with linear tactics; but since they came from different states, the maneuver methods differed from unit to unit, which led to confusion on the battlefield. For example, at the battle of Brandywine, American units successfully positioned their line to face a British attack on their flank, but inexpert maneuvering left a gap between two units. The Redcoats saw the opening, poured through it, and broke the American line. The next month, Washington attacked at Germantown with an innovative but complicated battle plan that fell apart when Continental commanders could not successfully coordinate their maneuvers. Ever since his time as a Virginia militia officer in the 1750s Washington had believed American forces should consist of disciplined soldiers that fought with European methods combined with tactics that suited American terrain.[4] The lessons of the first three years of the Revolution reinforced his thought and convinced him, many of his senior officers, and Congress that the Continental Army had to match the British in discipline, mastery of linear tactics, and the structure of a European army in order to consistently win the war's major battles.

In keeping with this thought, and after multiple consultations with

Congress, Washington began reforming the Continental Army in early 1778. He appointed Gen. Fredrick Von Steuben, a colorful veteran of the Prussian army of Frederick the Great, as the Continental Army's inspector general with the responsibility of ensuring proper training for battle. Steuben developed a method for uniform maneuver across every regiment and captured the training program in *Regulations for the Order and Discipline of the Troops of the United States, Part I*. The "Blue Book," as soldiers called it, was a comprehensive manual on soldier skills, disciplined musket firing, use of the bayonet, battlefield maneuvers, and the proper duties of sergeants, officers, staffs, and commanders.

With congressional support, as well as the expertise from an influx of volunteer officers from foreign armies, Washington also built branches that were standard in any European army, such as proper corps of engineers and cavalry, mounted police units to maintain order and guard prisoners of war, and a regiment of artillery artificers to maintain the army's cannon, munitions, equipment, and small arms. The Quartermaster General Department gained specialized companies that maintained wagons, assisted engineers with fortification construction, and built roads on the march. And almost daily, Washington wrote to state governors for more soldiers. Many of the reforms would take months to implement, but by the spring of 1778 the supply system was more efficient, the size of the army had doubled, and, thanks to Gen. Steuben's training, the soldiers had become more capable, and confident.

While the Continental soldiers suffered at Valley Forge, congressional diplomats in France convinced King Louis XVI to officially recognize the independence of the United States and enter an alliance for military support. The entry of France into the war placed Britain's other colonies around the world at risk, which could compel King George III to give up fighting the rebellion in order to defend the rest of his empire. America learned of the alliance in April 1778, and many citizens believed it would lead to a speedy victory. Britain sent three representatives, known as the "Carlisle Commission," to America that summer to concede on almost every point of grievance that had led to the rebellion, short of recognizing the independence of the United States. Confident of ultimate success, Congress refused to meet with the commissioners.

The alliance with France at first seemed to have the effect Americans hoped for. Howe resigned in the spring of 1778, Clinton became the king's commander in America, and the first orders he received from London were to evacuate Philadelphia, consolidate his army in New York City, and send

5,000 soldiers to the West Indies and 3,000 men to Florida to defend against French attack. Clinton reluctantly obeyed the order and moved his force across New Jersey to New York. Near Monmouth Court House in late June the Continentals attacked the rear of the British column and the two sides fought to a draw. Washington penned the British in New York City, and in mid–July, a French fleet under Vice Admiral Count d'Estaing arrived off New Jersey to assist the Americans. On the Ohio frontier Colonel George Rogers Clark seized the British outposts of Kaskaskia and Vincennes, securing American interests in the west. With a French fleet offshore, Clinton's force surrounded by a sound Continental Army, and the frontier under control, many Americans thought that Britain would evacuate New York and that the end of the war was in sight.

Those hopes for a quick end to the war dissolved by autumn. Washington planned to retake New York with the assistance of the French fleet, but Clinton blocked the move and the attack never took place. Then Washington sent a force of New England militia and Admiral d'Estaing's fleet to retake Newport, Rhode Island, but mismanagement and bad weather led to an embarrassing defeat for the new allies. The British became resurgent in the fall with raids in New England and New York. Guerilla war between Crown forces and American militias raged in New Jersey, and in December Clinton prepared to seize the city of Savannah, Georgia. At the end of 1778 it was clear that the war would entail at least one more campaign in the next year.

It was in this situation — with the Continental Army in the midst of reforms, with America in an alliance that had not yet proven extremely profitable, with the power of Britain diminished but not broken, and with Congress pushing for a strategy that would lead to victory — that Washington received Congress's ideas about invading Canada. After the general accepted their invitation to visit Philadelphia he wrote to his wife, Martha, to come meet him, and he departed Middlebrook on December 21 to meet with Congress and lay out the plans for 1779.

I

Committee of Conference

Philadelphia, January 1779

On December 22, 1778, General George Washington rode into Philadelphia and to the house of his friend Henry Laurens, a delegate in the Continental Congress. Many Philadelphians did not know that the general was in their city until the *Pennsylvania Packet* announced his presence on Christmas Eve, which fell on a Thursday that year:

> On Tuesday last arrived here, GEORGE WASHINGTON, esquire, Commander in Chief of the Armies of the United States—Too great for pomp—and as if fond of the plain and respectable rank of a free and independent Citizen, His Excellency came in so late in the day as to prevent the Philadelphia Troop of Militia Light-Horse, Gentlemen, Officers of the Militia, and others of this city from shewing those marks of unfeigned regard for this GOOD and GREAT MAN which they fully intended and especially of receiving him at his entrance into the State and escorting him hither.[1]

Called to Philadelphia to plan strategy for the coming year, Washington did not know how long he would be in the city, and he made Henry Laurens' home his lodging for the stay. Philadelphia was still recovering from occupation by the British army, which had ended six months earlier, and the situation there provided a backdrop for the general's meetings with Congress. Philadelphia was nearly ruined from the occupation. Prices on basic goods skyrocketed due to inflation (tea sold for $60.00 a pound), and the city's working classes lived in poverty. British troops used houses for barracks, storehouses, and even stables, cutting holes in the floor and

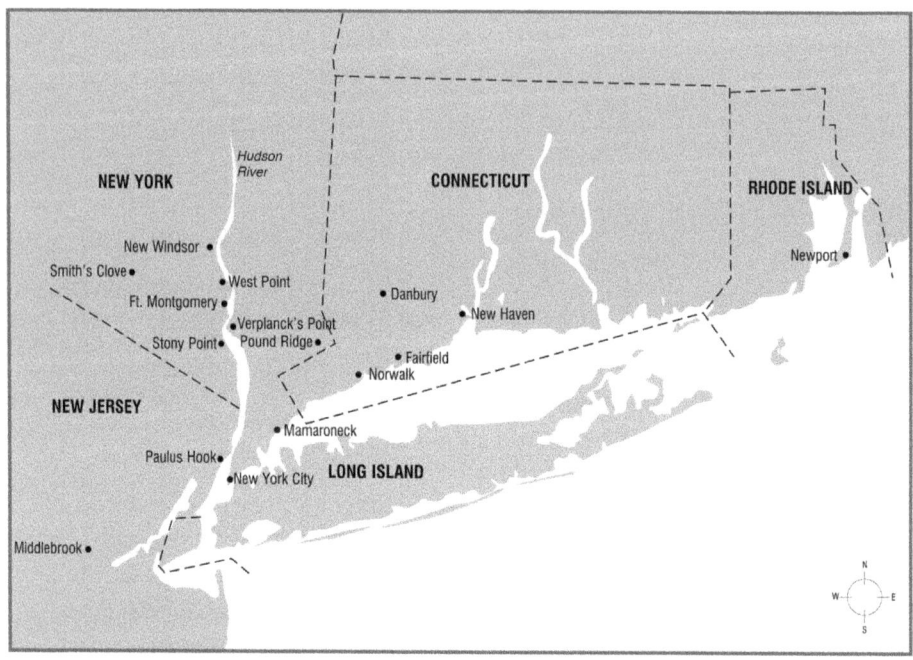

In the summer of 1779, George Washington and Henry Clinton maneuvered against each other in southeastern New York, along the Hudson River, and on the shores of Connecticut (map by Eleana Nicolaou).

shoveling dung into the cellars.[2] As they departed the city, Redcoats indiscriminately vandalized property and caused damages valued at over $180,000 dollars. Capt. John Andre, an aide to Gen. Sir William Howe, the British commander, stole books from Benjamin Franklin's house as well as a portrait of the famed inventor. Some Philadelphians vented their anger at neighbors they suspected of supporting the Crown, as in the case of John Roberts of Merion and Abraham Carlisle of Philadelphia, who were charged with aiding the British. Many people thought that the charges were thin and that the State sought their conviction to make examples of the two men, who were both Quakers and reputed to be harmless and gentle. Several Philadelphia clergymen, at least three signers of the Declaration of Independence, and a few Continental Army officers all signed a request that the men receive lenient treatment, but in the charged atmosphere after the occupation, Pennsylvania's Supreme Executive Council found Roberts and Carlisle guilty and hanged them both on November 4.

Congress had convened at York, Pennsylvania, during the occupation, and when the members returned at the end of June they found that British soldiers had used the Pennsylvania statehouse, later famous as Independence Hall, as a hospital. A pit outside the building served for the disposal of garbage, dead horses, and even dead men. Congress convened nearby at College Hall, but only long enough each day to conduct the most pressing business, as Henry Laurens wrote, because of "the offensiveness of the air in and around the State House....[The British] left it in a condition disgraceful to the Character of civility....I cannot proceed to a new subject before I add a curse on their savage practices."[3] Philadelphians cleaned and repaired their city, and on July 9 Congress gathered to sign the Articles of Confederation, the first charter for governing the United States of America. It was not until August that the state house was clean enough to receive Le Sieur Gerard, minister plenipotentiary to the United States from His Most Christian Majesty, the King of France, an event for which the congressmen wore their finest clothes and hosted a public dinner complete with music and cannon salutes.

Commerce and wealth returned to Philadelphia in the late summer. The military commander of the city, Brigadier-General Benedict Arnold, made his headquarters in the same mansion General Howe had used, courted a beautiful Loyalist named Peggy Shippen and lived luxuriously. Released from British occupation, wealthy Philadelphians enjoyed an active social scene. Martha Washington came from Mt. Vernon to join General Washington, and prominent citizens feted the couple almost every evening. Congressional delegate Samuel Holten noted in his diary that on New Year's Eve he dined with the general, Martha Washington, "M'r de Miralles, a Spanish Gentlemen ... 7 other ladies ... about 40 other Gentlemen of the first character." He also wrote that the entertainment was grand and elegant."[4]

In December the *Pennsylvania Packet* advertised a selection of teas, chocolate, brown sugar, raisins, rum, whiskey, English cheese, Port wine, salt, "and many other articles" for sale at Mr. James Talbot's shop; Joseph Sims and his son offered coffee, sugar, and molasses at their store; and the team of Fisher and Roberts sold Madeira, Port, French brandy, and West Indies rum. Dr. Baker, a traveling surgeon-dentist from Virginia, opened for business during a visit to the city. Citizens sought to hire such skilled help as a wet nurse, journeymen fullers, nailers, and an accountant. Mr. Erasmus Kelly announced the opening of his primary school and promised to "pay great attention to the morals and education of fine children as shall be committed to his care."[5] The extravagances and availability of goods glossed over the fact that Philadelphia's working classes still had not recovered from the effects of the high inflation, and their anger smoldered near the end of the year. In January the sailors of Philadelphia would strike for higher wages, dismantle ships on the wharves, and riot until Gen. Arnold sent in Continental troops to restore order.

The *Packet* also advertised several sales of African slaves, as well as the rewards offered for the return of others who had run away from their owners in the City of Brotherly Love. After ten days in the city Washington confided to a friend, "I have seen nothing since I came here ... but abundant reason to be convinced, that our Affairs are in a more distressed, ruinous, and deplorable condition than they have been in Since the commencement of the War.... Speculation, peculation, and an insatiable thirst for riches seems to have got the better of every other consideration and almost of every order of Men."[6]

This bleak outlook surely weighed heavily on Washington's mind as he met daily with the special "Committee of Conference" that Congress had formed to manage military matters. The committee members were composed of delegates James Duane, Jesse Root, Meriwether Smith, Gouverneur Morris, and Henry Laurens. Within a week the general convinced the committee to shelve their plans for an invasion of Canada and they moved on to discuss plans for 1779. The strategic situation they faced was not promising. The American and British armies were almost matched in numbers but several factors prevented America from being fully prepared for a summer campaign. The economy had plummeted — eight Continental dollars were worth only one dollar of gold currency — and America neared national bankruptcy. The depreciated money severely diminished the purchasing power of Continental Army supply officers and the army still suffered from shortages that Washington called "truly embarrassing" and "deplorable."[7] Even the general's headquarters camp was, as he wrote, "reduced to an alarming extremity for the want of forage.... The country is in a great degree exhausted, and our money is of so little value, that it affords hardly any temptation to the farmers to furnish what they have."[8] Despite the expected support from France, few shipments of uniforms and weapons arrived in 1778 and Washington called the army's clothing supply "scant and inadequate" and said that a regular issue of uniforms was "impossible."[9] He soon wrote about cannon, "We want them much everywhere."[10] With the embarrassing failure of the French-American expedition at Newport fresh in his mind, Washington believed that another offensive with France while the army was in such dire straits of supply could lead to "fatal effects."[11]

The enlistments for 3,000 men were also due to expire in the spring, which would reduce the Continental Army to 16,000 men, too few for an offensive campaign.[12] The army could recoup troop losses through new levies, but it would take time to raise the new soldiers and train them for action. Washington would soon write in frustration to his friend Benjamin Harrison: "[T]he whole strength and resources of the [British] Kingdom will be exerted against us this Campaign; while we have been either slumbering and sleeping or disputing upon trifles, contenting ourselves with laughing at the impotence of G. Britain which we supposed to be on her knees ... instead of devising ways and means to recruit our Battalions, provide supplies, and improving our finances, thereby providing against the worst and a very possible contingency."[13]

The situation compelled Washington to present three options to Congress: to attempt to push the British out of New York and Newport; to send an expedition into the Niagara region to subdue the Iroquois Confederacy; or to remain on the defensive, continue the Continental Army improvements, and react to British moves.

Washington supported the strategic value in attacking New York and Newport but considered the option unrealistic since the assaults would require, by his estimate, 26,000 Continental soldiers, "a larger number than we have ever had in the Field," as he wrote.[14] Although he also supported the necessity of an expedition against the Iroquois in New York, Washington admitted that a full offensive to secure America's northern frontier would also require more manpower and material than were available and that such an offensive was a distraction from the primary war objective of defeating Clinton's main army.

In mid–January Washington recommended that Congress adopt the option of remaining on the defensive, explaining that the strategy would give America a chance to "consolidate our [military] System. The Army tho' small should be of a firm and permanent texture." He went on: "The main Body of the Army must take a position so as to be most easily subsisted, and at the same time best situated to restrain the Enemy from ravaging the Country."[15] On January 20 Congress learned that the city of Savannah had fallen to the British, and many congressmen began to think that 1779 was not a year to take chances and risk further losses. The Committee of Conference agreed that, for the coming year, America would consolidate its gains and continue to reform the army. Washington left the door open for action in two ways. He allowed for "eventual preparations" for defeating the Iroquois Confederacy in the Niagara region, and regarding

Clinton's main army, "If [the British] should hereafter weaken themselves still more so as to give a favorable opening, we should endeavour to improve it."[16]

The Committee of Conference met with Washington a few more times on other military issues but the general's stay in Philadelphia was his longest absence from the army since he took command at Cambridge. After he requested permission to return to his troops, the committee concluded business on January 31. Washington left for Middlebrook two days later and he had every reason to be satisfied with the results of his trip; he had presented his views to Congress, thwarted the efforts to invade Canada, and secured a strategy for the next year that would allow time to strengthen the Continental Army. He returned to his headquarters and focused on training his army while his intelligence service watched for signs of a British offensive.

II

"He Could Fight as Well as Brag"

Middlebrook, New Jersey, February 1779

    The Continental Army had come a long way from Valley Forge. Almost all aspects of the winter camps around the village of Middlebrook, New Jersey, were evidence of a force that was healthier, more competent, and more formidable than it had been a year earlier. The soldiers wore better uniforms thanks to the improved Quartermaster Department and shipments from France. The Commissary Department provided adequate provisions. Each camp was a neat city of log huts with fireplaces, chimneys, and hinged doors and windows, built by the soldiers themselves in December, and arranged by regiment in streets with officers' huts at the front and kitchens to the rear. Work details kept the areas clean and cleared of rubbish. Other soldiers drilled, constructed roads and bridges, repaired equipment, or foraged for food. On Sundays, when only the most essential work took place, soldiers attended religious services, played games, fished, skated, played music, and held sporting or marksmanship matches.

    Dr. James Thacher, a surgeon in a Virginia regiment, noted that the winter was "remarkably mild and moderate" with barely any snowfall or even frost.[1] Only 764 soldiers from the New Jersey camps required army hospital care in February, a quarter of the amount hospitalized a year earlier at Valley Forge.[2] General Washington encouraged furloughs as morale-building breaks, and 1,486 soldiers were home on respite from army life.[3] Officers often performed plays, held dinners, or hosted matchmaking events with the daughters of local farmers or businessmen, as Dr. Thacher recorded of his regiment's New Year's Day celebration: "The table was amply furnished, and the guests did not separate till evening, when we were requested to resort to General Muhlenburg's quarters. Here we were introduced to a number of ladies assembled, to unite with gentlemen in the ball-room; a very elegant supper was provided, and not one of the company was permitted to retire until three o'clock in the morning." Dr. Thacher also wrote how on February 4 the army celebrated the anniversary of the alliance with France, the celebration opened by a sixteen-gun salute from the Continental artillery, followed by an "elegant dinner," a fireworks display, and a "splendid ball" attended by General and Martha Washington, though the general opened the ball by dancing with "the lady of General Knox."[4] Beyond the camp gaiety, soldiers also manned redoubts that guarded against the British patrols that sometimes made isolated attacks on camps to test their defenses. But located in the rolling, defensible hills of New Jersey, the camps were as strongly protected as they were comfortable.

General Washington enjoyed some of the social functions but did not permit himself the luxury of a furlough. Every day he toured the camps and observed the soldiers training or working. At midday he usually dined for up to two hours with several officers or the distinguished visitors that frequently visited the camp. Though the headquarters was comfortable, Washington avoided signs of ostentation. Dr. Thacher attended one dinner that included "his excellency with his lady, two young ladies from Virginia, and the gentlemen who compose his family [the general's aides] and several other officers." The doctor noted "the table was elegantly furnished, and the provisions ample, but not abounding in superfluities." Colonel Alexander Hamilton, Washington's primary aide-de-camp, managed the "civilities" of the table, and Thacher was somewhat awed by Washington, who, he wrote, always commanded "veneration and respect." "He is feared even when silent," said Thacher, "beloved even while we are unconscious of the motive.... In conversation his excellency's expressive countenance is peculiarly interesting and pleasing; a placid smile is frequently observed on his lips, but a loud laugh, it is said, seldom, if ever, escapes him. His is polite and attentive to each individual at the table, and retires after the compliments of a few glasses."[5] After meals Washington usually rode for exercise and worked for a few more hours. His work day ended with darkness, and then he relaxed with "Lady Washington," as Martha was called, or with his aides or generals.[6]

Washington's first matter of business every day was to read his correspondence, and he responded with several letters every day, many of which addressed the progress on the recommendations he had made to the Committee of Conference in Philadelphia. One was to build the Continental Army with a "firm and permanent texture,"[7] and on February 6 his general orders to the army authorized subordinate commanders to reenlist soldiers for "the continuance of the war" and offered every enlistee "a bounty according to the circumstances of his present engagement, but not to exceed in any case 200 dollars."[8] Washington and Gen. Steuben worked together to finalize the content of the "Blue Book" for distribution throughout the army.

In keeping with his recommendation for "eventual preparations" for defeating the Iroquois Confederacy in the Niagara region, Washington proposed expeditions in the New York and Pennsylvania frontier by Brigadier-General Phillip Schulyer. In mid–February Washington received a letter from Brigadier-General Anthony Wayne, who asked the general for command of the Corps of Light Infantry, a group of hand-picked soldiers that would be formed in the next campaign. It was not unusual for senior officers to petition the commander-in-chief for commands, but the request from Wayne required special consideration. Wayne was no ordinary officer, and the unit he asked to command, the Light Infantry, was one of the most dashing of Washington's efforts to form the Continental Army into a sophisticated force.[9]

Like many of Washington's planned improvements, a corps of light infantry was a standard part of most European armies. During the seventeenth century, when armies were developing firearms and linear tactics, France employed a group of soldiers that operated separately from the main army as partisans. By the mid–eighteenth century the concept had developed into companies of "chasseurs"— picked men who deployed forward of the main battle line in loose formations, used natural cover and concealment whenever possible, and engaged the enemy with the tactics of woodland hunters. Spain copied the concept with companies they called *cazadores*, the German states developed *jager* or "hunter" battalions, and Britain organized "light infantry" companies in every battalion, so named because they were originally more lightly equipped than other soldiers. On campaign British commanders grouped their light companies into separate battalions to be used on the main battle line as an elite force, or they employed them as assault troops, tasked with carrying out the most difficult raids or attacks. Regiments assigned their most intelligent, skilled, and fit soldiers to the duty. Light companies made up a large portion of the raiding force that Gen. Thomas Gage sent to Lexington and Concord on April 19, 1775, when hostilities opened. The loose, irregular tactics of the light infantry were particularly useful in the rugged terrain of America, and British light troops often outclassed the rebels in woodland fighting during the early campaigns.[10]

Regardless of Redcoat skills at light infantry tactics, many American troops were excellent marksmen with the rifled musket, which had spiral grooves in the barrel that gave spin to the musket ball and greatly improved the weapon's range and accuracy. But the weapons were also slow to load, and riflemen could only fire one or two shots a minute versus the three or four from a standard musket. Nevertheless, skilled American riflemen could hit targets, such as British officers, at ranges well over 100 yards, twice the range of standard muskets. Gen. Washington capitalized on this American skill with the organization of ad hoc light units, often armed with rifles, to harass British formations with their long-range, accurate fire. During the Philadelphia campaign in August 1777, Washington informed Congress of the following: "Sensible of the advantages of Light Troops, I have formed a Corps under the command of a Brigadier, by drafting a Hundred from each Brigade, which is to be constantly near the Enemy and to give them every possible annoyance."[11]

The corps performed well at the battle of Brandywine under the command of Brig. Gen William Maxwell of New Jersey. Col. Daniel Morgan's Rifle Corps, also formed in 1777, included a light infantry battalion. Morgan's sharpshooting riflemen contributed significantly to the American victory at Saratoga by picking off British officers at the battles of Freeman's Farm and Bemis Heights. The formation of a proper light corps along the British model was among the first topics that Washington discussed with Gen. Steuben at Valley Forge. On January 28, 1778, Washington sent Congress his recommendations for a thorough reorganization of the Continental Army, which included establishing one light company in every infantry regiment. Combining the light companies on campaign, wrote Washington, "would compose the flying army; and, in conjunction with a body of [cavalry] would become extremely formidable and useful."[12]

It was in August 1778, while the Continentals hemmed in the British on Manhattan, that Washington formed "a Corps of Light Infantry composed of the best, most hardy and active Marksmen and commanded by good Partizan Officers," under Virginia's Brig. Gen. Charles Scott.[13] Scott's orders were to protect the main army from a surprise attack, become the "master of all the roads leading to the enemy's lines," and "keep up a constant succession of scouting parties ... to penetrate as near the enemy's lines as possible."[14] As the light infantry operated as a single group only while on campaign, Scott's corps disbanded in the winter of 1778.

In February 1779, as the army refitted in winter quarters, Washington and his senior officers expected to form another light corps for the summer campaign. By then, the Light Corps had gained the reputation as an elite unit because of the dangerous missions Washington expected it to perform, as shown in his instructions to Scott. And since the corps answered directly to Gen. Washington, its command was a high honor that some senior officers coveted. For reasons unknown, Washington did not consider assigning the corps to Scott again. So when he received the letter from Gen. Anthony Wayne asking for command of the Light Infantry, Washington weighed Wayne's background, military record, and character to determine if he was the right man for the job.

Anthony Wayne was a man who was lucky to fall into a military life. Born in Chester County, Pennsylvania, on New Year's Day 1745, he was named for his paternal grandfather, Anthony, who was a native of Yorkshire, England. Grandfather Anthony Wayne moved to Ireland and as a Protestant served as a cavalry commander under William of Orange at the Battle of the Boyne in 1690. He came to America in 1722 and bought 380 acres in Easttown Township in Chester County, Pennsylvania, that became the family estate of Waynesborough. His two sons, Isaac and Francis, joined him from Ireland two years later. Wayne's father, Isaac, was a prosperous farmer who was active in the Chester County church, was a member of the county provisional assembly, and fought as a militia officer during the French and Indian War.

Young Anthony Wayne was a middle child with an elder sister, Hannah, and a younger sister, Ann. His childhood was uneventful, though he often clashed with his strong-willed father, who intended to raise Anthony to be a gentleman farmer. At school Anthony was an unremarkable student but apparently a natural soldier one who organized his fellows in mock battles. Not until he was sixteen, after his father threatened to pull him from school and put him to work at Waynesborough, did Wayne apply himself to studies with diligence. He excelled in mathematics at the Philadelphia Academy and returned to Easttown at the age of eighteen. Wayne was described as a young man of middle height with dark, penetrating eyes and an amiable manner.

Chester County was becoming rapidly settled and Anthony earned frequent employment and a good reputation as a surveyor. His circle of friends included the prominent gentlemen of southeastern Pennsylvania, including Benjamin Franklin. In 1764 Franklin and Wayne collaborated in an association that speculated land in Nova Scotia, but the venture failed and convinced Wayne that leadership was an extremely difficult task. In 1766 he married Mary Penrose, or Polly, as she was known, the daughter of a Philadelphia merchant. They returned to Easttown and four years later their first child, Margaretta, who Wayne called Peggy, was born. In the early 1770s he continued as a surveyor, opened a tannery, and prospered as a respected farmer and businessman. In 1774 he bought the family estate from his father and settled there with his small family.

As tension between America and Britain grew in the mid–1770s, Wayne sided strongly with the colonial cause. As early as 1774, he vowed to oppose English oppression, even with armed force, and ran for a seat in the provincial assembly. Britain had passed the "Intolerable Acts," which attempted to crush the rebellious Massachusetts Colony earlier that year, and the First Continental Congress was preparing to meet in Philadelphia. With conflict in the air, Anthony once addressed an audience during the election and asked if Pennsylvanians would allow their sister colony to be bullied into submission. He won his seat in October and continued agitating against British policies. After hostilities opened in the spring of 1775 Wayne raised over £100,000 to equip the Chester County militia and organized a regiment of volunteers with his own funds. But with its Quaker traditions Chester County was reluctant to take up arms against Britain. In January 1776 the Pennsylvania Assembly finally agreed to send troops for Washington's Continental Army, and they gave Wayne a colonel's commission and command of the Fourth Pennsylvania Battalion.

The role of army colonel suited Wayne. The Fourth Pennsylvania's first mission was to join America's invasion of Canada being led by New York's Gen. Phillip Schuyler. The regiment departed Philadelphia by ship for Albany, New York, in early May, along with five other regiments organized into a brigade under New Hampshire's Gen. John Sullivan. Wayne wrote, "Whatever may be my fate I can answer for this, that my children will never have reason to blush for the conduct of their father."[15] The brigade reached Ft. Ticonderoga, south of Lake Champlain, and encountered the remnants of the army that had retreated after the unsuccessful siege of Quebec. They reached the village of Sorel on the south bank of the St. Lawrence River in June; but since the Canadian invasion had ended, the troops were without a mission.

Sullivan, who was an aggressive officer, learned about a force of

300 British troops at Trois Rivieres, forty-five miles away, and ordered Wayne's regiment and another commanded by Col. William Irvine to join a force of 1,000 Continental soldiers and attack the Redcoats. The Americans moved in on June 9, became lost as they approached the position, and then suffered under cannon fire from British ships on the St. Lawrence. The British troops counterattacked. Wayne formed his Fourth Pennsylvania into a battle line, drove the British back, and was slightly wounded in his right leg. The other American regiments could not stand under the fire from British ships and infantry and retreated back to Sorel. The battle was an overall disaster for the Americans but Wayne had performed well in his first combat test.

In November 1776 Gen. Horatio Gates, commander of the Continental Army's North-

Brigadier-General Anthony Wayne. He was an excellent combat leader who instilled a winning attitude in the men he commanded. In early 1779 he asked Washington for command of the Corps of Light Infantry, the Continental Army's elite assault force (Library of Congress).

ern Department, named Wayne the commander of 3,000 soldiers at Ft. Ticonderoga. The post was poorly provisioned and the men suffered greatly over the winter. Although while he worked to keep his soldiers supplied and motivated, Wayne thirsted to join Washington's army. Unbeknownst to him, he had earned the respect of Congress and Washington through his conduct under fire and in command at Ticonderoga. Congress promoted him to brigadier-general in February 1777, and two months later Washington ordered Wayne to join the main Continental Army in New Jersey and take command of a division of Pennsylvania troops. Wayne happily left Ticonderoga in May to join Washington's army at its camp at Morristown.

Soon after arriving in late May, Wayne proved his reputation and earned Washington's approval when he and his men drove off 700 Redcoats that approached the American camp. When Gen. Howe withdrew soldiers from their post at New Brunswick, New Jersey, to Perth Amboy, Wayne and Col. Daniel Morgan's rifle corps harassed the British rear guard all the way and again garnered Washington's praise. As Howe's army landed at the Chesapeake and advanced towards Philadelphia, Wayne recommended the creation of a corps of 3,000 soldiers to attack the enemy flanks, a concept he admittedly learned from reading a history of Julius Caesar's campaigns. Washington did not approve the idea, but Wayne's combative nature and military education were showing clearly.

When Washington met Howe's advance at Brandywine Creek on September 11, 1777, Wayne's division held the crossing site of Chadd's Ford against heavy fire from Gen. Knyphausen's Hessian troops and helped prevent the collapse of the Continental line as the Americans withdrew. A month later, at the battle of Germantown, Wayne and his soldiers fought furiously and drove the Redcoats back until confusion led to the collapse of the American attack. While the army wintered at Valley Forge, at least three times Wayne sent Washington plans for strikes at the British, but the commander-in-chief turned down all of them, and Wayne believed that his commander was overly cautious. In June 1778, when Clinton withdrew from Philadelphia and Washington held a council of war on how the army should pursue the British, Wayne and other officers urged Washington to attack Clinton's column.

This time Washington concurred, and on June 28, he sent Gen. Charles Lee to attack the British rear guard. Wayne's Pennsylvania Division was one of four under Lee's command. Lee moved tentatively, and his attack near Monmouth Court House faltered and turned into a retreat when the British counterattacked. Washington arrived on the battlefield, relieved Lee, and ordered Wayne to form a line to hold the British off while the rest of the American line re-formed. The heat of the day soared over 90 degrees and the parched soldiers sweltered, but Wayne's Pennsylvanians held firm and then pushed the Redcoats back, which allowed Washington to send the entire line forward, pushing the British from the field. Washington was pleased with how well the army fought and very happy with the performance of his generals, except for Lee, but he singled Wayne out for mention in his report to Congress for "good conduct and bravery thro' the whole action."[16]

Much of Wayne's success in combat came from his forceful and colorful personality. He studied martial literature and leadership concepts and was a strict disciplinarian who expected his subordinate officers to master the military art and earn the respect, fear, and love of their troops.[17] At Ft. Ticonderoga in 1776, troops of the Sixth Pennsylvania mutinied over their terms of enlistment until Wayne browbeat the leaders into surrendering. When a second mutiny threatened, Wayne jammed his pistol into their leader's chest until the man begged for his life, and the mutineers dispersed. He was a champion curser during an era when many officers took pride in their ability to use profane language. Prone to neatness and famous as a fastidious dresser, Wayne wore ruffled shirts under a blue uniform coat with white facings.[18]

Soldiers too, according to Wayne, always needed to look smart. Even on the way to Canada in early 1776 he took care to ensure his troops kept their soldierly appearance by staying shaved and washed, and their hair powdered. Out of earshot, some called him "Dandy Wayne." He was supremely confident in himself and his soldiers, and said that he preferred to lead actions that depended on the spirit and bravery of his soldiers.[19] Those who observed Wayne in battle saw that he was cool under fire, maneuvered his men well, and seemed to come alive, with flashing eyes, a clear voice, and a mind that functioned like clockwork even in the most intense situations. Wayne constantly strove to get his men adequate pay, clothing, shoes and blankets, and even personally bought the material to make them uniforms at Valley Forge. His style, confidence, and care for his troops earned him the loyalty of his soldiers, and a winning attitude radiated through the units he commanded. Pennsylvania soldier Alexander Graydon thought Wayne was "as brave a man as any in the army" and "somewhat addicted to the vaunting style" but also admitted that he "could fight as well as brag."[20]

Gen. Washington also knew that there was one significant black mark on Wayne's record. Soon after the battle of Brandywine, Washington sent Wayne and his division to harass the Redcoats and slow their advance towards Philadelphia. Moving in on the British, Wayne camped his men near the town of Paoli, Pennsylvania, dangerously close to the enemy lines. Gen. Howe learned of Wayne's presence and ordered Gen. Charles Gray to drive the Pennsylvanians away. On the night of September 20, 1777, Gray's men stealthily advanced toward Wayne's camp, carrying their muskets unloaded and with bayonets fixed. Their attack caught the Americans off guard, and the fighting in the darkness was close, brutal and confusing. Maj. Samuel Hay of the Fourth Pennsylvania was in the thick of the fighting and wrote, "The annals of the age cannot produce such a scene of butchery. All was confusion....[T]he enemy rushed on with fixed bayonets and made the use of them they intended."

Wayne organized a fighting retreat that saved most of his division, but 200 of his men were killed and 100 wounded. Maj. Hay checked on the wounded in hospitals afterward and recorded this: "The scene was shocking—the poor men groaning under their wounds, which were all by stabs of bayonets."[21] The affair quickly became known as the "Paoli Massacre" in the press, and some officers wondered if negligence led to the defeat. Wayne requested a court-martial to examine the battle and clear his name. Though the court exonerated him and found him an "active, brave and vigilant officer" with the "highest honor,"[22] an undercurrent of doubt about his actions lingered among some senior officers. A second court-martial, also held at Wayne's request, again found him innocent of negligence. But Paoli remained an embarrassing defeat, and it was linked forever to Anthony Wayne.

Washington probably also knew that Wayne's reputation off the battlefield was not above reproach. His wife, Polly, was devoted to him and endured the difficulties of managing their estate in his absence, yet Wayne treated her coolly and enjoyed the company of other women while he was away from home. Wayne also carried on a feud with a fellow Pennsylvania officer, Brig. Gen. Arthur St. Clair. The argument between them stemmed from the fact that Wayne received his commission from Congress with command of the newly created Fourth Pennsylvania Battalion on January 2, 1776, and St. Clair received his commission on January 3, but with command of a battalion that existed *before* the organization of Wayne's. Under the military convention of the era, officers whose commissions predated others were "senior" to officers of the same rank, but those who commanded organizations that were "older" were also senior to others with earlier commissions. This made St. Clair technically senior to Wayne, and since Congress based promotions on seniority, Wayne considered St. Clair's ranking a significant affront to his honor.

The Scottish-born St. Clair was a veteran of the British army in the French and Indian War and, though he was not as an inspiring leader as Wayne, he fought bravely and competently at Trenton and Princeton. Nevertheless, Wayne intensely disliked serving under St. Clair. In August 1778, he sat on a court-martial when St. Clair was accused of prematurely evacuating Ft. Ticonderoga after Wayne had departed the post. Wayne sympathized with St. Clair's position and voted for his exoneration. But Wayne also believed that St. Clair held him responsible for the loss at Paoli, another insult to his honor. When Congress appointed St. Clair the commander of the Pennsylvania Division in late 1778—the same division that Wayne had led at Brandywine, Germantown, and Monmouth — Wayne was relegated to command of a mere brigade within St. Clair's division. To serve under his rival was too bitter a pill for Wayne to swallow. In February 1779 Wayne sought and received a furlough in Philadelphia, and it was from there that he wrote to Gen. Washington: "I therefore wish to be indulged with Command in the Light Corps — if it can take place without prejudice to the Service."[23]

The commander-in-chief considered Wayne's request at his headquarters at Middlebrook. Washington did not record his thought process, but he surely knew that command of the Light Infantry required an officer with personal bravery as well as the intelligence and reliability to maneuver independently from the army's main battle line. Wayne was already famous as a daring combat commander. The Paoli affair may have caused Washington to question if he was capable of independent operations, but the Light Infantry operated at the personal direction of the commander-in-chief, and Wayne performed well when under Washington's direct command, as he had shown at the battle of Monmouth. Command of the elite Light Infantry was a position that some officers coveted. Daniel Morgan, the tough and cantankerous Virginia colonel who led the Rifle Corps, was also dissatisfied with his opportunities in the Virginia line and considered himself the most qualified officer in the Continental Army to lead the Light Infantry. But command of the Light Infantry called for a brigadier-general, Morgan was only a colonel, and Virginia already had its full allotment of brigadiers, as restricted by Congress.[24] Washington made his decision, and wrote to Wayne: "My opinion of your merit will lead me cheerfully to comply with your request as soon as the arrangements of the army and other circumstances permit formation of the Light Corps."[25]

The Light Infantry would not take form as a separate corps until a campaign developed, and Wayne remained on furlough in Pennsylvania for the winter. Washington continued his efforts to build the Continental Army, but he remained concerned about if, how and where the next major British summer offensive would occur. It was highly unlikely that Britain would remain idle for the entire campaign season and let the rebellion gain strength. Clinton was sure to strike somewhere, and the Royal Navy gave him the ability to land forces almost anywhere along the seaboard. Washington received accurate reports on British activities from a spy in New York City, but he had no information about Britain's intentions for the year. Gen. Washington needed his spy to work harder.

III

The Culper Ring

New York City, March 1779

The spy Gen. Washington relied on for information about the British in New York City was a twenty-nine-year-old civilian named Abraham Woodhull. But just at the time the general needed him to get more information on British intentions, Woodhull was getting nervous. At his home in the town of Setauket, on the north coast of Long Island, Woodhull played the part of an American merchant with the utmost loyalty to King George III. Every few weeks he traveled to Manhattan ostensibly on business and conversed with British soldiers and noted the details of the military situation. Then he returned to Setauket, captured his observations in long letters, and hid the messages at a secluded bay. Boatmen, sent from a contact on the rebel-held coast of Connecticut, retrieved the letters and delivered them to couriers to be sped to army headquarters. Woodhull knew spying carried the death sentence under the Articles of War, and on every trip into and out of the city he endured questioning from suspicious Redcoat sentries. After six months of leading a double life that could lead to his death, he wrote to Maj. Benjamin Tallmadge, the Continental Army officer who managed Woodhull's activities, that he led "a life of anxiety to be within ... the lines of a cruel and mistrustful enemy."[1] Tallmadge passed Woodhull's concerns to Washington, saying, "Whenever your Excellency may wish him to discontinue his present correspondence, he will ... fully quit the employment, as he proposes no advantages to himself from the undertaking."[2]

That Woodhull could conduct his espionage without discovery was especially impressive considering that he operated in British-occupied New York City, an environment characterized by misery, brutality, and mistrust.

In the mid–1770s New York City consisted of buildings and homes that extended one and a half miles north from the lower tip of Manhattan. Visitors to the city admired its cobblestone streets, flat stone sidewalks, and neat English and Dutch architecture. Already a major port and trade center, hundreds of ships from New York's docks took American goods to London, Ireland, mainland Europe, Madeira, the Azores, and the West Indies. They returned with such luxury goods as coconuts, rum, mahogany, cotton, silk, coffee, manufactured carriages, furniture, drugs, dyes, indigo, and snuff. Sadly, ships also returned from the African coast with cargoes of slaves. The city had significant Jewish and black minorities. Philadelphia was larger in population, but New York City was known as the most cosmopolitan city in North America.

British forces under Gen. Sir William Howe entered New York City on the heels of withdrawing Continental troops in the autumn of 1776 and immediately met disaster. A fire, which began at the city docks and spread north and west, burned for ten hours and destroyed nearly a third of the city's housing before citizens and British soldiers extinguished the flames. Despite the destruction the 25,000 British and Hessian soldiers of Howe's army moved in over the next few months and established garrisons all over the island of Manhattan, on Staten Island, Flushing, Brookline, Harlem, across the Hudson in New Jersey, and at Kingsbridge, the crossing over the Bronx River on the north tip of Manhattan. At least 1,500 Redcoats and Hessians, including cavalrymen, moved into New York City proper. Gen. Howe occupied the house at No. 1 Broadway for his headquarters, with his deputy, Sir Henry Clinton, in the house next door.

The disaster of the fire did not prevent some aspects of New York City from profiting from the occupation. Since many of the residents, possibly as much as 16 percent, remained loyal to King George III and welcomed Crown forces, business boomed at Loyalist-oriented taverns.[3] At the Manhattan docks, shipbuilders benefited from contracts with the Royal Navy and outfitted privateers that went to sea to raid rebel commerce. The city was under martial law, and a military commandant, with a small group of civilian officials, operated New York's infrastructure, maintained a night watch and enforced regulations. Gen. Howe entered into an extravagant lifestyle with an active social scene that included fox hunting, golf, billiards, horse racing, saltwater bathing parties, concerts, and a biweekly "Garrison

Assembly" where Howe's officers, including a young Horatio Nelson, danced with local girls. British officers also operated the "Theatre Royal" with performances of Shakespeare, Garrick and Sheridan. And, of course, the city's prostitutes thrived.

But British occupation became a burden that the city could not sustain. In addition to the soldiers, the population of New York City swelled from 25,000 residents in 1776 to 33,000 as Tory refugees, escaped slaves, and indentured servants (the Crown offered freedom to slaves of rebels but not to those owned by Loyalists) flocked in for Crown protection. Many British soldiers were already quartered in what few boardinghouses and private homes remained after the fire. The population surge overwhelmed the city. Another fire in 1778 further reduced available housing. Refugees built "Canvas Town," a city of tents without sanitation, located west of Broad Street amidst the burnt ruins of the fire. Here crime became rampant and people managed to scrape out miserable lives. Wood also became scarce and there were reports that the city's poor burned animal fat for warmth and cooking. Yellow fever, cholera, and smallpox were common. Under such desperate living conditions, robberies and assaults became daily occurrences. But corruption also prevailed in the occupation government, the police were ineffective, and the courts were usually lenient on soldiers even in robbery, assault, rape, and murder cases.[4]

Nor could British authorities feed so many so mouths. The military supply system shipped provisions for the city from the port of Cork in Ireland, but due to corrupt contractors many shipments of meat arrived spoiled or underweight. Since some goods that did not spoil easily, such as wine, olives, cheese, mustard, nuts, spices and confections, arrived edible, a black market developed where New Yorkers traded the luxury goods for meat and poultry from the American-held areas outside the city. Known as the "London Trade," the practice was so widespread that few officials of either side interfered with it, as long as it did not involve military items.[5] But despite the London Trade and the "Cork victualars," by the middle of 1778 New York City had only five weeks of food left and British authorities considered abandoning the city. Ships from Cork arrived with enough supplies for six months, but more corruption in the supply system whittled the stores down to last only three months. Food costs rose 800 percent and the city remained on the brink of famine.[6]

Prisons for captured Continental Army soldiers, set up in three former sugar warehouses, were some of the most shocking aspects of the occupation. Supervising the prisons was a sixty-year-old provost marshal named

William Cunningham, an infamous bully and drunk who had once been roughed up by some rebels and took his revenge on the prisoners in his charge. Under the military conventions of the time the Continental Congress sent the British occupiers funds to purchase food and clothing for every prisoner. But Cunningham skimmed much of the money for himself, and the Yankee captives suffered without adequate water, food, heat, medical care, or clothing. Diseases were rampant and many prisoners froze or starved to death. Hundreds of Americans also languished in the unheated, rotting hulks of useless ships anchored in Wallabout Bay in east Manhattan. Every morning guards at all the prisons collected the bodies of the dead. In Britain after the war, Cunningham was convicted of forgery and sentenced to death. On his way to the gallows he confessed to purposefully murdering as many as 2,000 Americans by starvation, hanging, or poisoning.[7]

In addition to the internal strife, the open combat of the Revolution surrounded New York City. Across the Hudson to the west in New Jersey, British troops skirmished with American militias. To the southeast, Long Island was under Royal control but Yankees from Connecticut raided the coast, taking prisoners and destroying supplies. Covering half a million acres north and east of New York City and home to 28,000 people (24,000 whites and 4,000 blacks), Westchester County was the most contested area.[8] British lines ran along the southern edge of the county while Continental forces, headquartered at Peekskill, controlled the northern part. The area in between became a no-man's-land where armed bandits and troops of the opposing sides foraged for food, recruited more members, punished suspected enemies, and skirmished.

Units composed of Americans that remained loyal to King George were particularly effective in controlling the areas that surrounded New York City. The practice of enlisting provincial units to augment regular forces dated to the French and Indian War. Soon after Gen. Howe landed on Staten Island in June 1776, Oliver De Lancey, a colonel of the New York militia and French and Indian War veteran, raised a brigade of 1,200 soldiers to fight alongside the British. In August 1776 Howe also commissioned Robert Rogers, famous as the commander of Rogers' Rangers during the French and Indian War, as a lieutenant-colonel with authorization to raise a new battalion officially called the Queen's American Rangers but unofficially known again as Rogers' Rangers. Rogers' service to Britain particularly irked Washington, who discussed capturing the Ranger with Connecticut governor Jonathan Trumbull. "Rogers is an Active instrument in the Enemy's hands," Washington said, "and his Conduct has a peculiar claim to our notice."⁹

By 1779 there were several Loyalist units such as the King's American Regiment, the Loyal American Regiment, the Volunteers of Ireland, the King's Rangers, the New York Volunteers, and the British Legion — that were relentless raiders of the areas around New York City. During a two-week period in 1777 they seized more than 500 cattle from local farms, and Oliver De Lancey's men earned the nickname "DeLancey's Cowboys."¹⁰ When Westchester County farms became barren after constant raids, Loyalist units expanded their foraging into other counties on the banks of the Hudson as far north as Fishkill. Washington's spy Abraham Woodhull reported that DeLancey's men swept through eastern Long Island in November 1778 collecting cattle and sheep. "They make no distinction between Whig & Tory," he said, and "abuse all to a general degree and no relief can be obtained."¹¹

"Patriot" units were no kinder to their countrymen. The destruction in Westchester began in 1776 when American forces withdrew through the area and burned the courthouse and most of the residences in the town of White Plains without regard to the allegiance of the owners. Washington even directed his commanders to raze the area to prevent British troops from living off the land. "The Article of Forrage is of great Importance to them," he said. "[N]ot a Blade should remain for their use, what cannot be removed with should be consumed without the least hesitation."¹² In early 1779 Washington's commander of the Hudson River defenses, Maj. Gen. Alexander McDougall, ordered his troops to summarily hang any civilian caught stealing livestock on behalf of the British. Armed bands of Americans known as "skinners," because of their reputation for taking the very shirts off their victims' backs, roamed Westchester County beyond the control of Continental commanders, threatening and beating civilians in order to find their valuables.

Dr. James Thacher, the Continental surgeon that recorded dinner at Washington's table at Middlebrook, passed through Westchester County with his regiment and observed, "[T]he miserable inhabitants who remain, are not much favored with the privileges that neutrality ought to secure to them. They are continually exposed to the ravages and insults of infamous banditti.... These shameless marauders have received the names of *Cow-boys* and *Skinners*.... [T]hey have become a scourge and terror to the people." One resident told Thacher how a group of raiders (their allegiance was not further identified) forced him to disclose the location of his hidden money by hanging him by the neck until he was "apparently dead," reviving him, and then repeating the process.[13] The thirteen-member "Commission for Detecting and Defeating Conspiracies," operated by the rebel New York government, also ejected from the area anyone who did not support their cause. The Committee operated a ring of informants and on the first day it convened, in August 1776, the members named 111 citizens in southeastern New York as suspected British sympathizers. Its own militia company rounded up the unfortunate citizens suspected of crimes.[14]

As the location of Gen. Clinton's headquarters, the American intelligence service would have to operate in New York City to keep Gen. Washington informed about British plans and capabilities. But the deplorable conditions, constant conflict, and dozens of nervous sentries made it extremely difficult to set up an intelligence network inside New York City. And as Washington worked to establish such a system, there was little theory or instruction on how to conduct military intelligence operations to guide him.

Gathering intelligence was not a significant problem for Washington during the first campaign when the Americans besieged British forces in Boston and could directly observe enemy activities. When the theater of action shifted to New York in the summer of 1776, Washington created a special unit of scouts under Lt. Col. Thomas Knowlton, a veteran of Rogers' Rangers in the French and Indian War and Bunker Hill. But since Howe's army had the capability to strike on Long Island, Manhattan, or New Jersey, intelligence about British intentions and capabilities—information that was beyond the observation skills of "Knowlton's Rangers," as they were known—became essential for an effective defense. Washington needed spies.

Working against Washington was the commonly held opinion that military spying was an illicit pursuit. Espionage conducted in diplomatic circles among the courts of Europe, including the employment of secret agents, was an age-old and well-accepted practice. The observation of enemy military units by soldiers in uniform was also accepted as traditional and routine scouting. But *spying*, either by soldiers who sneaked behind enemy lines in civilian garb or civilians paid to send intelligence reports, was considered to be work beneath the dignity of gentlemen and fit only for unsavory characters. Soldiers also knew that spying was punishable by death. When Washington asked the army's division commanders to seek volunteers to go behind British lines to gather information during the New York campaign, few soldiers answered the request. Those soldiers that the Americans managed to sneak behind British lines returned with information that was vague, exaggerated, or reported too late to be valuable.[15]

One soldier who responded to Washington's request was Nathan Hale,

A hangman prepares to execute the captured American spy Nathan Hale, center, on Manhattan Island in 1776 under the supervision of a British officer, left. In a few minutes Hale would suffer a slow, agonizing death. Much of Gen. Washington's information about the British movements in 1779 came from a group of American spies like Hale in and around New York City that operated under the constant threat of disclosure, capture, and the noose (painting by Don Troiani, www.historicalimagebank.com).

and his famous case illustrates the difficulties and dangers of spying behind enemy lines. The twenty-three-year-old Hale was a recent Yale graduate and captain in Knowlton's Rangers who was eager for more action than his scouting duties offered. After he volunteered to go behind British lines, a sloop dropped Hale at a secluded bay on the north side of Long Island. He disembarked with orders to head west toward British lines on the western end of the island, collect information on troop strengths and dispositions, and then work his way out and report to Gen. Washington. As a "cover," he dressed in civilian clothes and masqueraded as a schoolteacher, carrying his Yale diploma to back up the claim.

But Hale had no training in the spy business. Loyalists quickly spotted him as an imposter as he asked probing questions about military matters and made notes on Redcoat units. Robert Rogers, the famed Ranger commander, captured Hale and took him to Howe's headquarters. The evidence against him was clear: he had admitted his mission to Rogers, was captured in civilian clothes behind enemy lines, and carried a notebook full of incriminating notes. Howe signed Hale's death warrant without a trial. The next day, Sunday, September 22, he was hanged from a tree on Manhattan. He almost certainly did not say, "I only regret that I have but one life to give for my country," as tradition tells us. But one witness recorded that Hale was calm and composed, said some well-thought-out words about the duty of officers to obey their commanders, and went to his death with dignity. The hangman's placement of the noose was inexpert, which failed to snap his neck immediately, and Hale suffered an agonizing death. His body was left swinging for a few days to set an example and some soldiers hung on the body a board that had "General Washington" crudely written on it. It is unclear when Washington learned about the fiasco, but when he did, the lessons from it and the other failed attempts that summer were clear: obtaining intelligence on the British was a difficult process that if done improperly would lead to the death of those involved.[16]

For the next three months, after the Continentals evacuated Manhattan and retreated across New Jersey to Pennsylvania, Washington received intelligence from scouts, soldiers or civilians. He wrote to Congress: "The intelligence we obtain respecting the Movements and situation of the Enemy is far from being so certain and satisfactory as I could wish."[17] To regularly gain accurate information about Britain's intentions, Washington decided to leave traditional scouting as the responsibility of military units and to build a proper network of civilian agents to spy behind enemy lines. In February 1777 he enlisted the help of Nathaniel Sackett, who operated the informants for New York's Committee for Detecting and Defeating Conspiracies. Washington also assigned Captain Benjamin Tallmadge, a promising twenty-three-year-old cavalry officer, to help Sackett send messages by army couriers and to deal with local military commanders.[18]

Together, Sackett and Tallmadge created an effective spy operation. Tasked with "obtaining the earliest and best Intelligence of the designs of the enemy" by Washington and provided with $500, Sackett recruited people of various backgrounds to enter New York City, act as Loyalists, befriend the British leadership, and send back information.[19] He even posed as a Loyalist for a time to recruit one agent. Sackett's operatives had varying levels of success—at least one disappeared completely—but the most valuable aspect of the operation was that Sackett developed tradecraft the spies needed in order to avoid detection, such as methods for clandestine communication. Tallmadge helped him process the messages for army headquarters and learned much about the intelligence business. The operations continued until the spring of 1777, when Washington dismissed Sackett over an issue that remains a mystery and Tallmadge returned to duty with the Second Light Dragoons. But Sackett's methods formed the basis for an effective American intelligence system.[20]

Washington's intelligence service began to coalesce into an organization that could regularly crack into New York City in August 1778, when he received a letter from Caleb Brewster, a Continental Army artillery lieutenant on duty at Norwalk, Connecticut. Like Nathan Hale, Brewster volunteered to spy for Washington because he craved action. His offer was a windfall. Washington was preparing to launch a combined French-American attack on British-held Newport and Admiral d'Estaing, commanding the French fleet, implored him to have "intelligent Spies" to gain information on the capabilities of the Royal Navy to offer opposition.[21] Washington told Brewster, "By every devise you can think of, have a strict watch kept upon the Enemy's Ships of War, and give me the earliest notice of their Sailing from the hook."[22] Brewster was fearless, a former mate on a whaling ship, toughened by years at sea, and he made an ideal spy for naval activities. On August 27 he sent Washington a report that detailed the British forces that were headed toward Newport. Washington combined Brewster's information with reports from another agent, and in early September, he was able to send d'Estaing the locations of all known British warships and tell him, "Our intelligence has in general been as good as could be expected from the situation of the Enemy."[23]

But a single capable spy was not enough, and Washington called upon Gen. Charles Scott, commander of the Continental Army's Light Infantry posted in Westchester County, to manage intelligence activities and build on Brewster's success by recruiting more spies in and around New York City. Unfortunately Scott often focused more of his attention on his regular command duties and Washington continued to have problems getting regular, reliable information. Washington brought Benjamin Tallmadge back to assist Scott, and soon the major recommended Abraham Woodhull as a new contact to work with Brewster. Tallmadge, Brewster, and Woodhull had grown up together in Setauket as supporters of the American cause. But whereas Tallmadge and Brewster entered Continental service, Woodhull continued working as a merchant in Setauket and entered the London Trade after the British occupied Manhattan. Woodhull was jailed in Connecticut after he was caught smuggling, but he was released after Tallmadge put in a good word for him. Tallmadge probably knew that Woodhull held a deep grudge against the British because they captured and killed his elder brother Nathaniel, a Continental general, in 1776. Possibly leveraging Woodhull's bitterness, Tallmadge talked him into spying.

After consultations with Tallmadge, Washington decided to establish a network of spies in New York City with Woodhull as the chief operative. Interception of the network's correspondence by British patrols was a constant danger, so Washington, Scott and Tallmadge assigned aliases to protect the identities of the participants: Tallmadge wrote under the name "John Bolton" and Woodhull was "Samuel Culper." The latter name was an inside joke—the name "Culper" came from Culpeper County Virginia, where Washington had worked as a surveyor. Tallmadge's younger brother was named Samuel, and the reverse initials of Samuel Culper were the same as Charles Scott's. Brewster was absolutely fearless and continued using his own name on correspondence. Scott soon bowed out of the intelligence business, and Washington appointed Tallmadge as intelligence chief.[24]

Tallmadge, Brewster and Woodhull formed the core of what was known later as the "Culper Ring," which directly responded to Washington's intelligence questions and acquired information that was normally accurate and timely. For example, in November 1778 Washington requested information on the enemy units around New York, their commanders, whether they were building fortifications, their state of provisions, and whether signs existed of movement toward Rhode Island.[25] Woodhull replied five days later with a detailed list of Crown forces and warned that Gen. Archibald Campbell was departing the city with 3,000 troops (it was the British expedition to take Savannah).[26]

In early 1779 Washington's primary intelligence concern became the identification of British campaign plans for the year. In late February Woodhull provided the strength and locations of all the Crown regiments, but no information on British intentions.[27] Caleb Brewster came closer to addressing Washington's concerns when he reported the British building several flat-bottomed barges usually used for amphibious landings, and said, "It is thought by the inhabitants that they will move to New London [to seize] the Continental frigates."[28] Possibly spurred by Brewster's intriguing report, in March Washington asked Tallmadge to get information on the movements and strength of enemy regiments, reinforcements from England, and the sentiments of Loyalist troops and refugees. Always suspicious of British moves to reinforce Rhode Island or attack Connecticut, he asked about the depth of Hell Gate and if ships of war could pass through it. He wanted Woodhull to get close to British army headquarters and "mix with, and put on the airs of a Tory to cover his real character, and avoid suspicion." Washington wanted no exaggerations in the reports and cautioned that in all his communications he should be careful in distinguishing matters of fact, from matters of report."[29]

By that time Woodhull was feeling the strain of spying. He was under constant threat of discovery and his trips into and out of Manhattan took him through some of the no-man's-lands, where roving thieves, guerrillas, and British patrols could rob or apprehend him at any time. Redcoat guards at the ferry to Manhattan routinely questioned him and required him to show a passport on every trip. He implored Tallmadge to destroy any reference to his real name and lamented about the difficulties of answering Washington's questions. "I can discover not movement afoot at present," he wrote, "their excursions are always very sudden and seldom begin to move before dark. And it will be ten to one if ever it will be in my power to give you early intelligence of their excursion. All I can say is that you must be everywhere upon your guard."[30]

In April, Woodhull seemed to cover his bets, reporting signs of a possible evacuation of the city, troops preparing for a raid, more building of landing craft, and a British peace offering.[31] But Washington considered Baltimore, Annapolis, or Philadelphia to be possible targets for the next Crown offensive and he could not be on guard everywhere, as Woodhull suggested. Washington told his friend Benjamin Harrison, "Britain will strain every nerve to distress us this Campaign; but where, or in what manner her principal force will be employed I cannot determine."[32]

Despite his growing reluctance, in late April Woodhull gained access to what he called "private letters" and told Washington that 800 soldiers with light artillery and landing craft were loading on transports with five days' provisions under command of a Gen. Matthew. "Most of the People judge they are going to Southward," he said.[33] Just as Washington directed, Woodhull's information indicated an impending amphibious operation that was actually the opening move of the summer campaign. Now Washington knew the British were getting ready to move, but he didn't know where they would land.

IV

"Chicane Might Draw Him into It"

New York City, April 1779

    Gen. Sir Henry Clinton was a dejected and discontented commander of his army's dismal occupation of New York. Forty-seven years old in 1779, Clinton was a veteran of the Seven Years' War, had thirty-three years of army service, and had been in America since 1775. Clinton was usually downcast and melancholy, a disposition possibly caused by the 1772 death of his wife, whom he loved dearly. His experiences in America only lowered his spirits. As Howe's deputy commander he saw action against the rebels at Bunker Hill, Long Island, Charleston, and Newport; but the two officers grated on each other, possibly because of Clinton's prickly character. He prosecuted the war, which he later called "a most unaccountable madness [that] seized both countries," with little enthusiasm.[1] Like many king's officers, Clinton originally had a low opinion of American soldiers and even less respect for Washington after the British out-maneuvered the Yankees at New York in 1776. But the battles of 1777, especially Washington's victories at Trenton and Princeton, convinced Clinton that the Continentals were experts at hit-and-run raids and that they could defeat British offensives, by retreating into rugged terrain, mobilizing local militiamen, and enjoy the support of a rebellious population.[2]

    After Howe's resignation in 1778, Clinton's assumption to command of all British forces in North America came at a time when defeating the American rebellion was Britain's second priority after protecting the Empire from French attacks. As if to confirm the diminished importance of the American war, London ordered Clinton to remain on the "strict defense," mount no major offensive for the remainder of the year, and send 8,000 troops to defend Florida and the West Indies.³ Sir Henry believed that he could defeat the rebellion in one campaign with 30,000 soldiers. But instead of being permitted to pursue his strategy, he was relegated to merely defending the British-held ports of New York, Savannah, and Newport, with barely half of the force he believed was required. In late 1778 Clinton reviewed the state of the war and his chances for success, and later wrote, "I did not derive much satisfaction from either." The mere thought of a summer campaign gave him "anxious solicitude."⁴ Convinced that he "had to be relieved from a situation of so little hope and so great a responsibility," in November Clinton requested relief from his command. While he waited all winter "in daily expectation of the King's leave to return home"⁵ Clinton sent raiding parties into Connecticut, launched the expedition to seize Savannah, and watched for vulnerabilities among the various Continental Army winter camps. Restricted from larger offensive moves by London's orders, he would take no further action nor plan for a summer campaign until he received the king's answer or instructions from Lord George Germain, the American secretary.

Washington's opponent in the campaign of 1779, Lieutenant-General Sir Henry Clinton. A veteran British army officer and an able strategist, Clinton was unhappy in his command in America and was usually in a state of melancholy. He launched the campaign around the Hudson in an attempt to subdue New York and New England and destroy the Continental Army in battle (Library of Congress).

Unfortunately for Clinton, his request for relief arrived in London amidst rumors that Spain was preparing to enter the war on America's side; the king was extremely reluctant to change commanders in the face of the new threat. At the same time, Joseph Galloway, a prominent

Loyalist from Philadelphia, was convincing the king and his ministers that Americans were tiring of the war and that the Loyalists could defeat the rebellion as long as the British army supported them. The success of Clinton's autumn raids and the recent victory at Savannah seemed to support the possibilities of British victory. Instead of relieving Clinton, in January the king, his advisors, and Lord Germain chose a strategy for 1779 that required Clinton to move out of New York in the summer and strike hard at America's army, population, and economy. Germain wrote out a set of lengthy orders for Clinton; but the fastest transatlantic crossing took up to eight weeks, and the instructions would not reach New York until the spring.

Clinton's inactivity while waiting for orders was a significant frustration to New York's Loyalists, who depended on Britain's success. William Smith, the Royal chief justice of New York, had the confidence of Tory leaders and senior British officers and in April he noted the prevailing belief among Loyalists that "the Spirit of the Rebellion is [abated], and Nothing wanting to extinguish it but an Attack on Washington's Division in Jersey or Putnam's in the Highlands or Posts near them."[6] The Loyalist New York newspaper *Rivington's Royal Gazette* also reported that the rebellion was near failure and that American soldiers were "sickly and discontented; that two regiments in the neighborhood of Washington's headquarters had mutinied, and that the most part of the men only wanted an opportunity ... for deserting to the British."[7] On April 24 Smith noted that Loyalist leaders were in a "general Anxiety" for orders from England.[8] As if in answer to their concerns, the same day that Smith made his diary entry a Royal Navy frigate arrived at the New York wharf with a load of supplies and a packet of letters for Gen. Clinton from Lord George Germain.

Clinton's heart surely sank upon opening the sheaf of letters. Instead of granting his request to return to England, the instructions from Germain told him, "I will state to you the outlines of a plan for the future conduct of the war in North America ... which His Majesty has thought fit to approve." Germain buttered Clinton up with a few sentences about how the king relied on the general's "wisdom, zeal for his service and great military abilities" to execute the next campaign and then got to the point. "It is most earnestly wished," he wrote, "that you may be able to bring Mr. Washington to a general and decisive action at the opening of the Campaign" (British officials usually referred to Washington as "Mr." since they did not consider their American opponent to be a legitimate military officer). Germain went on: "[B]ut if that cannot be effected it is imagined that ... you may force him to seek safety in the Highlands of New York or the Jerseys, and leave the Inhabitants of the open Country at liberty to ... renounce the authority of the Congress, and return to their allegiance to His Majesty." Since Virginia and New England supplied much of the material for the rebellion, Germain directed Clinton to send strong raiding forces, "the one to act on the side of New England and ... the other in the Chesapeake Bay, and by entering the rivers and inlets ... seize or destroy their shipping and stores, and deprive them of every means of fitting out privateers, or carrying on Foreign Commerce." He promised to send Clinton 6,000 more soldiers for the campaign.[9]

In addition to dashing his hopes for relief, the requirements of the orders stunned Sir Henry. In essence, Germain expected Clinton to crush the very formidable Continental Army, subdue all of New York, and destroy the commerce along hundreds of miles of coastline in the Chesapeake Bay and Long Island Sound. After fighting in America for five years Clinton knew that the objectives were almost impossible to accomplish, even with the 6,000 reinforcements that Germain promised. He later responded to Germain with much validity: "To force Washington to an action upon terms tolerably equal has been the object of every campaign during the war. The difficulty of attaining that object in so strong a Country ... by this time needs no illustration."[10]

But Clinton's frustration with the orders was short-lived, and something clicked in his mind as he considered them. Through long service he had developed the ability to analyze terrain for tactical advantages. For example, in June 1775, soon after he arrived in Boston, Clinton assisted Gen. Howe in planning the attack on Breed's Hill. Howe wanted a conventional frontal assault against the rebel position, but Clinton analyzed the terrain and recommended a flank attack that would cut the Americans off and enable the British to win with minimal casualties. Howe ignored his advice and ordered the frontal assaults. After three attacks the British won the field but suffered nearly 50 percent casualties. When Howe landed on Long Island a year later, Clinton scouted the rebel lines, identified a weak point, and developed a plan for another flanking maneuver combined with a frontal assault that would cause the American line to buckle. This time Howe grudgingly approved the concept. Clinton led the flank march himself and routed the Americans; but Howe, possibly remembering the high casualties of Breed's Hill, held the men back from pursuit. Clinton's plan had worked, even though two days later the American army escaped across the East River to Manhattan.

IV. "Chicane Might Draw Him into It"

With his knowledge of military geography, Clinton saw that the Hudson River was the key to securing the region. In the age of sail, when rivers were the roads of commerce, the Hudson was a superhighway. A million and a half years before the Revolution, glaciers carved its 300-mile course from what would become the Adirondack, Catskill and Taconic mountains and gave it a deep riverbed that extends into the Atlantic — the lower portion of the Hudson is actually an ocean estuary that allows tides and salt water sixty miles inland. Its width, depth, and slow current made the river navigable by large sailing ships all the way to Albany, 160 miles from New York harbor. The width of river also forms a natural barrier between New York and New England. (Part of the reason Britain seized New Amsterdam from the Dutch was to acquire control of the Hudson and unite her southern and northern colonies in America.) In the seventeenth and eighteenth centuries the Hudson was the New York colony's primary route for shipping goods and timber from inland farms to the port at Manhattan.

When conflict opened in 1775 British strategists considered New England to be the ideological seat of the rebellion and made mastery of the Hudson a key objective, as Clinton expressed, "as long as a British army held the passes of that noble river and her cruisers swept their coasts, the colonists would have found it impossible to have joined."[11] Gen. Howe's capture of New York City in 1776 gained Britain control of the lower Hudson, and Gen. Burgoyne intended to seize the entire river and split the colonies with his invasion from Canada in 1777. The effort failed with Burgoyne's defeat at Saratoga, but the Hudson remained an important objective for Britain.

The Americans also recognized the strategic importance of the Hudson and as early as May 1775 the Continental Congress made plans to control the river. The New York Provincial Congress followed suit three months later. Washington observed, "New York and the Hudson's River are the most important objects [the British] can have in view, as the latter secures the communications with Canada, at the same time it separates the Northern and Southern Colonies."[12] The area around West Point was essential to holding the Hudson, because a sharp bend in the river, strong tides and variable winds there forced ships to slow and become vulnerable to cannon fire. Fort Constitution (named for the English rights that the colonists fought to defend) was the first fortification on the Hudson, built in the autumn of 1775 on Martlaer's Rock, a small island in the stream of the bend at West Point. Five miles south on the west bank of the Hudson, Americans built Fort Montgomery, named for Gen. Richard Montgomery, who died leading the attack on Quebec, and Fort Clinton, named for the governor of New York, George Clinton. Both forts were star-shaped, earthen works with sixty-seven cannon and 700 soldiers between them. A giant chain, floated on a log boom, stretched from Ft. Montgomery to Anthony's Nose on the Hudson's east bank to block the passage of British ships.

Though Congress, Gen. Washington, and the New York Congress all appreciated the importance of the river, the citizens of the Hudson highlands did not completely support the rebellion, and Governor Clinton was unable to obtain the materials he needed to build the forts properly. Continental generals Nathaniel Greene and Henry Knox inspected the forts in 1776 and determined that they were inadequate to defend the river. By October 1777 the needs of the Philadelphia campaign siphoned off most Continental soldiers from the Hudson highlands, and the river fortifications became significantly undermanned. The town of Peekskill on the east bank was an important Continental depot but was lightly defended. Redcoats burned the village and its stores in March and September 1777. In October the same year Gen. Clinton attempted to assist Burgoyne's invasion by leading an expedition up from Manhattan to destroy the American river defenses. A furious battle between Clinton's troops, Forts Montgomery and Clinton, and two American frigates in the river raged through the night of October 6. The Americans fought stubbornly but both forts fell before midnight. The next day British troops burned Fort Constitution after its garrison fled. Clinton had destroyed American defenses on the Hudson in two days; but once Burgoyne's army surrendered, Clinton's force was too small to hold both the river forts and Manhattan. He withdrew to New York City, under the belief that his victory was complete.

But the ease with which the British swept through the Hudson fortifications energized Washington to more thoroughly ensure the river's protection. In March 1778 he appointed Major-General Alexander McDougall overall commander of the Hudson defenses. At West Point, Gen. Thaddeus Kosciusko, a Polish volunteer and experienced military engineer, built the star-shaped Fort Arnold and Fort Putnam, a massive stone bastion. He rebuilt and improved Fort Constitution and added a huge chain across the river, floated on sixteen-inch thick log booms Americans eventually called "General Washington's Watch Chain" and Redcoats termed "the Yankee Pumpkin Vine." Continental soldiers also rebuilt Forts Montgomery and Clinton. Fort Independence protected the waters around Peekskill, five miles south. The southernmost defenses on

IV. "Chicane Might Draw Him into It"

the river protected King's Ferry, a crossing site along a major road between New England and New York frequently used for Continental supplies and troops. On the eastern end of the ferry at Verplanck's Point, Yankees built Ft. Lafayette, an earthen work manned by seventy soldiers. A blockhouse with thirty troops guarded the western end of the crossing at Stony Point. By the middle of 1778 the Hudson was still the key to controlling the northeast, and it was the most fortified waterway in America.

Gen. Clinton's intelligence system kept him informed about the strength of American river defenses. Like most officers of the age, Clinton began the war without the training or traditions needed to acquire and employ intelligence. But while garrisoning New York City in 1777 as Howe's second-in-command, Clinton was surrounded in hostile territory where warning of attack became essential. Suspicious rebel organizations, such as New York's Committee for Identifying Conspiracies (that Washington leveraged for spies), inhibited the recruitment of agents, but the Loyalist units had natural contacts in their home counties outside the British lines. The system gave Clinton effective informants all around Manhattan, in Philadelphia, northern New York, Connecticut, and even the Allegheny region. (Clinton did not know that one of his operatives in New Jersey named Elijah Hunter was actually a double agent who was under Washington's control, supplying the British with false information.) However, the intelligence operation was too large for Clinton to manage by himself. Reports came in daily, but mixed with all the other correspondence for the commander of all British forces in North America, they often went unread.[13]

In May 1779 Clinton appointed his aide-de-camp, Captain John Andre, as his intelligence chief. The twenty-seven-year-old Andre had come to America in 1775 as a lieutenant in the Seventh Regiment of Foot, was captured in Canada, and spent a year in Pennsylvania on parole. Released in 1777, he served as an aide to Gen. Charles Gray, who commanded the British attack on Anthony Wayne's camp at Paoli, and Gray recommended him as an aide for Clinton in November 1778. In the active social scene that British officers enjoyed in occupied Manhattan, Andre wrote verse, enjoyed the theater, and authored plays that were popular with American and British audiences. Intelligent, energetic, and ambitious, he organized Clinton's intelligence system with an "intelligence book" that stored all the incoming reports from Loyalist refugees, interrogations of American deserters, and statements from escaped British prisoners in a readable chronological order.

Andre also developed his own spy network and ensured that agents communicated in cipher codes, which increased their safety. He asked his operatives for information on rebel troop locations and strengths, the state of their supplies, and American intentions. One of his contacts was a prominent Loyalist in Philadelphia named Joseph Stansbury. In May, Stansbury told Andre about a promising, if somewhat suspicious, offer to spy that he received from a Continental officer exceptionally famous for his bravery but now disgruntled with his situation, Maj. Gen. Benedict Arnold. Andre told Clinton about Arnold's offer and they opened a correspondence with him to see where it would lead. Clinton still handled correspondence from his closest spies, and Andre still handled the myriad duties of an aide-de-camp, but the British intelligence system reached new levels of efficiency. In the spring of 1779 the information available indicated that the main camps of the Continental Army in New Jersey were "too strong and his numbers too respectable to be rashly attempted," as Clinton wrote, and that some of the American forts on the Hudson south of West Point were lightly defended.[14]

With Germain's instructions before him, Clinton looked at his map and contemplated the situation. Strategically, he believed that the best course for winning the war was to shift the main theater of action to Georgia and the Carolinas, where Britain could rely on the support of the more numerous Loyalists to break the unity of the rebellion. Before that could happen, he would have to eliminate the main Continental Army and secure New York. But Clinton considered that a direct attack on Washington's fortified camps was unlikely to succeed and decided "by indirect maneuvers to draw him forward ... and then move against him while in motion, or force him into a general and decisive action...." Clinton was unwilling to move too far from his supply base at Manhattan, so he needed to bait Washington into New York.[15]

A conversation with Royal Navy commodore Sir George Collier helped Clinton finalize his strategy. Collier was the new commander of the King's American Squadron, appointed after three years of action in American waters as commander of the frigate HMS *Rainbow*. He took over a fleet that he called "wretched," after the wear and tear of four years of combat duty, and "a nominal command" with half the ships he needed to protect British commerce.[16] But Collier was an aggressive officer, had a low opinion of the rebels, and knew the American waters and how to employ his ships along the coast. He was one of the few king's officers in America that Clinton respected.

Collier believed that "the way which seemed most feasible to end the rebellion was cutting off the resources by which the enemy carried on the war, that these resources were principally drawn from *Virginia*." Collier may have ranked the Old Dominion's importance too highly, but he convinced Clinton that "an attack on that province would ... drive the rebels to infinite inconveniences and difficulties."[17] Clinton told Collier that he could not spare many troops for such an expedition but agreed to release as many as possible for raids on the Chesapeake Bay to destroy American shipping, "retard" an expected levy of 2,000 men bound for Washington, and "destroy considerable magazines ... and a quantity of naval stores which that province had provided for supplying a French fleet."[18] Collier later wrote, "Where people have the same object in view matters are easily adjusted and settled."[19]

Clinton planned that, once the Virginia raids succeeded and handicapped Washington's army, British troops in New York would move up the Hudson to lure the Americans out of their strong positions. The key to baiting Washington out of New Jersey was King's Ferry, the crossing site for the King's Highway, which ran from Massachusetts to New Jersey. Though two other Hudson ferries also operated (one just below West Point and another at Fishkill), King's Ferry was the most frequently used crossing site north of Manhattan and a vital link in the Continental Army supply line to New England. Thanks to his intelligence system and a personal reconnaissance of King's Ferry in late 1778, Clinton knew that only 100 soldiers defended the crossing in two rudimentary forts. And in late May, an American deserter reported that the forts guarding the site had only four cannon and the garrisons were poorly provisioned.[20] King's Ferry was an easy target, and Clinton hoped that cutting the American supply line would force Washington to attempt to recover the site, "risking a general action on unfavorable terms."[21] A conversation Clinton once had in London with Lord Germain illustrated his thinking. When Germain asked him if Washington would ever risk his army in a major battle, Clinton replied, "Knowing we wished it, he [would be] a fool if he did; but chicane might draw him into it."[22] With reinforcements due from England, an aggressive naval commander, and a ferry across the Hudson that was both important and vulnerable enough to bait the Americans, it appeared to Clinton that all the elements for a triumphant campaign against Washington were falling into place. He wrote later that he was "not altogether secretly without hopes that the American war might possibly be yet finished in one campaign."[23]

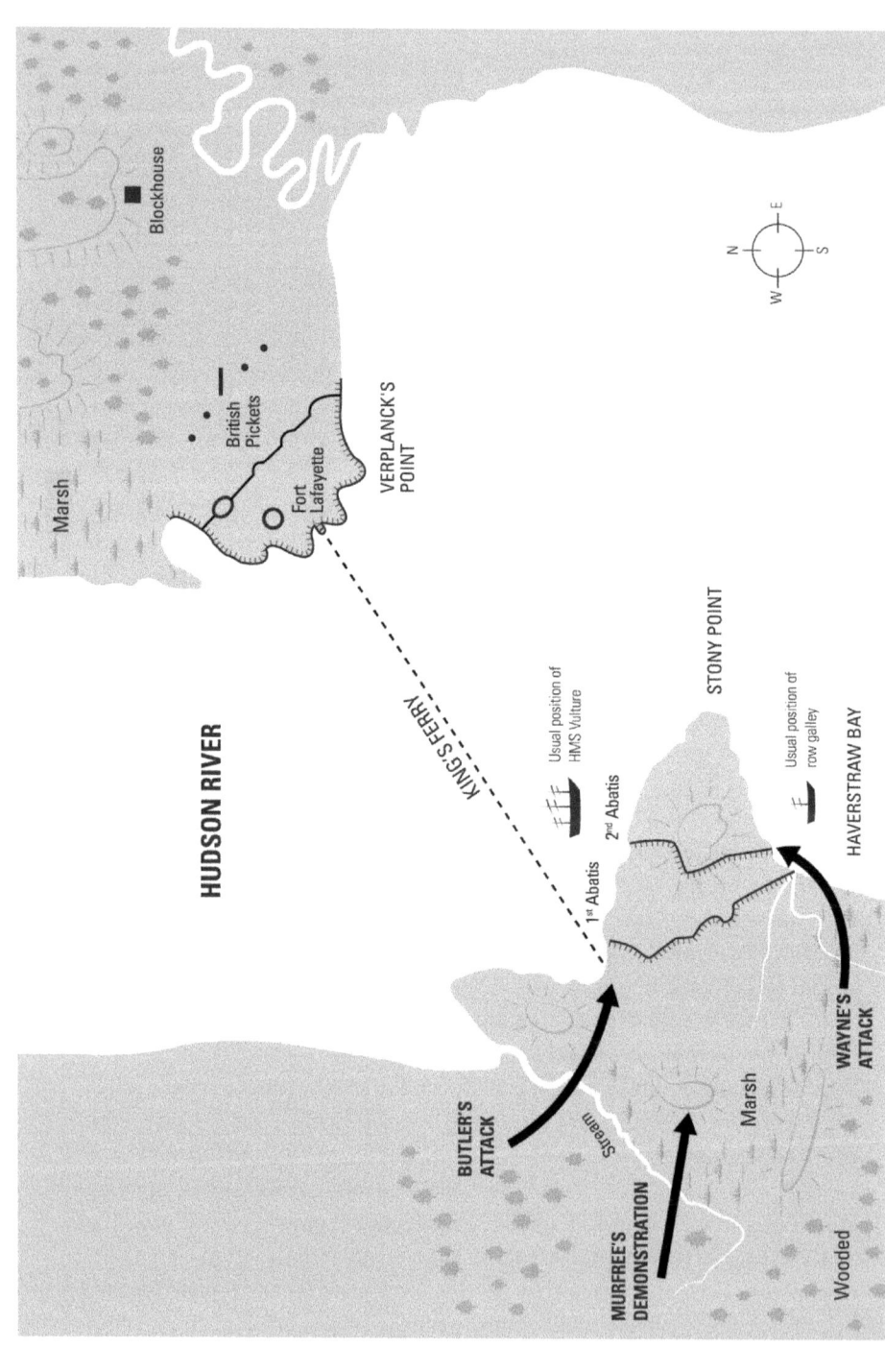

On May 5, the Virginia expedition, the opening move of the campaign of 1779, departed New York harbor (the same force that the spy Abraham Woodhull reported). Commodore Collier in HMS *Rainbow* commanded the Royal Navy contingent of seven warships. Twenty-eight transports carried the raiding force of 1,800 soldiers from the Forty-second Regiment, the Guards, Volunteers of Ireland, and Hessian Regiment of Prince Charles, all under the command of Maj. Gen. Edward Matthew. Five days later the squadron arrived at the mouth of the Elizabeth River near Portsmouth, Virginia, the first target of the raid.

Collier sailed up the Elizabeth River to a point half a mile from Portsmouth and Ft. Nelson, which was intended to protect the port with a garrison of 100 soldiers. The Royal Navy gunboats and frigates opened cannon fire on the shore, and a red flag from the *Rainbow*'s mast signaled for Matthew's troops to begin landing in flatboats (the boats that Woodhull and Caleb Brewster reported being built through the winter). Collier remembered: "The sight was beautiful and formed the finest regatta in the world." The first division of Matthew's force landed without opposition and the flatboats returned to the transports to land the second division and field artillery. Collier and Matthew planned to take Ft. Nelson the next morning.

"Everything was prepared for the attack," the commodore wrote, "but the enemy, with great cowardice, abandoned it in the night and fled, leaving the thirteen stripes *flying*."[24] Matthew's force occupied the towns of Portsmouth, Gosport and Norfolk, where they found a Continental frigate and two French merchantmen burning, set alight by the retreating Americans. In raids all along the Elizabeth River over the course of the next two weeks, Matthew and Collier destroyed or captured 137 ships and seized tons of artillery, gunpowder and provisions that had been bound for the Continental Army. Collier wanted to permanently garrison Portsmouth for a naval base but Clinton's orders called for Matthew to return to New York when the raids were successful. Collier acquiesced to returning, and the ships headed back to New York City.

Opposite: The British capture of this crossing site in the summer of 1779 threatened American control of the Hudson River as well as the Continental Army's supply chain to New England. Gen. Clinton ordered the ferry site fortified, and believed that Gen. Washington would commit the bulk of the Continental Army to re-taking the area (adapted by the author and Lara Dalinsky from the 1784 British army map *A Plan of the Surprise of Stoney Point by a Detachment of the American Army commanded by Brigr. Genl. Wayne, on the 15th July 1779*, held at The Society of the Cincinnati, Washington, D.C.).

Collier's squadron sailed into New York harbor on May 28, and the next phase of the offensive was already underway. The same day, Clinton sent fifteen regiments under the command of Maj. Gen. John Vaughan — nearly half of the forces in the New York City area — out from Kingsbridge, at the northern tip of Manhattan, on a sweep into the no-man's-land of Westchester County. There was no opposition from the American militia or the Skinners that so bravely preyed on civilians, and within a day Vaughan's troops controlled the southern five miles of the county from Eastchester to Phillipsburg (near what is now Yonkers) on the Hudson. Vaughan set up headquarters at the Georgian mansion known as Phillipse Manor Hall, the former home of Frederick Phillipse III, a Loyalist who had been forced to flee the area.

When Collier's ships came into New York harbor, Clinton ordered the transports that carried General Matthew's infantry regiments, as well as the frigates *Camilla* and *Raisonable*, to continue up the river and join Vaughan's force. On May 30 Gen. Clinton and Capt. Andre also sailed up the Hudson to the Phillipse House, where they boarded the *Camilla* with Commodore Collier and then continued up the river with 1,150 soldiers under Gen. James Pattison to take King's Ferry. Clinton remembered, "the wind being fortunately fair, our progress was quick."[25]

Clinton planned a three-pronged attack to take King's Ferry; Pattison's force, consisting of the Seventeenth, Sixty-third, and Sixty-fourth regiments of infantry and a detachment of Hessian Jagers, would land on the west bank of Haverstraw Bay, south of King's Ferry, and move north to seize the blockhouse at Stony Point and the ferry's western end. From southern Westchester County the navy transports would also take a second force under Gen. Vaughan consisting of 2,800 soldiers from the Light Infantry, Grenadiers, Hessian Grenadiers, Thirty-third Regiment, part of the British Legion, the Loyal American Regiment, and Maj. Patrick Ferguson's rifle corps and land at Teller's Point on the east bank of the Hudson. Vaughan would then move eight miles north to take the eastern terminus of the ferry and Fort Lafayette. Collier's warships would sail up the river in between the two forts and bombard both positions.

Pattison's landings began at 4:00 P.M. the next day, three miles south of Stony Point, and his men headed north for their objective. Clinton accompanied Pattison's column and recalled, "As soon as our little fleet came into view, the enemy's troops ... set fire to a large blockhouse at Stony Point and, evacuating their works, drew up on the hills with some show of an intended resistance. But, as the King's troops approached nearer, they fell back and left us the possession without a conflict."[26] Gen. Pattison said, "The Troops had no sooner gained the Heights of Stony Point, than Measures were taken to land the Artillery. The Moon favored this Operation, and admitted of its being carried on during the Whole Night." He described the terrain of Stony Point as "very craggy, and of uncommon steep Steep Ascent."[27] It took fifty-eight men with ropes to get four cannon and three mortars to the crest of the hill.

Gen. Vaughan landed at Teller's Point on the evening of May 31, and his column moved quickly toward Fort Lafayette. At dawn the next day, the cannon on Stony Point, the *Camilla*, the sloop of war *Vulture*, and a row-galley (probably the *Cornwallis*) from Collier's squadron opened fire on Fort Lafayette. Gen. Vaughan's troops surrounded the fort on the land and cut off any avenue of escape for its garrison of seventy soldiers. The cannon of Fort Lafayette fired back; but Clinton, who observed the action with Gen. Vaughan's corps, wrote that — with the "well directed and incessant fire" from Stony Point and the presence of Vaughan's infantry — the garrison of Fort Lafayette was "obliged to surrender at discretion."[28] Clinton sent Capt. Andre under a flag of truce to demand the fort's surrender. The American commander, Capt. Thomas Armstrong of the Fifth North Carolina Regiment, later explained that the British cannonade killed many of his gun crews, that the artillery on Stony Point dominated the area, and that his little fort was "entirely inclosed by land and water without the least Hope of Relief from any quarter."[29] Armstrong asked Andre if the British would permit his garrison to march out of the fort with the "honors of war" where they could fly their colors, terms that were justified under the Articles of War since his garrison had resisted to the best of its abilities. Andre offered him no terms except that the Americans would be treated as prisoners of war, not traitorous citizens in rebellion.

With his garrison surrounded and outnumbered twenty to one, Armstrong had no choice but to accept the terms. The Americans surrendered at mid-day on June 1, as the capitulation accords stated: "On the Glacis of Fort La Fayette, June 1st, 1779. His Excellency Genl. Sir Henry Clinton, and Commodore Sir Geo. Collier grant to the garrison of Fort La Fayette Terms of Safety to the Persons and Property (contained in the Fort) of the Garrison, they surrendering themselves Prisoners of war. The Officers shall be permitted to wear their Side Arms. John Andre, Aid de Camp."[30] Small numbers of American militia remained near King's Ferry, and, Gen. Pattison wrote, "the militia were impertinently troublesome by coming down in small Bodies, and firing upon our Jager Post, but five or Six of them having been dropt by our Rifle Shot, they thought fit to disappear, and have given us no further Disturbance."[31] Commodore Collier later wrote with satisfaction that the British were "masters of King's Ferry."[32]

On June 4, taking half of the force at King's Ferry with him, Clinton returned to Phillipsburg to be ready to strike at the Continental Army if it moved. What he called "a respectable force" of nearly 2,000 troops remained at King's Ferry under Gen. Vaughan's command, and they had much work to do to hold on to the crossing.[33] The existing defenses of Ft. Lafayette at Verplanck's Point consisted of a wooden palisade, earthen parapets, a ditch, and a wooden blockhouse, all of which were not strong enough to withstand a determined assault, as the British proved during their own attack. Commodore Collier noted that the defenses at Stony Point "were not half completed" and the Americans had burned the position's only blockhouse.[34] The two sides of King's Ferry were almost indefensible in their current state, and Vaughan's soldiers went to work improving the fortifications.

After stopping at Phillipsburg, Clinton went back to New York City, where he met with his Loyalist confidant William Smith on June 7. Smith was familiar with the general's usual downcast disposition so he was surprised to see Clinton "very happy on having seized the Mouth of the Highlands."[35] Clinton later wrote that he believed British control of King's Ferry "being on the great communication [line] below the Highlands between the southern and eastern colonies ... the inhabitants as well as their army must by the loss of it be thrown forty miles back and obliged to cross the mountains twice by a circuit of at least ninety [miles]" and that he "fully expected" the Americans to risk their army in an action to retake the crossing site.[36] Clinton also confidently expected to push into New Jersey or New England from King's Ferry, and he plied Smith for detailed information on the terrain along the upper Hudson. Two days before he had departed New York City to take the expedition up the Hudson, Clinton had confidently told Smith that the rebellion was "in the basket" and that he expected "to be presented soon with the Heads of some of the Rebel leaders."[37] With the successful raid in Virginia and the capture of King's Ferry, the campaign was unfolding exactly as Clinton planned.

V

"A Very Interesting Crisis"

Middlebrook, New Jersey, May 1779

Though the Culper Ring warned Washington about the beginning of the British offensive, the spies failed to alert their commander about Clinton's attack on King's Ferry. After Gen. Matthew's expedition to Virginia departed, the Culper agent Abraham Woodhull sent a somewhat belated summary of the regiments that formed Matthew's force and some updates on Redcoat units around Manhattan; but he had no information on Clinton's preparations to move up the Hudson. Woodhull still feared discovery by the British, writing, "I am very observant of them and think I am in continual danger." He curtailed his operations in May.[1]

Washington became so concerned for intelligence from New York that he enquired if Lewis Pintard, the civilian commissary for American prisoners in New York, could act as an agent in the Culper Ring. Pintard refused to take part in any espionage activity.[2] Elijah Hunter, the double agent who provided information to both sides, filled the gap on May 21 when he told Washington that he recently had met several times with Gen. Clinton, Gen. William Tryon and Capt. Andre and that the British officers were "very petulant" for detailed information about the Hudson forts and had asked his opinion on whether a British attack in Connecticut could lure the Yankee garrison at West Point away from the river.[3] Hunter did not tell Washington what answers he provided to the questions, but his letter was warning that Clinton planned an offensive along the Hudson.

In a candid letter to his brother that same week, Washington said that the Continental Army was "illy enough prepared Heaven knows," to defend against a British offensive. He called the army's ammunition supply "far from being sufficient."[4] The army also lacked enough wagons to transport baggage, tents, entrenching tools, ammunition and provisions. Gen. Steuben's "Blue Book" with the army's new regulations had been recently completed and was still being distributed, and Steuben was inspecting each regiment to gauge its readiness to take the field. The dispersed camps that had served so well as winter quarters now left the army too spread out to defend the Hudson River Valley. The Middlebrook encampment with the Pennsylvania, Virginia and Maryland divisions, and the Continental Artillery, a total of 8,230 soldiers, was fifty-five miles from the Hudson. Another 2,340 Connecticut troops and the Continental cavalry were thirty miles from the scene at Redding, Connecticut.[5] The army was also short on a good portion of the new recruits expected for the summer because the British raid into Virginia had compelled Washington to leave all of the state's troops, as well as all soldiers who were on furlough there, to remain in the Old Dominion, just as Clinton intended. Washington lamented to Gen. Horatio Gates: "This is no small deduction from our force here and will proportionably embarrass [hinder] our measure."[6] If the British suddenly moved up the Hudson, it would take the divisions in New Jersey five to six days to march to the area. The only force that prevented Clinton from seizing control of the river were 2,000 soldiers of the Highlands Department that manned the Hudson fortifications of West Point and Forts Clinton, Montgomery, and Lafayette, and the blockhouse at Stony Point, all under the command of Maj. Gen. Alexander McDougall.

The forty-eight-year-old McDougall had come to America from Scotland at the age of six. His first employment was assisting his father on the family dairy farm outside New York City, but at fourteen he went to sea as a merchant seaman and rose to captain his own ship. During the French and Indian War McDougall commanded two privateers that raided French shipping, but he retired from the seafaring life at the end of the war. He converted his assets to purchasing land, and though he was prosperous, McDougall spoke with a rough Scottish burr and had rough country manners that prevented him from being fully accepted into New York's genteel society. Nevertheless, as tensions with Britain grew he was a leader of New York City's Sons of Liberty and was jailed twice for authoring broadsides that railed against the Crown. In June 1775 Congress commissioned him a colonel in the Continental Army with command of the First New York Regiment, and in 1776 he applied his sailor's skills when he planned Washington's retreat from Long Island. He fought at the battles of White Plains and Germantown, and Washington appointed him the commander of the Highlands Department in 1778. In the spring of 1779 McDougall's headquarters were at Peekskill, five miles north of King's Ferry on the east bank of the Hudson.

Several areas along the Hudson, including West Point, the river forts, and the Continental supply depot at Fishkill, were possible targets for a Clinton's attack. Washington could not move his army until the British intent was clear, but he instructed McDougall to improve West Point's defenses and he placed Brig. Gen. Samuel Parson's brigade of Connecticut troops at Redding under McDougall's command. In New Jersey, Gen. Steuben inspected the Pennsylvania Division commanded by Gen. Arthur St. Clair, the officer whom Anthony Wayne feuded with over rank, and pronounced it ready for action. On May 28 Col. Alexander Hamilton, Washington's aide-de-camp, told St. Clair "recent intelligence indicates the probability of the enemy being on the front of some important movement [so] get your division ready to march as soon as possible."[7] An officer in St. Clair's division wrote, "The day after tomorrow we shall decamp — our destination up the [Hudson] River; where then I know not, but Heaven and the dear genius of Freedom will be our guides."[8]

Intelligence confirming the British objectives then flooded into Continental Army headquarters. On May 29 Col. Israel Shreve, commander of the Second New Jersey Regiment, informed Washington that a captain from his unit described as "a very intelligent person" recently had returned from New York City through a prisoner exchange and reported that for several days British soldiers had been loading "a great number" of provisions and artillery shells aboard transport ships and that "all the shipping in the harbor are ordered to be in readiness to sail upon the shortest notice."[9] The same day as Shreve's report, McDougall sent Washington a summary of his interrogation of Corporal Patrick Rogers, "a native of Ireland" who deserted along with two comrades from the Loyalist unit called Lord Cathcart's Legion. Rogers said that the previous evening he heard officers read orders for Crown forces to march through Westchester County, and that six regiments had embarked from New York on the twenty-seventh to sail up the Hudson. "It was given that they were going to attack some Fort up the River," reported the eager Rogers. McDougall added, "The Enemy's march to [White Plains] is very probable but I have had no advice of the appearance of the Enemy on the River."[10] Nevertheless, McDougall ordered Gen. Parsons to move to Peekskill, alerted Connecticut governor Jonathan Trumbull of the impending British incursion towards his border, and suggested the governor keep his militia ready for action with six days' provisions.

By that time it was clear that Clinton was moving through eastern New York and toward the Hudson fortifications. The same day he received Shreve's and McDougall's intelligence, Washington ordered St. Clair to march his Pennsylvanians north for the Hudson Highlands and block the British advance towards West Point. Soldiers on furlough were ordered to immediately rejoin their units. On June 1 Washington directed the entire army in New Jersey to be "in the most perfect readiness to march at the shortest notice."[11] Maj. Gen. Alexander Stirling's Virginia Division departed camp the next day. "If you cannot procure waggons for the transportation of your heavy baggage," Washington told Stirling, "you will prepare to move without it."[12] As he had with St. Clair, Washington authorized Stirling to take any measures necessary to block an attack on West Point. The divisions headed due north from Middlebrook towards Pompton, New Jersey, and then straight north from there for the town of Smith's Clove, New York, west of West Point, where they would consolidate before marching the final twelve miles to the Hudson. The Maryland Division under Maj. Gen. Johann De Kalb, a Bavarian volunteer, was scheduled to depart on June 3. The Yankee divisions would make one of their longest and most rapid marches of the war up to that point, and Washington called this major repositioning of his army to maintain control of the Hudson "a very interesting crisis."[13]

To move rapidly, Washington ordered that "the army should divest itself of every article that can be spared, and take the field as light as possible."[14] Gen. Knox, Washington's artillery commander, took only light field guns on the march and left the heavy cannon to be brought along later by oxen. Washington also told his commanders that despite the haste of the march they were to "observe an exact conformity to the new Regulations for the order and discipline of the army."[15] The regulations required that daily marching begin at dawn with a cannon shot fired from each division headquarters, followed by drummers beating the call "general," which signaled the men to pack their tents and equipment. The light infantry companies fanned out along the designated route to scout for the whereabouts of the enemy. After the light troops advanced three or four miles down the road, a group of regular infantry companies followed as the advance guard, packed closely in column formation of four to five men abreast. About three hundred yards behind the advance guard marched the main body, with infantry companies in another tight column. In wooded country, "flankers" moved out 100 yards on both sides of the road to prevent the division from being surprised. Three to four hundred yards behind the main body came the rear guard and a detail of cavalry to collect "strollers"—men who fell out from the march. The division's wagons, if they had them, rolled behind the rear guard.

During a forced march the column did not halt until dusk. Scouts selected a level campsite, the cavalry monitored the roads in the direction of the enemy, and the regiments planted their flags in a "color line," behind which the men pitched their tents after the wagons arrived. The process was repeated every day until the army reached its destination.[16] During the march to the Hudson the lack of wagon transport slowed the army's pace, and when McDougall told Washington that his posts on the river were short of supplies, Washington replied that McDougall had to hang on until the army could reach him. He sent Brig. Gen. Duportail, a French volunteer and trained military engineer, ahead to assist in improving West Point's fortifications, and he assigned the Second Continental Dragoons, camped in Connecticut, to McDougall's command. He reassured the Scot: "My anxiety on the present occasion would be extreme were it not for the perfect confidence I have in your care and exertion."[17]

Washington received a report about the loss of King's Ferry on June 2, and three days later McDougall confirmed the account, saying, "While the enemy is master of the River he can subject us to many Embarrassments, and it is devoutly to be wished a junction of the Army was formed." As a postscript McDougall also addressed Clinton's move into Westchester County, and said, "If the enemy continue in his present direction, Westchester will be ravaged of all its stock by this—and great bodies of militia cannot be kept together at this season." He sent no good news. Enemy ships sailed back to New York, he was told, to get fresh troops and heavy artillery and "from this it would seem that West Point is his objective."[18] On June 5 Col. William Malcolm, posted on the west bank of the Hudson with the New York militia, wrote to Washington: "The enemy's fleet consisting of about 70 sail—many of them very small—are at King's Ferry—a body of their troops are on the east side [of the] river [and] a very few at Stony Point."

Malcolm said that Redcoats pushed into the countryside and "burnt a few houses—but have got no stores at all." He understood that Fort Montgomery stood between the British and West Point and emphasized his determination: "Your Excellency may be assured that everything in my power will be done for the defense of the garrison."[19] Washington sent the colonel his agreement on the importance of holding Fort Montgomery, stated his confidence that the New York militiamen could defend the area, and asked Malcolm to keep him informed of any further developments. The next day Washington moved his headquarters from Middlebrook and joined the divisions marching north. Before leaving, he sent a summary of the situation to Congress; all the troops that wintered at Middlebrook were marching rapidly north with St. Clair's Pennsylvanians in the lead, followed by Stirling's Virginians, and De Kalb's Marylanders bringing up the rear. McDougall defended West Point with five New England brigades and North Carolina troops. He told Congress that "the very great difficulty of procuring horses and waggons and the scarcity of forage have unavoidably retarded our preparations," but that the army would "press forward with all diligence and do every thing in our power to disappoint the enemy."[20]

Rushing towards the Hudson and strung out over miles of roads, the army was vulnerable to being attacked piecemeal. Washington needed intelligence about enemy movements more than ever, and he called on every available agent. To the spy John Mercereau, who operated on Staten Island, he pointedly demanded, "The particular Regiments that are on the Island, their exact quarters, whether at their forts, and if not at what distance from them, are matters I wish to be solved in."[21] He asked Col. John Neilson of the New Jersey militia to find out "the number of men on Staten Island, where they are stationed, whether collected, or at different places, if works are thrown up at each post, and their respective force in men. These things I want ascertained without delay."[22] Culper Ring spy Abraham Woodhull reported that the British expected a fleet to arrive from England in June with 10,000 reinforcements.[23]

But to defend the Hudson, Washington needed specific information about the location and strength of enemy units close to the river. From a temporary headquarters at Ringwood, on the New York-New Jersey border, he told Maj. Henry Lee, commander of a separate unit of cavalry and scouts, to scour the country on the west bank of the Hudson for signs of enemy activity, "their situations, movement and designs and give me the earliest advice of every occurrence." Washington warned the major: "Your utmost vigilance and attention will be necessary as you will be entirely detached and unsupported, and will act in a very disaffected country, the inhabitants [of which] will give the enemy every kind of intelligence."[24]

Washington and his aides arrived at Smith's Clove on June 9 and set up headquarters at Smith's Tavern. The divisions of St. Clair, Stirling, and

De Kalb reached the Clove two days later. Col. Christian Febiger, the thirty-three-year-old commander of the Second Virginia Regiment, said that his unit arrived at Smith's Clove with "men and horses almost fatigued to death."[25] Washington deployed the army in an arc facing east and south, towards the British. As called for in the new army regulations, each division sent scouts down the roads that led to the enemy, sergeants inspected the soldiers' arms and equipment to see if they were still serviceable after the long march, and at Washington's expressed order, all officers familiarized themselves with the area and possible avenues for enemy attack. Two cannon fired from De Kalb's division were the signal for an alarm, "upon which the troops will get under arms as expeditiously and as light as possible."[26] Col. Febiger summarized the army's situation: "We are within 8 miles of the enemy, nothing but a mountain separates us, and we know not when or where [they] might move next."[27]

But by that time the crisis was lessening. The majority of the Continental Army was within a day's march of the Hudson and could contest any further British advances. Brig. Gen. Samuel Parsons, McDougall's commander at West Point, also told Washington that his garrison was "in high spirits and are very desirous to receive the Enemy attack." Parsons hedged his assertion a little by adding that he could not promise that his men would successfully hold West Point but would do all they could "to secure that honor to themselves and their country."[28] Despite Parsons's only partially comforting statement, on June 9 Washington told Gov. Clinton of New York and Col. Malcolm, the militia commander, that they could release their soldiers "with my warmest thanks, for the zeal and alacrity with which they have turned out upon the present interesting occasion."[29]

Though West Point and the Highlands were thoroughly defended, the British still threatened to control the Hudson as long as they held the King's Ferry crossing at Stony Point and Verplanck's Point. "[The British] continue fortifying and no doubt mean to keep possession of those posts," Washington wrote Congress, "The natural strength of the ground with very little help of art will make them inaccessible to us in our present circumstances. The advantages of holding them will be important to the enemy, the inconveniences to us great.... The extent and difficulty of land transportation considerably increased, a new resort and sanctuary afforded to the disaffected in these parts of the country, and a new door opened to draw supplies distress and corrupt the inhabitants."[30] Merely stopping Gen. Clinton short of West Point was not enough. Washington would eventually have to force the Redcoats back into Manhattan to regain control of the Hudson.

VI

"Men That Will Support the Reputation of His Regiment"

The Hudson Highlands, June 1779

When Col. William Malcolm informed Washington about the British landings at King's Ferry and noted the importance of holding Ft. Montgomery, he suggested that "if a few companies of Light Infantry could be sent here it could be useful."[1] The general agreed that there was great utility in a light infantry force but admitted to Malcolm, "I have not made a detachment of this kind."[2] Brig. Gen. Anthony Wayne, whom Washington had designated to be the commander of the Light Infantry back in February, was on furlough in Philadelphia when the British offensive became apparent. Washington sent at least one letter recalling him to the army in May; but the message apparently never reached Wayne and the army moved north without him or a Light Infantry corps.[3] But in June British forces moved no further north up the Hudson than King's Ferry, and the Continental Army's pause at Smith's Clove gave Washington time to bring the Corps of Light Infantry together.

On June 12, Washington ordered each regiment at Smith's Clove to fill a quota, by either selection or accepting volunteers, to create a sixteen-company Corps of Light Infantry. The general orders required the thirteen Virginia regiments at Smith's Clove to provide 247 soldiers to form six companies. The eight Pennsylvania regiments and a Delaware Regiment sent 246 men for another six companies; and seven Maryland regiments provided 164 troops to form four companies. The regiments were also ordered to select one captain, a lieutenant, and three sergeants to lead each company. To meet the requirements, commanders could send the light infantry companies that were part of every regiment or choose soldiers from throughout their units. However, Washington told them to "be particularly careful in the choice of the men, which is a duty, the good of the service and the credit of their respective regiments equally demand; When it is considered that in every army the honor of a regiment and that of its Light Company are intimately connected, the officer commanding it cannot but be solicitous to furnish men that will support the reputation of his regiment."[4] Three days after Washington's order over 750 soldiers had either volunteered or been selected for the Light Infantry, enough to form all sixteen companies. The commander-in-chief's staff, probably Col. Alexander Scammell, the adjutant general, organized the Corps of Light Infantry like a typical brigade of infantry, composed of two regiments, each commanded by a colonel. Two battalions, commanded by a major or a senior captain, composed each regiment. Battalions had four companies, commanded by captains.[5] Scammell had the lion's share of work to organize the Light Infantry, but Gen. Washington personally named some of the senior officers.

Continental Army officers were usually members of the gentleman class that existed at the time, and this social status heavily influenced how they led their soldiers, interacted with brother officers, and acted in combat. Community leadership was the obligation of every gentleman in eighteenth-century American society, and the Continental Army mirrored this structure, appointing the natural community leaders as officers over the farmers and workers comprising the ranks of private soldiers and sergeants. With the status came obligations that were unwritten but well-known: a gentleman was expected to live with style but also meet his family and community responsibilities. Gentleman strictly followed a code of honor that required them to be honest, straightforward in their dealings, and execute their duties to the best of their abilities. Infractions against the code of honor could damage a man's reputation, bring into question his qualifications for his post, and destroy his status as a true gentleman. Officers jealously guarded their reputations against slights to a level that we would consider extreme today.

Dueling between officers over perceived insults came into vogue at Valley Forge. Gen. Anthony Wayne had a heightened sense of honor, and in January 1779 he challenged Gen. Charles Lee to a duel after Lee commented about Wayne in terms that the Pennsylvanian thought damaged "the Military Character of a Gentleman."[6] The situation blew over as both men cooled. Class differences kept many Continental officers distant from their soldiers while in camp, but in battle, honor required officers to lead men courageously by personal example. During the Revolution patriotic Americans expected gentlemen to be committed to the cause of American liberty. There are many facets to effective leadership, but the strength of belief that the officers had in the American cause, combined with their abilities to set stirring examples and earn the loyalty of their soldiers, was a significant factor in successful Continental Army officers' combat leadership. In June 1779, dozens of officers from different regiments and states came together to lead the Corps of Light Infantry, and the gentleman's code of honor was their common bond.[7]

Col. Richard Butler, a friend of General Wayne's from the Pennsylvania Line, took command of one regiment. Before the war Richard and his brother William operated a frontier trading post near Pittsburgh, and Richard first saw combat as a junior militia officer during Pontiac's Rebellion in 1764. When the Revolution began, Richard first served as the Continental Congress' agent to the Native American tribes on the frontier, and he gained a captain's commission in the Eighth Pennsylvania. He proved himself courageous as the second-in-command of Morgan's Rifle Corps at the battle of Saratoga, was promoted to lieutenant-colonel in 1777, and was in temporary command of the Ninth Pennsylvania when Washington selected him for the Light Infantry. Butler would turn thirty-six years of age on July 1. In addition to William he had three other brothers who served as Continental Army officers. Gen. Wayne still had not rejoined the army, so Butler took temporary command of the corps as it came together at Smith's Clove.

Three-year army veteran John Stewart, a major from the Second Maryland, gained command of a battalion of four companies of Maryland troops within Butler's regiment. A contemporary wrote that Stewart, who was six feet tall and handsome, had "a fine presence for an officer,"[8] but another, who said that he had a "natural vehemence" of passion, probably captured Stewart's personality best.[9] As a lieutenant in 1777, Stewart had been in charge of a detachment that became cut off during the withdrawal of American troops from Staten Island. He continued fighting even after his men were surrounded, but then he coolly walked toward British lines with a white handkerchief on the tip of his sword to surrender.[10] Captured, he escaped from a British prison ship, swam to the New Jersey shore, and rejoined his regiment. Stewart fought at Brandywine, Germantown, and Monmouth and earned the nickname "Crazy Jack." He was twenty-one years old in 1779.

Four companies of Pennsylvania troops, commanded by Lt. Col.

VI. "Men That Will Support the Reputation of His Regiment"

Samuel Hay, formed the second battalion under Butler. Thirty-nine years old, Hay had served in the Sixth, Seventh, and Tenth Pennsylvania regiments since January 1776. He was in the thick of the fighting on the terrible night at Paoli in 1777 and was a close friend of Gen. Wayne.

Gen. Washington named Col. Christian Febiger, the officer who described his fatigued soldiers and horses when they arrived at Smith's Clove, to command the second regiment in the Corps. Febiger was a native of Denmark and had received a military education at Copenhagen while in his teens. He served briefly with Danish forces in the West Indies on the staff of his uncle, the governor of Santa Cruz (now St. Croix), and had stopped in the North Carolina colony on the way back to Denmark. Febiger returned to America permanently in 1772, married Elizabeth Carson, the daughter of a Philadelphia merchant, and entered the lumber, fish and horse businesses in Boston and Salem. Ten days after the Lexington Alarm in April 1775 Febiger joined Colonel Samuel Gerrish's Massachusetts Militia Regiment and fought at Bunker Hill. Later the same year his regiment was part of the Canadian invasion and Febiger earned the respect of his fellow officers for his martial skills and gentlemanly behavior.[11] Captured by the British during the American attack on Quebec City, Febiger was released on parole in August 1776 and formally exchanged — allowing him to return to active service — in January 1777.

Colonel Christian Febiger. A veteran of Bunker Hill, Quebec, Brandywine, Germantown, and Monmouth, he did not want to leave his command of the Second Virginia Regiment when Washington appointed him to lead a regiment in the Corps of Light Infantry. Around his neck hangs a "gorget," an officer's badge of rank (Library of Congress).

He reentered the army as the second in command of the Eleventh Virginia (possibly from connections with other prisoners during his captivity), and fought with valor at Brandywine and Germantown. Congress promoted him to the rank of colonel and command of the Second Virginia, and after enduring the winter at Valley Forge, Febiger led his regiment well at the battle of Monmouth. He was, by all appearances, devoted to his wife and called himself "Old Denmark" in letters to her. In mid–June Febiger wrote to her: "Agreeable to orders of yesterday I am to take command of 2 battalions of Light Infantry for the present campaign." But he wondered why "His Excellency" Washington appointed him to the duty, saying "he knows I prefer my Reg't." Still, Febiger wrote that he was "determined on all counts to preserve the Dignity of my Reg't, which is at present in excellent order."[12]

Thomas Posey, painted by James Peale in 1795. A neighbor of George Washington's before the war, Posey fought at Saratoga and Monmouth before he took command of a battalion of light infantry under Col. Christian Febiger (reproduced by permission of the Society of the Cincinnati, Washington, D.C.).

Four companies from Virginia, commanded by twenty-five-year-old Maj. Thomas Posey, formed one of the two battalions in Febiger's regiment. A native of Fairfax County, Virginia (his father and Washington were friends), Posey had fought in a militia expedition against the Indians in 1772 and was a saddler in Virginia's Botetcourt County when community leaders asked him to head a company of riflemen for the Seventh Virginia in January 1776. Posey led his company well at Saratoga and Monmouth. He took temporary command of the Continental Army's Rifle Corps in July 1778 and successfully led the unit on an expedition to fight the Indians in New York. Promoted to major in December the same year, Posey had temporary command of the Seventh Virginia at the Middlebrook encampment. His wife and infant son had recently died of disease back in Botetourt County, and Posey was doubtless still grieving their loss when Washington chose him to lead a battalion of Light Infantry.

Lt. Col. Francois-Louis Tesseidre, the Marquis de Fleury, took command of the second of Febiger's battalions composed of two companies each from Virginia and Pennsylvania. Thirty years old, de Fleury had eleven years of service in the French army and was one of the many foreign volunteers in the Continental Army. European military tradition allowed officers to serve in other armies for experience, promotions and adventure, and many foreign officers began joining the American service in 1776. Congress welcomed the volunteers because they brought vital technical skills, especially in artillery and engineering, and Congress deeply desired European recognition. A trained engineer and veteran of France's campaign on Corsica, de Fleury volunteered for the Continental Army in 1777 along with the Marquis de Lafayette. He fought at Brandywine, wintered at Valley Forge, underwent Steuben's training program, served as a volunteer without pay in a corps of riflemen, and gained a commission as a captain in the Continental Engineers. As commander of an artillery company at Fort Mifflin on the Delaware River, de Fleury defended the post against British assaults and was wounded just as the fort was evacuated.[13] He also led a troop of cavalry, served as an assistant to Gen. Steuben, and commanded American troops in the battle for Newport, Rhode Island. Congress promoted him to lt. col. of engineers in November 1778. Gen. Washington called the Frenchmen "a young man of talents" and "brave, active, and intelligent."[14]

In many cases the junior officers of the Light Infantry were as experienced as their commanders. Twenty-seven-year-old Capt. Thomas Boude, commander of one of the Pennsylvania companies, was known as an "active and energetic" young gentleman.[15] He joined the Fourth Pennsylvania with Anthony Wayne in 1776 and was a veteran of Brandywine, Paoli, Germantown, and Monmouth. In the summer of 1779 Boude commanded the light infantry company of the Fifth Pennsylvania. He, his company lieutenant, James McCullough, and all forty-four soldiers of Boude's company volunteered for the Corps of Light Infantry.[16]

All of the officers in the assembled companies had served for at least two years in Maj. Posey's battalion, with the exception of Ensign Thomas Wallace, who had been a member of the Eighth Virginia since only June

2. Lt. James Gibbon from the Sixth Pennsylvania was twenty years old but had served since 1776 and was taken prisoner during the New York campaign. Surgeon Samuel McKenzie had served with the Second Pennsylvania since March 1776 and was captured at the battle of Trois Riviere, Anthony Wayne's first combat action.[17] Thirty-nine years of age, McKenzie was also close friends with Gen. Arthur St. Clair, the officer with whom Wayne feuded over seniority in rank.[18]

Once the volunteers for the Light Corps assembled, Adjutant General Scammell inspected the ranks to ensure that they met Washington's expectations. As the former commander of a New Hampshire regiment and veteran of heavy fighting in the Saratoga campaign, Scammell was a good judge of soldiers. He reported to Washington afterward that the Light Infantry "almost to a man are composed of proper sized well built men from five feet seven to five feet nine inches high, who have been in Actual Service two, three, and Some almost four years, a very few excepted, who are natives. Four only out of the sixteen companies were ordered to be exchanged for better men. The arms and accoutrements (except the 8th Va. Regiment) are in good order and complete. A few of the Men are in want of shoes who were absent at the last draught. The Baron Steuben is concerting measures with the officers of the Virginia and Pennsylvania Lines to have three incomplete companies filled up immediately."[19]

The fact that some of the men still needed shoes hints at the army's continuing supply problems. Scammell's report also shows that the soldiers were a little above the average age and height for the Continental Army. American soldier demographics varied during different periods of the Revolution; but in the middle years of the war, Virginia troops averaged between twenty-three and twenty-four years of age, Pennsylvanians averaged about twenty-six, and Marylanders twenty-three. The records of the Light Infantry are fragmentary but available information shows that the average age of the enlisted soldiers was twenty-five, and twenty-nine for officers. Most Continental soldiers stood between 5'6" and 5'8" tall, and if Scammell's observation that the Light Infantrymen were between 5'7" and 5'9", Gen. Wayne's men were slightly taller than most American troops.[20]

The Light Infantry enlisted men were also tough, seasoned veterans. Pvt. James Noble joined the Sixth Virginia in 1777 and was wounded at the battle of Germantown when he attempted to save his regiment's colors after the young officer charged to defend them abandoned his post. Noble returned to the Sixth Virginia at Christmas after nearly three months'

VI. "Men That Will Support the Reputation of His Regiment"

recovery in a hospital, and his captain informed him that he might as well have gone home, since they had believed him to be dead. Noble went on to fight at Monmouth. He had no record of his exact birth date but believed he was about nineteen years of age in 1779.[21] Pvt. Marshall Burton from the Eighth Virginia originally enlisted in an artillery company, transferred to the infantry, and then volunteered for the Light Infantry.[22] Pvt. John Bray, from the same regiment, was wounded at Brandywine.[23] Twenty-five-year-old Sergeant Robert Humble enlisted in the Tenth Pennsylvania in 1777, fought at Brandywine, Paoli, and Germantown, survived Valley Forge, and fought again at Monmouth.[24] Twenty-four-year-old Vincent Vass, a private in De Fleury's battalion, was from Spotsylvania County, Virginia, where he was fortunate to receive an informal education from a local widow. He signed on with the First Virginia Regiment in 1778 along with other soldiers who had the understanding that they would not serve outside their home state.

Vass recalled that when they received orders to join Washington's army in Pennsylvania, "the regiment refused to go, but after some confusion we were called up again and orders red,—them that was willing to go was to have furlow to go by home, their wages to be raised from $5 to 8, and a bounty of land.... On them conditions we agreed, my officers resigned & I did not go [home]—we marched off & joined General Washington's army at the Valley forge...." He remembered when an officer approached his battalion at Smith's Clove and asked for volunteers for the Light Corps: "We were drawed up—Major Stewart rode up and down the lines & said he wanted none men but what was willing to face death for their country. He talked very cleavour on the occasion, them that was willing step out 3 paces in front, my messmate Samuel Arnold & my self stepped out—we were told to take nothing with us but our arms and our canteens...."[25]

Pvt. Peter Francisco from the Sixth Virginia Regiment was literally the stuff of legend. Citizens of City Point, Virginia (now Hopewell), found him alone on the docks in 1765, a boy of about four or five who spoke a language that sounded like Portuguese and said his name was Pedro. A local judge rescued him from the poorhouse and raised him in Buckingham County, Virginia. When the Revolution began Francisco stood six and a half feet tall and weighed 260 pounds. In 1776 he joined the Tenth Virginia Regiment and later fought at Brandywine—where he was slightly wounded—Germantown, and Monmouth, where he was wounded again. He said that he "never felt satisfied, nor thought he did a good day's work, but by drawing British blood."[26]

The army adjutant general assigned quartermasters, forage-masters, fifers, drummers, and other support personnel in mid-June, and the Light Corps was ready for service. The possibility of an attack on West Point demanded that the corps move to the Hudson as soon as possible, and on June 21 Washington ordered Col. Butler to march the corps to a position near Ft. Montgomery to collect intelligence on British activities and "to oppose a movement of the enemy against the forts."[27] The Corps of Light Infantry assembled with their packs, blankets, and four days' provisions, and began their first march as a unit. The same day he gave Col. Butler his orders, Washington wrote to Anthony Wayne again in Philadelphia and ordered him to rejoin the army as soon as possible: "I wrote you upon this subject before we marched from Middle Brook," the general said, "but as you have not arrived, It is probable my Letter has miscarried or that it did not come to hand till very lately."[28] Washington was correct: Wayne never received his commander's previous letter and knew nothing about the situation on the Hudson. When Wayne received Washington's second letter, he made hasty good-byes to his friends, bid farewell to his wife, Polly, by sending her a brief note, and departed to join his new command.[29]

Also on the same day that Butler marched the light corps away from Smith's Clove, Washington called to his headquarters Capt. Allan McLane, an experienced and cunning scout who commanded a company of riflemen on the west bank of the Hudson. The general ordered him to begin observing the activities of the British at the height known as Stony Point.

VII

Little Gibraltar

King's Ferry, June 1779

    The Hudson River Valley, especially the area known as "the Highlands" that begins around Stony Point, is a rugged region that was the scene of conflict long before the Revolution. Native Algonquins, including the Mohawk, Raritan, Tappan, Rewechnoug, Rechgawawanck, and Rumachenank tribes, were there in 1609 when the explorer Henry Hudson, in the employ of the Dutch, sailed up the river and anchored his ship, the *Half Moon*, near the place that came to be known as Stony Point. The local Native Americans visited his ship once as guests in the daytime and returned at night, uninvited, as thieves. The crew of the *Half Moon* discovered the robbery in progress and fought the Indians off. The ship's cook cleaved off the hand of one native who tried to climb aboard a small boat.

    The Dutch East India Company acquired a charter for the area around Stony Point as part of the New Netherland Colony in 1629. But Europeans did not arrive in large numbers until 1640, when Captain David De Vries purchased the area south of the Highlands from the Raritan tribe and established a community to trade with Indians. War between the Dutch and the Raritans ended the De Vries enterprise. England acquired the colony in 1664 and Orange County, which included Stony Point, was incorporated in 1691. Stevanus Van Cortlandt bought the area that was directly across the Hudson from seven Native American chiefs in 1683 for the price of wampum, guns, blankets, coats, kettles, rum, beer, shirts, gunpowder, hatchets, saws, knives, and tobacco boxes. Ownership passed to Van Cortlandt's granddaughter and her husband, Phillip Ver Planck, and the area became known as Verplanck's Point. As charged by the New York Colony, Ver Planck drove the tribes of the Six Nations from the area.

Land speculation in Orange County began in the early eighteenth century, and King George II granted a charter for 1,000 acres around Stony Point to Richard Bradley and William Jamison. Four miles south, the village of Haverstraw (which was originally "Haverstroo" in Dutch, roughly translating to "oats straw") was founded in 1719 and had 654 residents in 1738. The King's Highway, a major artery between New England and New York, ran north to south through the county. King's Ferry was the road's crossing site on the Hudson.

By the time of the Revolution the families of Abraham Betts and Harrick Len owned the tracts that included Stony Point and its nearby shoreline. Haverstraw was the headquarters for the rebel militia that patrolled the west bank of the Hudson, but it was also home to the Smith family, who were prominent Loyalist landowners. In 1779 the area around Stony Point was heavily wooded and populated by families on scattered farms. It was the frequent target of Loyalist and patriot guerrilla bands that sailed up the Hudson and raided the county for provisions.[1]

Rock outcroppings on the banks of the river are common in the Highlands. Among them, Stony Point literally stands out as a granite spur 150 feet high and a half-mile long. The river also narrows and turns sharply there, forcing sailing ships to slow and tack back and forth to negotiate the curve. The slopes of Stony Point were steep, rocky and wooded. With a swamp fifty yards in width between it and the west bank of the Hudson, the height turned into an island when the marsh flooded at high tide. From a military standpoint, Stony Point nearly matched this description of a naturally strong defensive position from an eighteenth century military treatise; "A position on rising ground with steep banks is strong; and when on the side towards the enemy, there be a canal, river, lake, morass, quicksand, steep precipice, or narrow pass through which the enemy must defile before he can attack the camp, it is still stronger; indeed some positions of this nature are found that are impregnable."[2] Gen. James Pattison, the British artillery commander who seized Stony Point in June, described it as "by Nature exceedingly strong."[3] Even Gen. Washington called Stony Point "strong by nature and almost inaccessible by land."[4]

The British soldiers at King's Ferry needed every natural advantage that Stony Point presented because river crossing sites are difficult places to defend. The river splits defending forces and prevents them from supporting each other if attacked, and failure to control both sides of the site renders the crossing useless. Successful defense of a ford, bridge or ferry crossing usually requires a single commander to ensure unity of effort, long-range weapons that can fire across the river, and fortified infantry positions at both ends of the site. The British defenses of King's Ferry in early June had all of these. Under the command of Maj. Gen. Vaughan, the officer who seized Ft. Lafayette, 3,000 soldiers from the Thirty-third Regiment, light infantry, grenadiers, a Hessian grenadier regiment, the Loyal Americans, and Maj. Patrick Ferguson's rifle corps defended the eastern terminus at Verplanck's Point. Vaughan also commanded the defenses across the river, where another 1,000 troops from the Seventeenth, Sixty-third, and Sixty-fourth Regiments and Hessian Jagers held Stony Point. Since Stony Point towered over the area, cannon placed there could hit targets all around the crossing site, just as British guns had lobbed shells into Ft. Lafayette during the June 2 attack. Stony Point was the key to holding King's Ferry.

British troops began fortifying Stony Point and Verplanck's Point in early June. Under the direction of Capt. Alexander Mercer, Gen. Vaughan's chief engineer, soldiers improved the works at Ft. Lafayette on Verplanck's Point (since they were essentially the same location, the British came to use "Ft. Lafayette" and "Verplanck's Point" interchangeably for the fortifications on the east bank) with an earthen parapet, cannon batteries that could fire across the river, a log stockade, and a mobile barrier of wooden stakes called a *chevaux de Frize*. At Stony Point, also under the direction of Mercer and another engineer, a Capt. Traille, soldiers cleared the woods west of the hill for visibility and fields of fire. They then used the felled trees to construct an abatis from the north end of Stony Point, along the base of the hill overlooking the marsh and down to the south edge of the hill where it extended into the water. The abatis—logs buried in the ground with half their length pointing out at an angle to the height of a man and with the ends sharpened and facing the direction of the enemy—formed a barrier like the quills of a giant porcupine. Just behind the abatis on rock outcroppings soldiers built three fleches—earthworks, large enough to hold a dozen men shaped like a V with the point towards the enemy and open in the back. At Stony Point's south end, Fleche Number One contained a brass cannon that fired a twelve-pound shot and covered a causeway over the marsh. In the daytime a corporal and six soldiers manned the position with double that number at night. Fleche Number Two was a quarter-mile to the north of Fleche Number One, and was also just behind the abatis and manned in a similar manner with a mortar and six soldiers. Further north, Fleche Number Three held another mortar, an officer and fourteen soldiers in the daytime and thirty-four soldiers at night. In between Fleches Number Two and Number Three sat a three-pounder cannon in the open, positioned to fire on any attackers who broke through the abatis. Combined, these defenses constituted Stony Point's "Lower Works."[5]

Further up the hillside the slope leveled off to an area known as the "Table," where the engineers designed the "Upper Works." Here, soldiers built another abatis along the base of the Table, and behind it raised an earthen parapet, broken only by a small entry port on the north side and narrow ports called "embrasures" for cannon. On the Table's south side, a battery of two heavy cannon was sited to fire down the southern slope. In the center of the Table, near the post's flagstaff, sat a twelve-pounder cannon on a flat platform that could fire in any direction. Another battery with an eighteen- and twenty-four-pounder covered the northern slope. An eight-inch howitzer, with a sentinel standing by at all times to fire the gun at the first sign of an attack, was sighted to blast the lower abatis. In the center of the Table, a ten-inch mortar was positioned to lob high-explosive shells at attackers.[6]

Infantry support completed Stony Point's defenses. Outside the Lower Works, the soldiers of the Seventeenth Regiment and 120 Hessian Jagers patrolled the west bank of the Hudson and manned six picquets—stationary guard posts situated on hillocks with good visibility and manned by ten to twenty soldiers each to give advance warning of an attack. Attackers that succeeded in pushing back the Redcoats and Hessians would have to slow down as they encountered the lower abatis along the base of the hill. Any attackers that cut through the abatis faced a steep climb up Stony Point's rugged slope, and then they would have to negotiate through the second abatis and break through the parapet of the Upper Works. Musket fire from the 600 infantrymen of the Sixty-third and Sixty-fourth regiments that manned the works would sweep the open ground. And at every obstacle, British artillery pieces would catch Americans in interlocking fire.

Eighteenth century field cannon were exceptionally deadly weapons. The twelve-pounder guns mounted in the fleches at Stony Point, just behind the lower abatis, fired round shot, the traditional cannonball, which could tear through ranks and cut men in half at ranges up to 1,400 yards. The guns also fired case shot, a tin can containing sixty lead balls that turned the cannon into giant shotguns that could kill or maim dozens of men at close range. Well-drilled gunners could fire three rounds of case shot or two rounds of round shot every minute. The mortars mounted in Fleches Number Two and Three could lob explosive shells into the air at high angles to land in enemy columns. The guns behind the fleches could fire over the abatis in any direction. The distance from the guns in the Upper Works to the lower abatis and marsh was only 400 yards, a third of the guns' maximum range. Lt. John Roberts, adjutant of the Royal Artillery at Stony Point, said that the guns on the hill's southern side were so close to the abatis that they "could not have missed" when firing at attackers.[7] In addition to the ground-mounted cannon, the Royal Navy sloop of war *Vulture* anchored in the river in a position to sweep the northern approaches with its fourteen six-pounder cannon. On the south side, anchored in Haverstraw Bay close to where the lower abatis entered the water, the row galley *Cornwallis* covered the southern approaches with one twenty-four pounder and four four-pounder guns. With its natural defensive qualities, fortifications, artillery, veteran infantrymen, and naval support, British troops called Stony Point their "Little Gibraltar" with some justification. Gen. Clinton inspected the post in late June and called it "nearly perfected."[8]

Clinton expected an attempt to retake King's Ferry by a substantial portion of the Continental Army, but he was unwilling to launch a major attack on the American columns that were still moving to Smith's Clove because it would take his forces too far from his supply base at New York City. He considered a cavalry strike at the American camps in New Jersey, where the Continental heavy baggage and artillery remained under guard; but after a consultation with a senior cavalry officer, he said, "I was persuaded by him to drop my intention."[9] Instead, Clinton kept the bulk of his army at Phillipsburg in Westchester County, fifteen miles south of King's Ferry, to be in a position to strike at the Americans when they approached the crossing site. But as Washington kept his army at Smith's Clove, safe behind the barrier of the Hudson, Clinton realized that he needed more enticing bait to lure the Continentals into battle on the east side of the river.

Remembering Lord Germain's instructions to destroy American shipping and commerce in New England, Clinton looked to Connecticut, which was a base of supplies for the Continental Army and home to privateers that raided British shipping. Clinton recalled, "I thought it very probable that, if I should send a corps into Connecticut, the cries of that province might stir [Washington] from his position and ... possibly afford an opening either of attacking some part of his army."[10] Sir Henry planned for Maj. Gen. William Tryon, the former colonial governor of New York turned Loyalist commander, to take 2,600 troops to the Connecticut coast, "for the purpose of destroying public stores, privateers, etc., and doing the enemy every other injury he could consistent with humanity."[11] Commodore Collier would command the naval squadron transporting Tryon's forces.

Clinton could not detach all the men needed for Tryon's expedition and still maintain a strong force near the Hudson ready to strike at Washington, so he assembled the Connecticut raiding force with regiments from several locations. From the defenses of Newport, Rhode Island, he brought the Fifty-fourth Foot, Hessian Landgrave Regiment, and the Loyalist King's American Regiment back to the Connecticut expedition's assembly point at Whitestone, New York (near Flushing on Long Island's north coast). From his forces at Phillipsburg, he also sent the Twenty-third Regiment, light infantry, and grenadier companies from the elite Brigade of Guards to the assembly point. This shifting of units was a sensible way to assemble the raiding force but also forced Clinton to withdraw Gen. Vaughan, the Hessian Jagers, and the Sixty-third and Sixty-fourth regiments from King's Ferry to Phillipsburg to replace the regiments being sent to Connecticut. Lt. Col. James Webster — of the Thirty-third Regiment at Verplanck's Point and who Clinton called "an officer of great experience and on whom I reposed the most implicit confidence" — replaced Vaughan as the commander of the King's Ferry defenses.[12]

Though reduced, the defenses of King's Ferry remained formidable. Nearly 500 soldiers from Col. Webster's own Thirty-third Regiment, the Loyal Americans, and detachments from the Royal Artillery and Seventy-first Regiment still defended Verplanck's Point. Stony Point was still defended by fifteen artillery pieces, the *Vulture*, the row galley, one company from the Loyal Americans, and two grenadier companies from the Seventy-first Highlanders. The lion's share of the work in defending Stony Point went to the Seventeenth Regiment of Foot.

The Seventeenth Foot traced its lineage to the year 1688, when it was raised to support King James II. Campaigns in Spain, Nova Scotia, Gibraltar, and New York during the Seven Years' War were part of its battle history. The regiment was on duty in Ireland when rebellion began and it sailed for America in August 1775 with about 400 soldiers divided into ten companies of thirty-eight soldiers, two lieutenants, two sergeants, three corporals, and a drummer each. About 60 percent of its soldiers had served for at least four years, and 10 percent had between ten and twenty years of experience. At least twenty-five men had been in the service for over twenty years, and when the regiment went into the New York Highlands in 1779, it is possible that some of them had fought along the Hudson sixteen years earlier during the Seven Years' War.[13]

The regiment's first commander during the rebellion, Lt. Col. Charles Mawhood, led the Seventeenth through the New York and New Jersey campaigns. At the battle of Princeton in January 1777, American infantrymen surrounded the Seventeenth and closed in until Mawhood ordered a bayonet charge that broke the encirclement. Gen. Howe, Lord Germain, and King George III all praised the soldiers of the Seventeenth for their bravery, but the charge cost the unit 101 casualties out of its 240 men. The next two years brought more action in New Jersey and in the campaign for Philadelphia. The regiment had quartered north of Manhattan at Kingsbridge during the winter of 1778–79 and sailed up the Hudson as part of Clinton's expedition at the end of May.

At Stony Point, the Seventeenth consisted of approximately 380 veteran soldiers led by professional officers.[14] The thirty-one-year-old regimental commander, Lt. Col. Henry Johnson, served in the West Indies as a subaltern with the Twenty-eighth Regiment in the Seven Years' War, came to America with the same unit as a captain in 1775, and gained command of the Seventeenth Foot in 1778. Gen. Clinton considered him "a vigilant, active, spirited officer."[15] Most of the regiment's junior officers were veterans of three years' service in America and at least nine had more than four years' service. Capt. Francis Tew, for example, had held his rank since 1771, and an army historian recorded that he "had frequently been left for dead on the field, and could show more wounds, received in the German and American wars, than any other officer in the British, or perhaps any other service." The historian also wrote that Tew "supported several spinster sisters" in England.[16]

Lt. Col. Johnson also had command over the two companies of grenadiers from the Seventy-first Foot. Originally raised in October 1775 by Major-General Simon Fraser, famed veteran of the Seven Years' War, the regiment assembled at Sterling and Glasgow and sailed for America in May 1776. Americans captured one transport with several hundred Seventy-first troops after the ship unluckily sailed into the rebel-controlled Boston Harbor. The remainder of the regiment successfully joined Howe's army at New York. Though some men had served in the Seven Years' War, most soldiers of the Seventy-first, including its leaders, were new soldiers

A soldier of the Seventeenth Regiment of Foot, the unit that comprised the majority of the defenders of Stony Point. In the summer of 1779 the men of the Seventeenth Foot were veterans of four years of combat in America (painting by Don Troiani, www.historicalimagebank.com).

and arrived with only the training they had received on their transports. After fighting throughout 1776 and 1777 at Long Island, New Jersey, and Brandywine, the Seventy-first, also known as Fraser's Highlanders, became an excellent combat unit. In December 1778 most of the Seventy-first sailed to South Carolina with the force that attacked Savannah, but the grenadier companies remained in New York and became part of Clinton's push up the Hudson under Gen. Vaughan. The grenadiers wore kilts of the Fraser family tartan, red and white checkered knee-high hose, and tall black bearskin hats. In addition to their muskets, a pistol and broadsword of black steel was part of their official armament, though it is unlikely that many men carried these heavy accoutrements in battle in North America. There were 158 of these heavily armed Scots at Stony Point.[17]

Sixty-eight soldiers from the Loyal American Regiment were also under Johnson's command. Their formation illustrates the bitterness of the civil war between Americans. Beverly Robinson was a respected militia captain and landowner in Duchess County, New York, before the war. Though he disagreed with much of the Crown policy toward the American colonies, Robinson did not support armed rebellion and he refused an offer from the Duchess County leadership to command the county militia. When New York's Commission for Detecting and Defeating Conspiracies tried to force him to sign an oath of loyalty to the United States in February 1777, Robinson fled to the protection of British forces in Manhattan. His wife and children escaped soon after him and the committee seized Robinson's estate. Angered at the rebels, Robinson recruited the Loyal American Regiment, mainly from friends and former tenants of his lands. Four of his sons, Beverly, John, Morris, and Frederick joined as junior officers. During the Saratoga campaign, the Loyal Americans helped capture Fort Montgomery on the Hudson; in March 1779 they participated in a raid at Horse Neck, Connecticut; and in June the regiment sailed up the Hudson with Gen. Vaughan and helped seize Ft. Lafayette. Most of the Loyal American Regiment remained at Verplanck's Point, and Beverly's son Capt. Morris Robinson commanded the company assigned to Stony Point.[18]

Capt. Morris Robinson was twenty years old in 1779. He was seventeen when his family fled Duchess County and he and his older brother Beverly slipped through the American lines into Manhattan and immediately joined the king's forces. His fourteen-year-old brother, Frederick, also obtained a commission as an ensign in the Loyal Americans but transferred to the Seventeenth Foot. In June 1779 Morris and Frederick found themselves defending Stony Point in their respective units. Now sixteen,

Frederick Robinson had tremendous respect for the older officers in the Seventeenth, especially Capt. Tew and Lt. Col. Johnson, who, Robinson wrote, welcomed him "as his son." Frederick's first action had been in the raid on Horse Neck, in March, where he commanded a company, as, he wrote, "my captain having preferred flirting in New York to doing his Duty." Frederick admitted that he "was not a very able Warrior." When his company took fire at Horse Neck he struggled to climb over a stone wall until a "stout young Corporal," he recalled, heaved him over, saying, "Now, young gentleman, take care of *yourself*."[19]

Morris and Frederick Robinson probably considered it a stroke of luck that they served alongside each other at a post the British were turning into a fortress, but it is unlikely that either officer knew that the height's defenses were not as perfect as they seemed. Capt. Mercer, the engineer who designed Stony Point's defenses, said that the post could withstand any American attack; but he still left instructions for his replacement, Lt. William Marshall of the Sixty-third Regiment, to complete the works with the construction of another cannon battery, additional fleches, and improvements to the magazine where the garrison's ammunition was stored. Lt. Marshall's first inspection of Stony Point also revealed that both abatis required strengthening. He began work on the additional cannon battery but Lt. Col. Johnson wanted other projects done—a new embrasure cut into the parapet of the Upper Works to site cannon to fire down the river, and clearing of existing fields of fire—and refused to assign soldiers to complete the improvements that Mercer suggested.[20]

Johnson's reluctance to devote men to improving his defenses is perplexing. He may have simply disagreed with the engineer's assessment of his fortifications. It is possible that he considered the extra work an unnecessary burden on his soldiers, who also had to patrol outside the fortifications. Gen. Clinton's army was only a day's march away at Phillipsburg and ready to reinforce King's Ferry in case of attack, and Johnson may have considered further fortification superfluous when assistance was so close and available. The lack of support irritated Marshall. But despite the lieutenant's continued requests, Johnson did not detail men to improve the defenses until July 6.[21] Marshall later stated that Capt. Mercer's recommended improvements were only "fulfilled in part."[22]

Whatever Johnson's reasoning, it is also possible that the soldiers at King's Ferry felt that they were becoming a backwater of the campaign as Gen. Clinton's focus shifted to Connecticut. As the men at Stony Point toiled at building earthen fortifications in the summer heat, on Long Island the 2,600 men of Gen. Tryon's raiding force gathered and prepared to sail northeast into Long Island Sound, where they would land on Connecticut's coast in an attempt to bait the Americans into battle. At the same time, British patrols in eastern Westchester County were encountering resistance and ambushes from Continental cavalry posted near the Connecticut border. To eliminate the troublesome Yankee horsemen, Clinton decide to launch an early-morning raid to the town of Pound Ridge, New York, where they were to capture the rebel cavalry commander, a young major named Benjamin Tallmadge.

VIII

"Surrender, You Damned Rebel"

Pound Ridge, New York, July 1, 1779

    In the southeast corner of Westchester County, New York, seventeen miles west of King's Ferry and two miles from the border with Connecticut, lies the town of Pound Ridge. In 1779 the village had existed for thirty-five years. Captain Joseph Lockwood and eleven citizens from the town of Stamford, twelve miles to the south, had carved the settlement out of the wilderness of oak, hickory, and chestnut trees. North of the village a craggy four-mile long ridge known as the Stony Hills ran southwest to northeast, a fertile valley at its base. Four interconnected streams and ponds bordered the town to the east. Hills and valleys rolled to the southwest. Before Lockwood arrived, Native Americans of the Sagamore, Ponus and Wascussue tribes used the area's natural barriers to trap game; and European settlers gave the town its name from the Indian game pound, and the nearby ridge.

    The town's first public building, the Presbyterian meetinghouse built in 1760, was the figurative and physical center of the town, which consisted of about twenty dwellings and the shops for three carpenters, three shoemakers, a blacksmith, a grist mill, and a schoolhouse. Farms surrounded the village. A low hill to the south held a small graveyard. Roads that led to other towns gave Pound Ridge an almost triangular shape; one ran four miles west to Bedford, the High Ridge Road ran south to Stamford, the Salem Road went north to Ridgefield, and another road went southeast to Canaan. During the Revolution the citizens of Pound Ridge were solidly on the side of the rebels, and except for periodic American cavalry patrols the war did not come to Pound Ridge until June 28, 1779, when Maj. Benjamin Tallmadge and ninety troopers of the Second Continental Dragoons clopped into town.

Tallmadge's arrival was the result of Gen. Washington's continued consolidation of the American defense of the Hudson. During the first few weeks of the campaign, Washington gave orders directly to the seven divisions in the Continental Army as well as to the special corps, such as the artillery, cavalry, and light infantry. But the standard practice for a campaign was to streamline the command system by grouping the army's divisions into "wings" whose commanders, usually senior major-generals, answered directly to Washington. The army's pause at Smith's Clove gave Washington time to designate his wing commanders. Considering that the army was oriented southward, towards the British, Washington named Maj. Gen. Israel Putnam commander of the right wing on the west side of the Hudson, Gen. Alexander McDougall took charge of the center wing concentrated at West Point, and Maj. Gen. William Heath commanded the left wing on the river's east side.

With British troops raiding throughout Westchester County near the Connecticut border, Heath ordered the Second Light Dragoons to the area around Pound Ridge, "to afford protection to the country ... which will give great confidence to the distressed inhabitants."[1] In mid–June Washington reinforced the cavalrymen with 100 infantrymen from the Sixth Connecticut Regiment. At the end of the month, under pressure from Connecticut governor Jonathan Trumbull to protect the border area, Washington ordered Col. Stephen Moylan and the Fourth Light Dragoons to cross from the west side of the Hudson to "the neighborhood of Bedford" and take command of the Second Dragoons and the infantry. "The purposes of this command," he told Moylan, "are to protect the country and inhabitants, give countenance to the militia, and as far as it lies in your power, gain intelligence of the enemy's force, movements & designs, of which you will give me the most punctual information."[2] On the first of July Moylan's Fourth Dragoons were on their way to the area. The American post at Pound Ridge consisted of ninety soldiers of the Second Light Dragoons, 100 Connecticut infantrymen under Maj. Eli Leavenworth, and 100 local militia commanded by Maj. Ebenezer Lockwood. Tallmadge was in temporary charge of the Second Dragoons while the regimental commander, Col. Elisha Sheldon, was away.

The Second Dragoons had operated in Westchester County and

western Connecticut since the summer of 1778, so Tallmadge knew the area well and called Pound Ridge "pretty strong ground." He also knew that his soldiers were the only opposition in eastern Westchester County against the push of British infantry, cavalry, and Loyalist troops towards Connecticut. "The enemy have 6[00] or 700 horse & 200 infantry within a few hours march of us," he wrote. He said the British were making it "a capital object to surprise us. For this purpose they have moved more than once, & changing my post at different hours of the night has defeated their plan." Tallmadge also assured Gen. Heath that "every step in my power shall be taken to protect the country and annoy the enemy."[3] In June his dragoons skirmished with the British north of White Plains and at the end of the month he planned to lay an ambush along a local road where enemy cavalry frequently patrolled. Tallmadge cancelled his plans when he learned that Col. Sheldon was on his way back to rejoin the regiment; but his scouting, skirmishing and ambushing were in concert with everything that Washington intended for the Continental cavalry.

A mounted arm was not originally part of the Continental Army at the beginning of the war. In the eighteenth century, cavalry served two roles: shock effect and scouting. "Heavy" cavalry regiments charged infantry lines with lances in closely packed formations. "Light" cavalry, armed with sabers, pistols and short carbines, scouted the enemy and mounted fast raids. Dragoons were fast-moving, mounted infantry that fought either on horseback or on foot and also carried pistols and short carbines. Washington had little need for any of these types of units in the first campaign of the war when the Continentals surrounded the British in Boston. But during the New York campaign, when Gen. Howe introduced the Sixteenth and Seventeenth light dragoons, the Americans needed their own cavalrymen for scouting and to fend off probes from the British horsemen.

A mounted detachment from the Connecticut militia commanded by Maj. Elisha Sheldon conducted useful reconnaissance, and in November 1776 Virginia also offered the services of a newly raised cavalry regiment under Col. Theodoric Bland. Washington wanted to expand his cavalry capability. At his urging, in January 1777 Congress authorized the creation of four regiments of light dragoons with 280 officers and soldiers each as the Continental Army's reconnaissance force.[4] Washington, an excellent horseman himself, took great interest in his new dragoons. He instructed the officers in charge of the new regiments, Col. Bland of the First, Sheldon of the Second Regiment, Virginia's Col. Thomas Baylor of the Third, and Col. Stephen Moylan in command of the Fourth Regiment, to use only native-born Americans in their ranks to ensure loyalty and to have them ride dark-colored horses that would be less visible on scouting missions. The cavalry was considered a more prestigious arm than the infantry, and the formation of the regiments attracted some of the Continental Army's rising stars, such as Benjamin Tallmadge.

The son of a minister in Setauket, Long Island, Tallmadge had a pale complexion, dark eyes, and, in the words of historian Alexander Rose, "a disconcerting habit of cocking his head like a quizzical beagle."[5] A 1773 graduate of Yale and close friend of Nathan Hale's, he was teaching school in Wethersfield, Connecticut, when hostilities opened. In

Benjamin Tallmadge, in the uniform of the Second Continental Light Dragoons. The two epaulettes on his shoulders indicate his rank as a major. Underneath his unassuming features was a courageous cavalry officer and cunning manager of Washington's intelligence operations around New York City (portrait by John Ramage, courtesy of the Litchfield, Connecticut, Historical Society).

June 1776 Tallmadge joined the Sixth Connecticut Regiment and saw action at the battles of Long Island and White Plains. In December 1776, when the states were selecting officers for the new cavalry regiments, his commander recommended him as one of the "good men" and "fit for any post."[6] Tallmadge jumped at the chance to serve as a captain in the Second Continental Light Dragoons, commanded by Col. Elisha Sheldon, even though it meant taking a step backward in rank. "As these appointments were from General Washington," he wrote, "I felt highly honored and gratified."[7] He recruited a company from the men of Wethersfield, where he had taught school, and trained with them there over the winter of 1776–1777. Outfitted in dark blue coats with buff facings, buff breeches, high black boots with silver spurs, and brass riding helmets with horsehair plumes, Tallmadge's men cut dashing figures as they practiced charging and wheeling at Wethersfield. Despite Washington's directions to use dark-colored horses, Tallmadge outfitted his troop with dapple gray mounts. Tallmadge said his men "looked superb."[8]

It was while the Second Light Dragoons trained at Wethersfield that Tallmadge began assisting Washington and Nathaniel Sackett with intelligence operations. Like Abraham Woodhull, his cautious spy on Manhattan, Tallmadge held a grudge against the British for the death of his older brother, who had been captured and starved to death in one of the wretched New York prisons. When the campaign season returned in the spring of 1777 Tallmadge continued with his regular duties as a cavalry officer and was promoted back to the rank of major. The Second Dragoons lost ten troopers skirmishing and scouting during the Philadelphia campaign; and when the Continental Army moved into Valley Forge, Tallmadge recalled that his duties were to "scour the country from the Schuykill to the Delaware River, about five or six miles, for the double purpose of watching the movements of the enemy and preventing the disaffected from carrying supplies or provisions to Philadelphia."[9] He barely escaped when a detachment of British horsemen surprised one of his encampments at 2:00 A.M. one day. Another time, he arranged to meet a "country girl" at a tavern near British lines so she could pass him information about enemy activities in Philadelphia. While he and the girl talked his sentries spotted some British cavalry and Tallmadge went to the door in time to see Redcoats riding toward the tavern at full speed, capturing one of his outposts. "Having not a moment to reflect," he recalled, Tallmadge mounted his horse, swung the girl up behind his saddle, and galloped off. He wrote that "although there was considerable firing of pistols, and not a little wheeling and charging, she remained unmoved, and never once complained of fear after she mounted my horse. I was delighted with this transaction." Years later he wrote for his children: "My duties were very arduous."[10]

In July 1778 Washington posted the Second Dragoons in Westchester County, which helped put Tallmadge in a position to again assist with intelligence operations, what he called "private correspondence with some persons in New York," even though Abraham Woodhull was still nervous about disclosure.[11] In April 1779 Tallmadge visited Woodhull in Setauket to reassure the spy that Gen. Washington appreciated his efforts, but a storm prevented him from sailing back across Long Island Sound and two

British officers took up lodging in Woodhull's house. For five days Tallmadge hid in the woods while Woodhull sneaked food to him, constantly afraid of being discovered.[12]

In early June an informant told Col. James Simcoe, commander of the Loyalist Queen's Rangers, that Woodhull was engaged in some type of suspicious activities. Simcoe thundered into Seatuket with a patrol intent on apprehending Woodhull, but the spy had departed for New York City. Finding only Woodhull's father present, Simcoe "plundered him in a most shocking manner,"[13] as the spy reported later. Woodhull escaped apprehension only by convincing a local Loyalist to vouch for him to Simcoe, but the episode left him shaken. Nevertheless, Woodhull managed another trip to New York City and reported on June 8 that the British planned to "make a descent along New England, New London the most likely. I do not doubt that their next move will be there and if you hear again of their embarkation you may readily judge they will go there for they have a particular spite against that place on account of privateering."[14] Two weeks later he correctly added that British and Loyalist regiments had moved from King's Ferry to the town of Whitestone (now Flushing) on Long Island, where they joined others from Rhode Island and transport ships for "excursions" into Connecticut.[15] Both reports were correct warnings about British intentions. And fortunately for Tallmadge, a man named Luther Kinnicutt, a smuggler and spy for New York's Committee of Safety, came into Pound Ridge on the night of June 30 and said that though he did not know the date it would occur, a British attack on Pound Ridge was imminent.

At the same time that Kinnicutt conferred with Tallmadge, fifteen miles to the southwest at Mile Square, New York, the British raiding force intended for Pound Ridge gathered under the command of an up-and-coming twenty-four-year-old cavalry officer named Banastre Tarleton. Son of a middle-class Liverpool businessman, Tarleton had attended Oxford for two years and studied law at Temple. He was of middle height with a stout, powerful body, and in 1775 he purchased a commission as a cornet (the lowest rank of cavalry officer) in the Dragoon Guards regiment. Eagerness for action characterized Tarleton's military career. He volunteered to fight the American rebellion only six months after beginning service with the Dragoon Guards. Two months after landing with Howe's troops at New York in August 1776 he volunteered again for duty with the Seventeenth Light Dragoons. He gained a reputation for being audacious, energetic, and driven to make a name for himself. When the Light Dragoons

An engraving of Lt. Col. Banastre Tarleton, the audacious British cavalryman who led his troopers on the raid to Pound Ridge. The bottom panel shows Tarleton drilling his British Legion (Library of Congress).

caught Gen. Charles Lee at White's Tavern, New Jersey, in December 1776, Tarleton led his cavalrymen at full gallop to surround the tavern and personally helped capture the rebel general. He was an active scout and raider of American outposts and patrols during the Philadelphia campaign, and at the battle of Monmouth his company drove back the American flank with a charge. As Clinton's army withdrew to New York his troopers constantly rode on the flanks of the column, skirmishing with Yankee cavalry.

Tarleton chafed under the inactivity of winter quarters, and when not riding he filled his time by acting with the theater group organized by Capt. John Andre. He enjoyed the social life among the Loyalists and had at least one mistress. In January 1778 Tarleton learned that mere audacity did not ensure victory when his troopers caught Continental cavalry commander Capt. Henry Lee and a small party of soldiers at the Spread Eagle Tavern, about six miles from Valley Forge. Thinking they would repeat the capture of Gen. Charles Lee, Tarleton spurred his men in at top speed. But Lee's men fired back, dropped five dragoons from their saddles, and Lee shouted a ruse that American infantry were on their way. Lee's trick and hard fighting drove the British off, but not before a musket ball knocked the hat from Tarleton's head and three buckshot pellets pierced his jacket.

Nevertheless, his boldness in combat, as well as his refined social skills, made Tarleton a star of the inner circles of the British high command. In July 1778 Gen. Clinton created a new unit called the British Legion, composed of cavalry and infantry companies of Scottish, Irish, English, and American volunteers, with his adjutant general, Lord William Cathcart, as the unit commander and Tarleton as the second-in-command with the rank of lieutenant-colonel. Clinton later appointed Cathcart his quartermaster general, and Tarleton took command of the legion. Clad in short green jackets, they became known as Tarleton's Green Horse.[16]

Tarleton and his troopers spent the early winter of 1779 on Long Island and at Kingsbridge, north of Manhattan. As part of Clinton's push into Westchester County in May, the Green Horse skirmished with scattered rebels and camped on Valentine's Hill near the village of Mile Square near the Bronx River. In late June, after approving of the raid to capture Benjamin Tallmadge and the Second Continental Light Dragoons at Pound Ridge, Clinton reinforced Tarleton's British Legion with seventy troopers of Seventeenth Light Dragoons and detachments from the Queen's Rangers, the Hussars and Hessian Jagers, a total force of 200 mounted soldiers. The raid at Pound Ridge would be Tarleton's first independent command.

Tarleton's force departed their camp at Mile Square at 11:30 P.M. on July 1. It was raining heavily. Tarleton said that the "remarkably bad" weather made their march slow, and his column reached North Castle, eight miles west of Pound Ridge, at about 4:00 A.M. Here Tarleton received information—the source is unknown, but it possibly came from advance scouts—that the Continental dragoons and infantrymen still remained at Pound Ridge. Tarleton drove his men on. The most direct route to Pound Ridge was to head east on the Bedford Road, but he took the North Road, which intersected with the Salem Road, to approach the town from the north. The Green Horse neared Pound Ridge in the early morning, and Tarleton saw a civilian named John Crawford standing in a doorway and asked the man for directions to the town. Crawford, who was one of the few Loyalists in the area, gave Tarleton proper directions to turn south for Pound Ridge, probably with some degree of happiness about the presence of Crown forces in the area. But somehow Tarleton misunderstood Crawford's instructions and his troops took the Salem Road north towards Ridgefield. The rain had stopped, and just as dawn was breaking the Green Horse trotted through the sodden countryside ready to strike the Continentals—but heading the wrong way.

In their billets among the barns and outbuildings of the farm owned by militia commander Maj. Ebenezer Lockwood on the south side of Pound Ridge, the men of the Second Continental Dragoons were wide awake. Col. Sheldon had arrived the day before and Tallmadge informed him about the attack warning from the spy Kinnicutt. Sheldon posted vedettes—mounted sentries—to patrol the roads, and kept his men under arms all night with their horses saddled. The commander of the Connecticut infantry detachment, Maj. Eli Leavenworth, stationed his men on the Bedford Road. Maj. Lockwood's wife was seven months pregnant with their eighth child and though he was determined to move her to safety in Ridgefield the previous night, Sheldon convinced him that the British would not attack in such a heavy rain and implored them to wait until daylight to depart. Lockwood and his family sat up through the night, fully clothed and with their belongings packed. Just after daylight Sheldon allowed his men to unsaddle their horses and let the mounts graze.

North of the town Tarleton realized his mistake after riding half a mile, turned around, and headed south to Pound Ridge. Not long after Sheldon's order to relax the horses, the Yankee vedette that watched the northern approaches galloped into the headquarters and told Sheldon that a column of British horsemen was coming down the road. Sheldon quickly

VIII. "Surrender, You Damned Rebel"   97

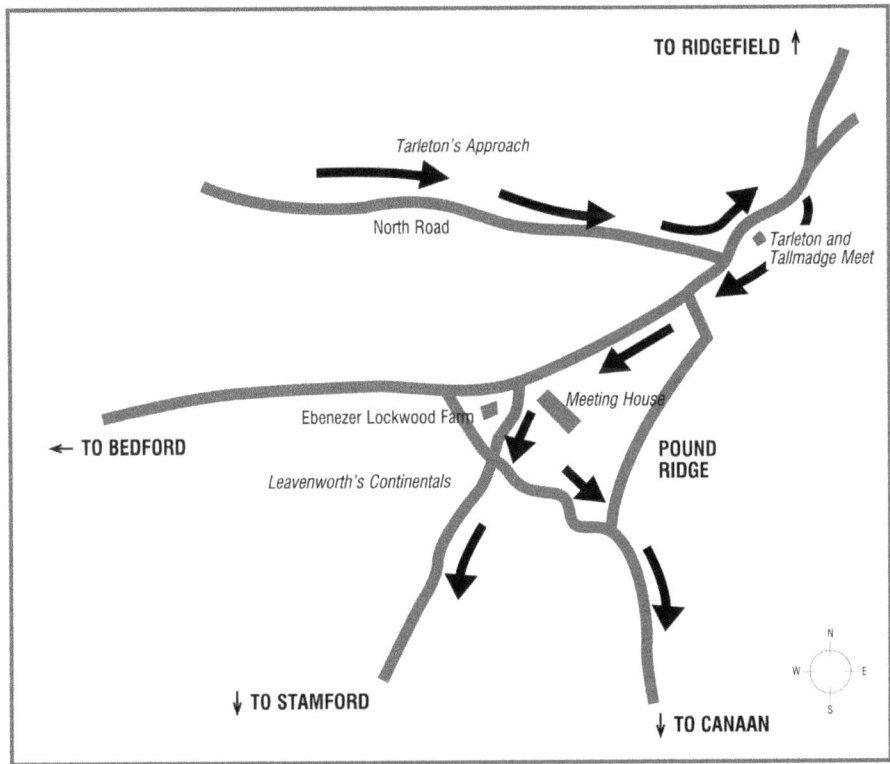

Tarleton advanced from the area of Bedford to the west and descended on Pound Ridge from the north, encountered Maj. Benjamin Tallmadge, and drove the Americans to the south (map by the author and Eleana Nicolaou, adapted from a map in *God's Country: A History of Pound Ridge, New York* by Jay Harris).

ordered the men to re-saddle their horses and sent Tallmadge out with a detachment to positively identify the column: Col. Stephen Moylan's Fourth Regiment of Light Dragoons was due to arrive at Pound Ridge at any time, so was the incoming group friend or enemy? Tallmadge received his answer a few minutes later when he and his men rode north through the town and ran headlong into the Redcoats heading south on the Salem Road, about half a mile from the Yankee camp. The officer leading the Seventeenth Light Dragoons, Tarleton's advance guard, shouted for Tallmadge to surrender and charged, his men shouting and their swords high. Outnumbered, Tallmadge wheeled his detachment around and rode for the American camp at top speed with the Redcoats close behind.[17]

Tallmadge and his men galloped back into the Lockwood farm and the rest of the American dragoons, alerted by the sounds of the clash on the road, opened fire but the British charged down the road with unstoppable momentum. The Yankees quickly mounted their horses and when the Redcoat cavalrymen thundered into the camp the fighting became hand-to-hand. Tallmadge recalled, "The onset was violent, and carried on principally with the broad sword."[18] Banastre Tarleton came up through the British column, formed his men near the village meetinghouse, and then ordered a charge at the American camp. Outnumbered two to one, Col. Sheldon withdrew his dragoons to the south, while the Continental infantry and Maj. Lockwood's militiamen withdrew to the west. Tarleton reported: "The Enemy did not stand the Charge, a general Route immediately ensued."[19] An American officer recorded: "The enemy pushed hard on our rear for more than two miles. In the course of which a scattering fire was kept up between their advance and our rear, and a constant charge with the sword."[20] A British dragoon closed on cavalryman John Buckhout, in the rear of Sheldon's group, and yelled, "Surrender, you damned rebel, or I'll blow your brains out." He fired a pistol shot that knocked off Buckhout's cap and scraped his scalp and shouted again:

A soldier of the Second Continental Light Dragoons. In their brass helmets with turbans and high black boots, Maj. Benjamin Tallmadge thought his men looked "superb." About ninety soldiers from the regiment, also known as "Sheldon's Light Horse," defended Pound Ridge from Banastre Tarleton's British Legion (painting by Don Troiani, www.historicalimagebank.com).

"There, you damned rebel, a little more and I should have blown your brains out." Buckhout called back, "Yes, damn you, and a little more and you wouldn't have touched me," and he spurred his horse away.[21] Yankee trooper Jared Hoyt received a saber blow on the head, swung his own sword in defense, and slashed his attacker in the face. Tarleton attempted to encircle Sheldon's men as they retreated, but the ground on the sides of the road was rough and broken and made a close pursuit too difficult for the horses. The British captured a few of the Americans whose horses had stumbled on the rocky paths, but they then abandoned the chase and headed back to Pound Ridge.[22]

The Americans recovered from the initial shock of the attack, regrouped, and fought back with guerrilla tactics. Maj. Lockwood's militia had retreated from Pound Ridge when the British had the advantage of surprise, but they returned and harassed the Redcoat column with musket fire. Tarleton discredited the militia counterattack, saying, "The Militia assembled again on Eminences and in Swamps, and before we quitted the Ground on which the first Charge was made they fired at Great Distances.... [T]he rest hovered almost out of Sight." But the resistance clearly angered him, as he continued: "The inveteracy of the inhabitants ... in firing from houses and out-houses, obliged me to burn some of their meeting and some of their dwelling houses with stores. I proposed the militia terms, that if they would not fire shots from buildings, I would not burn. They interpreted my mild proposal wrong, imputing it to fear."[23] The Tory newspaper *Rivington's Royal Gazette* reported that the Americans "were cautioned by the commanding officer [Tarleton] to desist from firing, on pain of their houses being consumed, but still foolhardily persevering in their hostility, he was constrained to carry his menaces into execution, and several houses were accordingly destroyed." No American account verifies the offer of clemency.[24]

Tarleton ordered his men to burn the house of militia captain Joseph Lockwood, the meetinghouse, and Maj. Lockwood's home. Militia fire drove the Redcoats away from the younger Lockwood's home; but the house of the elder Lockwood, where surgeons of both sides treated the wounded and the seven months pregnant Mrs. Lockwood still remained, was not spared. When two British surgeons protested the burning of their hospital, Tarleton simply ordered the wounded moved out. The Redcoats searched the house, found all of the baggage from Col. Sheldon's headquarters, took the colors of the Second Light Dragoons as a war trophy, and then set their torches, burning the house to the ground along with all

A dragoon of Lt. Col. Banastre Tarleton's British Legion in his distinctive green jacket prepares for action. Just after sunrise on July 2, 1779, "Tarleton's Green Horse" swept into the town of Pound Ridge and surprised the American soldiers in the town (painting by Don Troiani, www.historicalimagebank.com).

of the American equipment. Tarleton reported that the rebels "persisted firing until the torch stopped their progress; after which not a shot was fired."[25]

It is more likely that since Maj. Leavenworth was advancing toward the town with his Continental infantrymen, Tarleton realized that it was time to end the raid. He assembled his men and went back west toward Bedford while the main body of his soldiers withdrew north along the Salem Road, the way they had entered Pound Ridge, herding Maj. Lockwood's sixteen cows behind them. When they passed the house of John Crawford, the Loyalist whose directions the British misunderstood that morning, Tarleton ordered his house burned in retaliation for misleading his column. American dragoons and infantry pursued the Redcoats as far as North Castle Church but were unable to overtake them. Tarleton's force retraced their route back to the Bronx River and reached their camp at about 10:00 P.M., "extremely fatigued."[26]

The raid was an odd success for the British. The Americans lost only eight soldiers wounded, four captured, and four citizens taken prisoner.[27] And although Tarleton did not end the Second Light Dragoons activity in Westchester County nor capture Benjamin Tallmadge, his soldiers did seize the major's horse and saddlebags, which contained twenty guineas to pay Abraham Woodhull and some of Tallmadge's correspondence. In one of the captured letters, written on June 27, Washington described to Tallmadge a man named George Higday, "who I am told hath given signal proofs of his attachment to us, and at the same time stands well with the enemy."[28] Washington suggested that Tallmadge should investigate if the man was truly trustworthy and if so, add him as an agent in Bergen County. The captured letter confirmed British suspicions about the existence of an American spy ring in New York City, named at least one prospective agent, and associated Tallmadge with the operation.

Strategically, the raid was the beginning of Clinton's expansion of the campaign to draw the Americans into a major battle. While Tarleton rested his men and Tallmadge and Washington assessed the damage to their intelligence system, at the town of Whitestone on Long Island, Gen. William Tryon assembled 4,500 soldiers for the next series of raids on Connecticut's ports. Unless Gen. Washington soon offered Clinton an opening for combat, Connecticut was going to burn.

IX

"Too Pretty a Place to Burn"

The Coast of Connecticut, July 3, 1779

There was no respite from the British offensive. On July 3 Gen. William Tryon loaded his raiding force onto forty-eight transports and launched the expedition up Long Island Sound, escorted by the frigates *Virginia* and *Greyhound*, the sixteen-gun sloop *Scorpion*, and the gunboat *Hussar*. The twenty-gun frigate *Camilla*, flagship of the squadron, carried Tryon and his naval commander, Commodore Collier. The weather was fair but the winds light, so their progress eastward was slow. The residents of Connecticut's coast had been on alert since April, after Washington received Culper Ring reports about the building of landing boats, and rebel militiamen monitoring the sound lit signal fires as warnings about the Royal Navy presence. But the sight of British warships protecting transports was not uncommon — over 100 ships had sailed up the sound from New York on their way to attack Newport in 1777 — and none of the Connecticut residents knew the intent or destination of Collier's squadron. If the ships were a raiding force to destroy American privateers, several ports of Connecticut made logical targets.

Privateering was essentially piracy, legalized by a practice that was common for hundreds of years before the Revolution: governments at war expanded their naval forces by the issue of official "letters of marque" that authorized armed civilian vessels to seize enemy shipping and sell the captured cargos for prize money. The Continental Congress began issuing letters of marque in 1776, such as the one for the nineteen-gun *General Washington*, which authorized the ship to "by force of arms attack, subdue, seize, and take all ships and all other vessels, goods, wares and merchandizes, belonging to the Crown of Great-Britain, or any other subjects thereof."[1] The Royal Navy did not have enough ships to protect the entire British merchant fleet that sailed the Caribbean, North American, and African waters, and American privateers pounced on the unarmed ships. The supply ships sent from Cork in Ireland were favorite targets, and their losses contributed significantly to the poor conditions in New York City. As Gen. Clinton wrote, "Rebel privateers [had] grown so numerous and daring that I every hour dreaded to hear of the capture of the Cork victualars, to whose arrival alone we trusted for a supply."[2]

During the first full year of American privateering in 1777, Yankee raiders seized 461 British merchant ships with cargos that included, among other things, rum, sugar, provisions, mail, gold dust, wine, Hessian soldiers, uniforms, and slaves, whom the privateers rarely released from captivity.[3] The sale of such cargos could make the owners and crews of privateers wealthy after only a few voyages, and the seafaring citizens of New England found the practice a lucrative way to support the rebellion. The sea raiders based in the ports of New London, New Haven, and Fairfield made Connecticut's privateer fleet the fourth largest of all the thirteen states in rebellion, surpassed only by Massachusetts, Maryland, and Virginia. From smaller towns like Stamford and Norwalk, rebels raided the coasts of Long Island Sound in armed whaleboats. Thirty to thirty-five feet long, powered by either sails or oarsmen, armed with small cannon, and manned by crews intimately familiar with the coastline, whaleboats ravaged unarmed ships or settlements on Long Island and often did not discriminate between Loyalists or American patriots.

The town of New Haven ranked highly as a possible target for retribution by the Crown. Its 8,000 residents made it the largest city in Connecticut at the time, and 10 percent of its citizens engaged in seafaring trades, one of whom included Captain Ebeneezer Dayton, a privateer who captured seventeen prizes in 1776. With 108 vessels registered it was also Connecticut's second largest seaport, after New London. And many British leaders considered Yale College to be the "parent and nurse of the rebellion," in Commodore Collier's words. He added, "It was in this seminary that the arch-rebels *Hancock*, *Adams*, *Warren*, *Otis*, and *Deane* had their education."[4] The commodore was mistaken; the famous Patriot leaders John Hancock, Samuel and John Adams (it is not evident to which Adams Collier referred), Dr. Joseph Warren, and James Otis were Massachusetts men who attended Harvard. Of the "arch-rebels" Collier mentioned, only

Silas Deane was a Connecticut native and Yale graduate. But Collier was not entirely mistaken about the college's influence on the rebellion. Yale alumni formed the majority on Connecticut's Committee of Safety that instigated opposition to Crown policies, and other Yale graduates led the rebel movements in New Haven, Hartford, New London, Norwich, Windham, and Lyme.

The geography and layout of New Haven contributed to the port's vulnerability. Weeks before Gen. Tryon's departure, Capt. Patrick Ferguson of the Seventy-first Highlanders had surreptitiously scouted the Connecticut coast. His professional opinion as an experienced army officer was that the terrain and harbor at New Haven particularly suited British raiding. He reported that "under cover of arm'd vessels a brigade of inferior Troops could land & reimbark in the view of the most numerous & gallant army in the world, uninsulted."[5] When he ordered Gen. William Tryon to raid the Connecticut coast, Gen. Clinton brought all the British loathing for New Haven together and simply told Tryon this: "As New Haven is the only port in which the rebels have any vessels ... it is, in my opinion, better to begin there."[6]

Nine large blocks comprised the center of New Haven, where four churches, a courthouse, a prison and the buildings of Yale College surrounded the center block of New Haven Green. Residents lived in about 300 houses, many beautifully constructed with colonial-style architecture. Before the war many citizens opposed British policies but they did not rush to join the hostilities at Boston in April 1775. One exception was Benedict Arnold, a New Haven shop owner and militia captain who demanded powder from the town magazine and marched his company to join the fight at Boston without waiting for permission from the town leaders (he left hanging above his shop the sign that declared him as "B. Arnold, Druggist, Bookseller").[7]

Students at Yale, including freshman Noah Webster, formed their own militia company as support for the rebellion grew. The student-soldiers and two local militia companies turned out to honor Gen. Washington and Gen. Charles Lee when they stopped in New Haven on the way to Boston in June 1775. But a significant portion of the population remained loyal to the Crown and several men left town to join the Loyalist King's American Regiment. Tories who stayed often found that town leaders denied them some of their basic rights, including participation in religious services, until they signed oaths of loyalty to Connecticut. Yale students with Loyalist leanings endured harassment from their peers or summary dismissal by Ezra Stiles, who became the college president in 1778.

The year 1779 was the first that residents of New Haven decided to publicly celebrate the independence of the United States, but since July 4 fell on a Sunday, out of respect for the Sabbath the Puritan-descended citizenry planned to hold their gala, complete with a militia parade, on the following day. The town of West Haven, on the west side of New Haven Harbor, marked the Fourth with day-long church services where the Reverend Noah Williston offered prayers for the Continental Congress and Gen. Washington's army. Collier's Royal Navy squadron appeared on the horizon on the afternoon of July 4 but was still headed east, and, to the militia observing from the coast, the ships appeared to be bound for another destination. Yale president Ezra Stiles observed, "A lethargy seemed to have seized the inhabitants, who would believe the fleet would pass by in the morning."[8] The militia shore patrols continued while residents slept, relieved that the fleet was gone.

Part of a local artillery company, that night led by Lieutenant Aziel Kimberly, monitored the sound from the area known as Clark's Point, west of New Haven Harbor. One of Kimberly's soldiers on duty in the early morning hours of July 5 was twenty-year-old Thomas Painter, who had been a militiaman for only three months. Painter recalled that at about 2:00 A.M., "as it was a starlight night," he saw the Royal Navy squadron turn and head towards the shore.[9] Painter fired an alarm gun to alert the town and then ran to his uncle's house to tell him about the landing. The ships came in close and dropped anchor near Savin Rock at the western mouth of New Haven Harbor.

The boom of the signal gun led to the ringing of church bells and the long roll of militia drums, which woke Yale president Ezra Stiles, who had an inquisitive mind. A short list of his interests includes meteorology, astronomy, physics, silk cultures, horticulture, political science, philosophy, and languages. He wrote and spoke Latin fluently, and, seeking a deeper understanding of the Scriptures, he mastered Hebrew and sometimes attended synagogue services just for practice. Now awakened, Stiles climbed the steeple of the college chapel as soon as there was enough daylight to see more than a few hundred yards, looked towards the coast, and was shocked to see dozens of British ships anchored off the harbor. "All then knew our fate," he wrote later.[10] He quickly left his perch and sent his four daughters to the nearby town of Carmel. With his youngest son, Stiles gathered the college records, his silver tableware, and important belongings and sent them out of town on a cart. Then he dismissed the college students.

Despite the signal gun, drums and bells, at his uncle's house Thomas Painter found his relatives "extremely incredulous and unwilling to believe there was any real danger, for they had become accustomed to frequent and unnecessary alarms." Painter rejoined his militia company at the shore and later recalled, "a gun was fired from the [British] Commodore as a signal for landing, and instantly a string of boats was seen dropping astern of every transport ship, full of soldiers."[11] Painter and Stiles were both stunned witnesses to the landing of the raiding force commanded by Maj. Gen. William Tryon.

William Tryon was well-suited to command the raids meant to destroy Connecticut's commerce. He had been born in Surrey, England, as the maternal grandson of an earl and had served briefly as a junior officer in the British army, until he married into a wealthy family in 1757. Family influence garnered Tryon an appointment as lieutenant-governor of the South Carolina Colony, and in 1771 he became the royal governor of New York. He was in England when hostilities erupted and the day he returned to New York, June 25, 1775, crowds cheered his arrival from England. (That morning they had also cheered Gen. Washington on his way to Boston.) After the rebels seized New York City, Tryon was forced to attempt to rule the parts of the colony that were not in rebel hands from aboard the Royal Navy ship *Duchess of Gordon* until Gen. Howe took the city. His position as governor was restored, but with the city under martial law and many of the counties still under rebel control, Tryon had little function.

As the war continued without a decisive British victory, Tryon became convinced that the only way to end the conflict was to devastate the areas in rebellion, especially the property and livelihoods of the Patriot leaders, in a practice he termed "desolation warfare." Though he had no animosity towards Americans in general, Tryon obtained a major-general's commission to command Loyalist forces and he led his soldiers with the vehemence of a man who had a score to settle with the rebels, who he contemptuously referred to as "committeemen."[12] Over the course of two years, beginning in April 1777, his troops raided throughout New Jersey, southeastern New York, and western Connecticut (including a raid at the town of Horseneck, in which the Seventeenth Foot and Loyal American Regiment, the defenders of Stony Point, participated), destroying the property of prominent rebels, whaleboats, and tons of stores intended for the Continental Army.

Gen. Clinton and Tryon initially got along well, but by early 1779 Clinton considered Tryon's methods excessively brutal and Tryon believed that Clinton lacked aggressiveness. When Tryon proposed the formation of a corps of Loyalists to wage guerrilla war in Connecticut and plunder at will, Clinton rejected the idea as barbaric. The Loyalist confidant William Smith recorded that Tryon was "vastly mortified by being left at Home" during Clinton's new offensive.[13] But in late June, after Washington failed to be baited into attacking King's Ferry, Clinton decided to employ Tryon to draw the Americans into battle on the east side of the Hudson. Clinton's orders to Tryon did not direct the plunder or burning of the towns, nor did they expressly forbid the practices. Tryon interpreted his commander's conspicuous silence on the topics as permission to carry out his desolation warfare methods.[14] Smith wrote that when it came to coastal raids, Clinton "seemed fond of that Mode of War."[15]

The landings near Savin Rock at the New Haven harbor was a spectacle of the military might of the British Empire. The masts of Collier's fifty-three ships crowded the horizon. Red, white and blue British ensigns flew from every vessel. To cover the landings the warships *Camilla*, *Greyhound*, *Scorpion*, and *Virginia* anchored as close to shore as their draughts allowed, and their black cannon pointed menacingly toward the beach. Flat-bottomed landing barges, each packed with up to sixty soldiers and rowed by twenty blue-jacketed sailors, were lowered from each transport and then turned their bows toward the shore. As the boats touched the beach the soldiers poured out and formed their long ranks. Maj. Gen. George Garth, Tryon's deputy, commanded the first division to land. The soldiers of the Fifty-fourth Regiment of Foot, fresh from their occupation of Newport, stood resplendent in scarlet coats with white gaiters on their legs. The light infantry companies of the Guards and the Welch Fusiliers wore the traditional red coats with white facings. A detachment of Hessian Jagers in green jackets fanned out, hunting human prey. Royal Artillerymen wheeled four field guns out of the barges and onto the beach. Time and again the barges made the circuit between the beach and the ships until the 1,500 soldiers of Garth's force were on the shore. All along their ranks, the sun glittered off brass buttons, officers' rank badges, and bayonets. By 6:00 A.M. the British began marching north toward New Haven, about four miles inland. Three local Loyalists welcomed the king's soldiers and volunteered their services as guides. Militiaman Thomas Painter and some of his comrades fired a few shots at the British landings, but their company wisely withdrew from the beach.

Garth's column reached West Haven Green in mid-morning and halted for rest. The temperature climbed to near ninety degrees and the soldiers were already exhausted and drenched with sweat after their march. Garth issued orders against pillaging but soldiers ransacked nearby homes anyway. William Campbell, adjutant of the Foot Guards, became a one-man enforcer of civil behavior. Campbell had received a king's commission after serving in the enlisted ranks, a rare feat at the time, and so was accustomed to handling unruly troops. He intervened when soldiers caught the Reverend Noah Williston (who had offered the prayers for the Continental Congress on July 4) fleeing the British advance. Williston had broken his leg scaling a wall and the troops threatened him with death, but Campbell reportedly chastised them: "We make war on soldiers, not civilians."[16] He had the minister carried into his home and the regimental surgeon set the limb. Campbell returned to the Green and arrested other soldiers he caught looting civilian property. As the Redcoats continued their advance toward New Haven an American sharpshooter shot Campbell in the chest, close to the heart. Soldiers carried the wounded officer to a house on the side of the road but Campbell died within minutes. The next day residents of West Haven buried him in a shallow grave near the spot where he fell.

North of West Haven Green the American militia gathered, summoned by the church bells, alarm guns, and drum rolls. District commander Lt. Col. Hezekiah Sabin collected 150 militiamen along the road close to Milford Hill, southwest of New Haven, assisted by James Hillhouse, a twenty-five-year-old local attorney and Yale alumnus. One of their soldiers was Payson Williston, son of the clergyman that Adjutant Campbell saved, and another was Ezra Stiles, eldest son of Yale's president. George Welles, a senior at Yale and captain of the student militia, added his company of schoolmates to Sabin's force, along with fifty-one-year-old Professor Naphtali Daggett, Yale president emeritus. Continental Army colonel Aaron Burr, on furlough in nearby Eddington visiting relatives, helped organize the defenders who had retreated from landing beach, one of whom was Pvt. Thomas Painter.

The American militia was outnumbered ten to one, so Capt. Hillhouse concealed his men behind a stone wall and watched as Garth's soldiers marched north from West Haven in neat ranks. When the advance guard of the Redcoats came within musket range, the Yankee militiamen rose and fired. Yale student Elizur Goodrich wrote later about the action: "We fired on them several times, then chased them the length of three or four

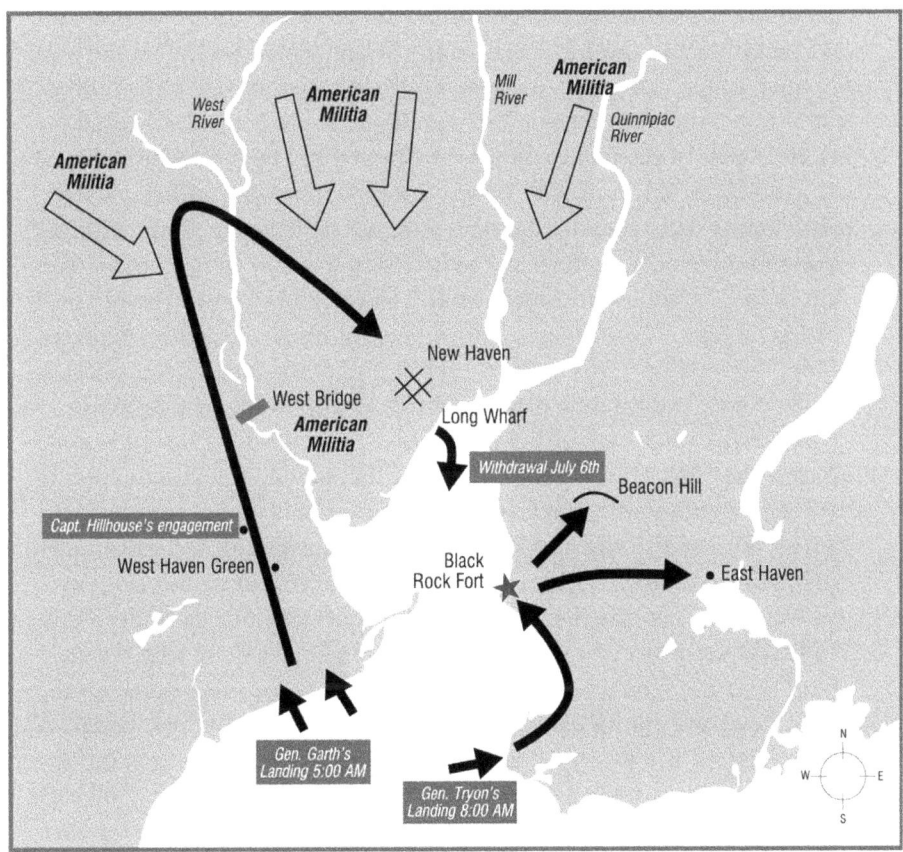

On July 5, 1779, Maj. Gen. William Tryon's men landed on both sides of New Haven Harbor and moved toward the town under stiff opposition from American militia units, including a student company from Yale College (map by the author and Eleana Nicolaou, adapted from a sketch by Ezra Stiles in *The Literary Diary of Ezra Stiles*).

fields as they retreated." The main body of the British column immediately formed a line of battle, counterattacked, covered the ground quickly and nearly surrounded the Yankees. Goodrich continued: "It was now our turn to run, and we did for our lives."[17] Retreating with the militia, Thomas Painter wrote that he ran through the fields "at the top of my speed, and the bullets after me like a shower of hail, which seemed to prostrate the grass around me."[18]

Professor Daggett fired only once before the militia retreated and left him behind. He later wrote that two British soldiers approached him, "the fury of infernals glowing in their faces. They called me a damned old rebel and swore they would kill me instantly. They demanded 'What did you fire upon us for?' I replied, 'Because it is the exercise of war.'" The soldiers stabbed at Daggett with their bayonets and the old professor begged for his life. "One of them gave me four gashes on my head with the edge of his bayonet to the skull and bone," he remembered, "which caused a painful effusion of blood. The other gave me three slight pricks with the point of his bayonet on the trunk of my body, but they were no more than skin deep." "A thousand times worse," Daggett wrote, was the physical beating he took. "I was knocked down once or more and almost deprived of life," he recalled.[19] The soldiers robbed him of his shoes, silver buckles, handkerchief, and tobacco box and marched him to the British column.

After he took care of his family and Yale college, Ezra Stiles rode around the New Haven area observing the action. He saw the scrape between the militiamen and Garth's soldiers and said that as a result of the Yankee musket fire the Redcoats "marched in a huddled confusion."[20] Garth pushed his men northeast toward New Haven; but at the bridge over the West River, on the most direct route, American militia under Capt. William Bradley tore up the bridge planking and opened fire with two field guns. Their fire forced Garth to divert his march two miles north up the Forest Road and Darby Pike to cross the West River at Darby's Bridge. A Redcoat guard still forced Naphtali Daggett to follow the column but the old professor was weak from blood loss. He wrote of it later: "When I failed, in some degree, through faintness, he would strike me on the back with a heavy walking-staff, and kick me."[21]

Capt. Bradley's militia split. Part of them crossed the West River to fire at the rear of the Redcoat column and part marched north to block Darby's Bridge. Other Yankee militiamen, led by Col. Aaron Burr, harassed the British left flank. The Americans initially prevented Garth's troops from crossing Darby Bridge but the Redcoat Light Infantry forded the river and wedged the Yankees off the crossing site. By this time Col. Sabin and Capt. Hillhouse had come up from the West Bridge with a two-pounder field gun and opened fire. Ezra Stiles remembered: "The northern militia and those from Darby by this time crouded in and pressed on all side— and some behaved with amazing intrepidity. One captain drew up and threw himself and his whole company directly before the enemy's column and gave and received the fire.... [T]he battle became very severe and bloody for a short time, when a number was killed on both sides."[22] The Yankees repulsed a British detachment sent to destroy a nearby gunpowder mill and halted Garth's advance north of New Haven at a tract of land known as Ditch Corner, but the Redcoats scattered the militia with a bayonet charge and continued toward the town.

Gen. Tryon reported that Garth's men were "under a continuous fire," but the American militia was outgunned and fought a fighting retreat to the northwest corner of New Haven, where Garth finally entered the town at about 1:00 P.M., "not without opposition, loss, and fatigue," as Tryon recorded.[23] The column reached New Haven Green, and Naphtali Daggett recalled as follows: "I obtained leave of an officer to be carried into the Widow Lyman's and laid upon a bed, where I lay the rest of the day and succeeding night, in such acute and excruciating pain as I never felt before."[24] Sixteen months later Daggett died from the effects of his beatings. Gen. Garth sent a message to Tryon that recommended immediately burning the town. "This place is almost entirely deserted," he reported, "and therefore merits the flames."[25]

Gen. Tryon was experiencing his own troubles with rebel resistance when he received Garth's message about burning the town. Tryon's division had landed on the east side of New Haven Harbor at about 10:00 A.M., after Garth's division was ashore. Just as with Garth's earlier landings, the barges rowed in 1,500 men from the Twenty-third Foot, two Hessian regiments, the Royal Welch Fusiliers and the King's American Regiment, the latter commanded by Col. Edmund Fanning, a 1757 graduate of Yale and Gen. Tryon's son-in-law. A fifty-man company of East Haven militia led by Captains Josiah Bradley and Amos Morris took position on the shore with three field guns and opened fire. An officer of the King's American Regiment stood up in his boat and shouted, "Disperse, ye rebels!"[26]—and a militia sharpshooter killed him with a single musket shot.

Tryon reported that the militia's field guns "annoyed"[27] his soldiers, and Commodore Collier disclosed a bit of the British fear of American sharpshooters when he wrote that the landing was opposed "by some companies of *riflemen*," whom he described as "excellent marksmen, with rifle-barreled guns" who "concealed themselves in the bushes."[28] The American fire forced Tryon's boats to split up. One-half landed at the Grove House Wharf to the west and the other half continued straight to unload troops on the beach. Collier was apparently relieved that the landing did not suffer more from the Yankee sharpshooters when he noted "several troops were wounded, but the troops got on shore with less injury than might have been expected."[29] The Redcoats pushed the American militia off the beach, captured one of the cannon, and moved inland towards New Haven, five miles distant.

Tryon's column was initially successful as the American militia continued to fall back ahead of them. Locals sniped at the column. The Redcoats retaliated by setting fire to the homes of militia captain Amos Morris, who commanded the troops that opposed the British landing: Morris' brother; and Joseph Pardee, who collected his valuables and family in an oxcart and barely escaped ahead of the British. Joseph Tuttle and his seventeen-year-old son were away from their family farm fighting with the militia. When the Redcoats approached their home, his wife buried their silver plates in her garden, loaded their six other children and some household items in a cart, and fled northward. The Tuttle house was in flames while it was still within her view. Before the day was over, the smoke from ten houses swirled into the sky above New Haven Harbor. Nineteen militiamen and armed citizens made a stand at Black Rock Fort, an earthen bastion on the west side of the harbor, but fired all of their ammunition. Charging Redcoats then surged over the walls and captured all of the fort's defenders, which included Joseph Tuttle, his son, and Capt. Amos Morris, whose houses were already charred ruins.

A deadly routine developed as the invading troops moved further inland. The American militia concealed themselves behind the fences that ran along the roads and when the British column came close, the Yankees rose from behind their cover, fired, and then fell back. Each volley forced the British to stop, deploy into a line of battle, counterattack, and re-form into a column formation to march down the road. Militia Capt. Josiah Bradley, one of the commanders at the beach with Capt. Morris, hid his men along one road and told them, "Wait until you can see their eyes and then fire and run."[30] Then another group of militia would emerge from the fences and loose another volley, followed by the same sequence of events. American artilleryman set up two field guns on the road, fired on Tryon's column, and then pulled the guns back a few yards after every shot. The pursuit of militiamen frustrated and exhausted the Redcoats. New England militiamen had used these classic guerrilla tactics at the opening battles of the war outside Boston on April 19, 1775, when they decimated the British ranks and shocked the king's officers with the intensity of their resistance. The methods were equally effective at New Haven.

By early afternoon the British column had advanced barely three miles from its landing beach. Tryon still had another two miles to go before he could cross the Quinnipac River and unite with Gen. Garth's division in New Haven, and the morning's slow advance gave the rebels time to entrench on Beacon Hill, south of the Quinnipac, and block the crossing.

A British infantry charge drove the Americans off Beacon Hill, but the Yankees maintained control of the bridge over the Quinnipac. Tryon sent a detachment one mile to the east to occupy the village of East Haven, but his troops again met stiff resistance that prevented them from controlling the town. Unable to advance further, Tryon held his position south of the Quinnipac and set up headquarters on Beacon Hill.

The messenger bearing Gen. Garth's note that recommended burning New Haven probably reached Tryon on Beacon Hill. In response, Tryon took Leavenworth's Ferry across the Quinnipac to New Haven and convened a council of war with Garth, Commodore Collier, and Col. Fanning of the King's American Regiment to decide how to proceed with the raid at New Haven. Musket shots still cracked sporadically and the officers agreed that strong rebel forces remained outside the town. At some point during the conference Tryon and Garth decided not to burn New Haven. Legend states that Loyalist leaders, including Col. Fanning, asked the British commanders to spare the town, and that Garth consented, saying, "'Tis too pretty a place to burn."[31] But in his report to Gen. Clinton, Tryon attributed the decision to their belief that the gathering rebel militia would soon outnumber the British force as well as outgun them with heavy cannon. The officers agreed that, for the evening, Garth's division would occupy New Haven while Tryon's division held Beacon Hill. Tryon also remembered that Gen. Clinton's orders had emphasized that it was "not advisable to stay any time.... [Y]our business must be done in 24 or 48 hours."[32] With the rebel militia gathering and his commander's orders in mind, Tryon decided his force would depart the next morning.

Before the soldiers settled in for the evening, one of Garth's officers walked onto New Haven Green and read aloud from an open address from Tryon and Collier to the residents of Connecticut. "Your town, your property, yourselves, lie within the grasp of the power whose forbearance you have ungenerously construed into fear," the broadside declared, and went on: "Can the strength of your whole province cope with the force which might at any time be poured through every district in your country? You are conscious it cannot. Why, then, will you persist in a ruinous and ill-judged resistance? We hoped that you would recover from the frenzy which has distracted this unhappy country; and we believe the day to be near come when the greater part of this continent will begin to blush at their delusion."[33] Tryon's soldiers also went to the New Haven wharf and read a proclamation that offered freedom to all slaves that joined the British. Ezra Stiles wrote that few slaves, if any, accepted the offer.

General Tryon and Commodore Collier distributed this broadside to the citizens of New Haven, which chastised them for rebelling against King George III and urged them to return to Crown allegiance. The citizens of New Haven responded by sniping at Tryon's troops throughout the night (Library of Congress).

Tryon and Collier were overly optimistic in their expectations for the residents of New Haven to repudiate the rebellion. Collier recalled, "Such inhabitants that remained in their homes had a sentinel at their doors granted them, to prevent any irregularities. But even this mark of indulgence was treated with the *baseness and treachery* inherent in these people. The very sentinels placed as their *safeguards* were villainously shot and murdered from the upper windows! Their inveteracy extinguished even their feeling of humanity, if they ever possessed it."[34] Several balls whistled past Collier as he surveyed the town with a party of officers.

Some unknown citizens left casks of West Indian rum out near the Green, possibly in an effort to curry favor from the Redcoats. Exhausted from the day's combat in the sweltering heat, frustrated by fighting the elusive American militia, and fueled by free rum, British soldiers vented their anger on the civilian population, as a contemporary newspaper recounted: "New Haven was delivered up ... to promiscuous plunder; in which, besides robbing the inhabitants of their watches, money, plate, buckles, clothing, bedding, and provisions, etc., they broke and destroyed household furniture and other property to a very great amount."[35]

It is possible that a Patriot newspaper exaggerated British actions, but at least nine New Haven residents filed affidavits that documented atrocities. Among them was Elias Beers, who told how his sixty-one-year-old father, Nathan, helped and bandaged a wounded British officer, "for which the officer offered his thanks upon his departure." Minutes later, three Redcoats rushed toward the elder Beers as he stood in his doorway and pointed their muskets at his chest. "One of the pieces only went off," remembered Elias, but Beers knocked the weapon down and the ball entered his hip. Beers crawled to his bedroom, but another group of soldiers entered the house, dragged him from bed, "demanded his money, kicked and otherwise abused him."[36] The soldiers stabbed him with their bayonets, and Beers died a week later. At least two women were raped and others were otherwise assaulted. Redcoats quenched their thirst at a well owned by seventy-four-year-old Benjamin English and then bayoneted the old man to death after he reproached them for behaving like ruffians. Loyalist John Kennedy welcomed the king's troops but soldiers still looted his home and stabbed him to death when he protested. Troops shot militia Capt. John Gilbert in the knee and then beat him to death. Possibly most shocking was the fate of Elisha Tuttle, who suffered from epilepsy and a mental illness that may have been linked to the time the British and Indians had burned his home and killed his family on the frontier of New York.

When the British entered New Haven, Tuttle seized an old, unloaded musket and pointed it at them in a fit of revenge. Neighbors intervened and implored the soldiers to understand that Tuttle was a "distracted delirious person," but the Redcoats mercilessly beat the man and since he could not respond satisfactorily to their taunts, cut out his tongue with a bayonet. Tuttle died from his injuries three days later.[37]

Outside New Haven the countryside was in arms. Near the town of Wallingford, militia colonel Street Hall rode from farm to farm and called for his soldiers: "Turn out! The British are in New Haven!"[38] Lt. John Holbrook went to join his militia company and his father advised him, "You are going to fight the enemies of your country; now remember that I had rather see you brought back wounded in front than in running from the enemy."[39] North Guilford resident Lyman Beecher recalled, "I remember that day we were plowing, when we heard the sound of cannon toward New Haven. 'Whoa!' said Uncle Benton; stopped team, off harness, mounted old Sorrell, bareback, shouldered the old musket, and rode off to New Haven. Deacon Bartlett went too; and Sam Bartlett said he never saw his father more keen after deer than he was to get a shot at the regulars."[40] Militia from the towns of Hamden, North Haven, Meriden, Derby, Guilford and others also answered the alarm. By nightfall on July 5 about 1,000 militiamen had assembled outside of New Haven, along with some Continental Army soldiers from a nearby camp under General Artemus Ward, who took command of the group. Lt. Holbrook scouted New Haven and recommended an immediate attack after he saw the drunken British troops. Gen. Ward declined, waiting to see what the next day brought.

At dawn on July 6 the British raiding force set fire to six port buildings and seven vessels suspected to be privateers and then marched to the New Haven wharf and Black Rock Fort to embark for their ships. A dense fog covered the area and the British movements caught most American militiamen off guard. Gen. Tryon reported that "there was not a shot fired to molest the retreat,"[41] but a few militiamen, like Capt. Jedediah Andrews, sniped at the Redcoats as they departed. The last British vessel slipped its cable from the wharf in the afternoon, and the row galley *Hussar* loosed a few parting cannon shots at Black Rock Fort as it sailed out of the harbor. The Redcoats took with them twelve prisoners and left behind twenty-seven Americans dead and seventeen wounded, in addition to the destruction of the seven ships, ten private houses, six shops, and three barns, a loss estimated at the time to exceed £25,000, over $5,000,000 in modern money. Four Loyalist families also left with Tryon. The records of British losses are contradictory, but a fair estimate is that Tryon's force suffered nearly 100 casualties, probably forty-four killed or missing and around the same number wounded.

Yale College president Ezra Stiles returned to New Haven soon after the British departure. He had "a mixt sense of joy and sorrow" because the Redcoats left the college buildings relatively undamaged but the rest of the town was a scene of "plunder, rapes, murder, bayoneting, indelicacies towards the sex, insolence and abuse and insult towards the inhabitants in general."[42] Stiles also knew that New Haven remained largely intact and that the British could still return to finish destroying the town. But on board the frigate *Camilla*, Gen. Tryon referred to Gen. Clinton's instructions, which stated that after he struck at New Haven, "your next object seems to be Fairfield."[43]

X

Desolation Warfare

Fairfield, Connecticut, July 7, 1779

Twenty-five miles west of New Haven on Long Island Sound, farmers around the town of Fairfield were in the midst of the wheat harvest. The Reverend Andrew Eliot described the time as "a season of extraordinary labor & festivity, which promised the greatest plenty that had been known for many years.... Never did our fields bear so ponderous a load; never were our prospects ... so bright."[1] The bountiful fields were indicators of Fairfield's prosperity, a town that had, in the words of a local historian, "fine churches, new courthouse, and stately mansions."[2] Fairfield was also the location of the Penfield Mills that supplied flour for the Continental Army and home port to the privateers *Defence* and *Oliver Cromwell*. The nearby town of Stratford operated a gunpowder mill.

These industries made the area a lucrative target for British raids, but the only measure townspeople made for defense was to man the tiny Black Rock Fort at Fairfield Harbor with twenty-seven militiamen under Capt. Isaac Jarvis. On the morning of July 7 Jarvis' men saw Commodore Collier's Royal Navy squadron sailing southwest on the Sound, looking like they were bound for New York City. A thick fog covered the coast later that morning but when the mist cleared at about 10:00 A.M. the lookouts were shocked to see the king's ships anchoring four miles off the coast near Kenzie's Point. The soldiers fired three cannon shots to alert the town.

Collier's ships rode at anchor until about 4:00 P.M., when Gen. Tryon began landing southwest of Black Rock Fort with the flank companies of the Guards, the Hessian Landgrave Regiment, the King's American

Regiment, and two field guns. Capt. Jarvis' militia opened fire on the Redcoats with a twelve-pounder cannon. Though an eyewitness said that the Americans kept the gun firing "till it was so hot you could hardly bear your hand thereon," Tryon reported that the shelling had no effect.[3] Guided by local Loyalist George Hoyt, the column headed towards Fairfield, which was about a mile-and-a-half inland.

The squadron's day at anchor gave the local militia time to gather, and by the time Tryon's column began their march Yankee soldiers had concealed themselves along the road to Fairfield. Gen. Tryon reported that as his column marched towards the town it "received a smart fire of musketry"[4]; the Reverend Andrew Eliot wrote that the militiamen "gave them such a warm reception with a field piece which threw both round and grape shot.... The column, however, quickly recovered its solidity."[5] The Redcoats pushed through the fire and occupied Fairfield, forcing the militia to retreat to a hill overlooking the town, and from there they bombarded the British with field guns. At midday Gen. Garth's division landed and united with Tryon's force in Fairfield.

With no significant militia opposition, nothing prevented Tryon from putting his "desolation warfare" concept into action. Most residents had left the village with their valuables and livestock but the Rev. Eliot remembered "a few women, some of whom were of the most respectable families & characters, tarried with a view of saving their property. They imagined their sex & character would avail to such a purpose." But, he continued, "the Hessians were first let loose to rapine & plunder. They entered houses, attacked the persons of Whig & Tory indiscriminately; breaking open desks, trunks, closets, & taking away everything of value. They robbed women of their buckles, rings, bonnets, aprons and handkerchiefs. They abused them with the foulest and most profane language, threatened their lives without the least regard to their most earnest cries & entreaties. Looking glasses, china, and all kinds of furniture, were dashed to pieces."[6]

The soldiers distributed copies of the same Tryon-Collier proclamation they had read in New Haven. Tryon also had a local clergyman take a copy of the broadside under a white flag to Col. Whiting, commander of the Fairfield militia. Whiting responded:" Connecticut has nobly vowed to take up arms against the cruel despotism of Britain, and as the flames have now preceded your flag, they will persist to oppose to the utmost that power exerted against injured innocence."[7] Commodore Collier recalled "in spite of every argument that could be used to induce these infatuated people to return to their allegiance, they remained obstinate, and the lenity exerted towards New Haven served but to harden them the more towards their inveteracy and rebellion."[8]

Rebels fired at the Redcoats from house windows and Tryon ordered Garth to clear the sharpshooters out and put their houses to the torch, "which was done accordingly," wrote Collier.[9] Tryon unabashedly wrote how he ordered his men to burn "the greatest part of the village," beginning with the home of Mr. Isaac Jennings.[10] Two Loyalists from nearby towns helped the British troops set their fires, the flames spread to nearby structures, and the entire town became engulfed. The Rev. Eliot recalled that "General Tryon was in various parts of the town plot, with the good women begging & entreating him to spare their houses."[11] After another clergyman asked Tryon to leave some buildings intact as shelters for those who had lost their homes, and the general spared the churches and the Rev. Eliot's home. Eliot wrote that Tryon "was far from being in good temper during the whole affair. General Garth at the other end of the town, treated the inhabitants with as much humanity as his errand would admit."[12] The only militia defense came from Capt. Jarvis and his soldiers, at Black Rock Fort, who lobbed cannon shells at any British troops that moved within their sight. Jarvis and his men held out against British attempts to seize the fort, including bombardment from the row galley *Hussar*. One resident remembered "had [Capt. Jarvis] been a coward 10 more houses would have been burnt."[13]

With the town in flames, Tryon's work was complete and he withdrew his force to their landing beach at around 8:00 P.M. The Hessian Landgrave Regiment covered the withdrawal as a rear guard, and the Rev. Eliot wrote that the German troops "set fire to everything which General Tryon had left; the large & elegant meeting-house, the minister's houses, Mr. Burr's and several other houses which had received protection.... They may properly be called sons of plunder & devastation."[14] A thunderstorm began, and lightning flashes illuminated the pitiful burning village. As one resident recalled, "The conflagration of nearly two hundred houses illuminated the earth, the skirts of the clouds, & the waves of the Sound with a union of gloom & grandeur, at once inexpressibly awful & magnificent.... At intervals the lightning blazed with a livid & terrible splendor. The thunder rolled above.... Add to this the convulsion of the elements, the dreadful effect of vindictive & wanton devastation, the trembling of the earth, the sharp sound of muskets occasionally discharged, the groans here & there of the wounded & dying ... then place before your eyes crowds of miserable sufferers [and] you will form a just but imperfect picture of the burning of Fairfield. It needed no great effort of imagination to believe that the final day had arrived."[15]

The next morning, July 8, Tryon's men loaded once again into their transports and sailed over the horizon into Long Island Sound. Behind them ninety-seven homes, sixty-seven barns, eighteen shops, two schoolhouses, the courthouse, two meetinghouses, the jail and two churches still burned or lay in smoking ashes. Townspeople saved only twelve of Fairfield's houses.[16] Tryon reported the incidents matter of factly to Clinton, stating that he only regretted the burning of the churches, which, he explained, "took fire unintentionally by the flakes from other buildings."[17] The next day Maj. Benjamin Tallmadge and a detachment of the Second Continental Light Dragoons, sent from Pound Ridge, clattered into the town but found no British to fight. A militia captain named Sturges and 100 militiamen gathered at the home of Jonathan Bulkley, whose wife was the sister of George Hoyt, the Loyalist who guided the British to Fairfield. A witness recalled that Sturges "informed Mrs. Bulkley that he would allow her a short time to clear the house, & unless she left it would blow her to atoms."[18] Col. Whiting, the district commander who had indignantly replied to Tryon's broadside, arrived and ordered Sturges and his men to disperse under the threat of arrest.

Tryon's force sailed across the sound to the town of Huntington on Long Island, where his men rested, took on provisions, and on the afternoon of July 10 sailed back across the sound to a point five miles off the Bay of Norwalk, Connecticut, whose citizens should have expected a British raid. Norwalk was one of four Connecticut ports authorized to accept and sell prize cargoes from privateers, home to the owners of the successful privateer *Ranger* and the home of Captain Lemuel Brooks of the privateer *Gamecock*. Norwalk was also a key link on routes from military depots at Danbury and Fishkill that supplied the Continental Army and a source of provisions in its own right. One Norwalk merchant sent 22,000 pounds of flour, 240 gallons of rum and 281 quarts of salt to Washington's troops in a two-month period; another sent two hundred bushels of oats and corn in less than one month. The town also operated saltpeter works that refined potassium nitrate, a component of gunpowder. Norwalk had already experienced one narrow escape: in 1777 Gen. Tryon made the town the target of his first raid into Connecticut, but cannon at the mouth of Norwalk Harbor forced the Redcoats to land elsewhere and they raided Danbury instead.[19]

By this time, Gen. Washington had begun reacting to the British raids, though his somewhat tardy response was not the fault of his intelligence system — Abraham Woodull had sent two reports in June about British preparations to attack the Connecticut coast. But Washington was on an inspection tour of the Hudson River fortifications in the first week of July and he did not see Woodhull's second message, written on June 29, until he returned to headquarters on July 7, the same day Tryon landed at Fairfield. Washington immediately informed Governor Jonathan Trumbull that the British "probably have in view a sudden incursion into your State; perhaps New London may be the object."[20] He also ordered Gen. Horatio Gates, the victor of Saratoga and commander of the Continental Army's Northern Department, to "give all the aid in his power to the [Connecticut] Militia" and to send them a brigade of Massachusetts troops under Col. John Glover.[21]

Brig. Gen. Samuel Parsons, the Connecticut officer in command at West Point, had recently requested permission to travel to his home state to conduct some personal business, and Washington initially intended to deny his request. But with the coast under attack he ordered Parsons to Norwalk. "It is probable from different accounts the enemy have made an incursion into Connecticut," he wrote. "[I]f so you may be useful by taking the direction of the militia which may be assembling to oppose them, if you can arrive in time."[22] Washington put Glover's Brigade, already on the march towards Connecticut, at Parson's disposal. As soon as he received the order Parsons directed the militia companies along the coast to rendezvous at Norwalk and come under his command. He departed his headquarters immediately, rode to New Haven and Fairfield to survey the damage, and arrived at Norwalk on the night of July 9, where about 1,000 militiamen gathered. Parsons also asked Washington for reinforcements of 1,000 Continental troops.

Afloat off Norwalk Harbor on July 10, Tryon's division of the Fifty-fourth Foot, the Hessian Landgrave Regiment, the Jagers and the King's American Regiment loaded into their landing barges at sunset and rowed towards a flat grassland east of the harbor known as Cow's Pasture. There was no opposition and the Crown troops finished landing in the early morning hours of July 11 and marched toward Norwalk. Gen. Garth's division began landing at dawn. Scattered small groups of American militiamen appeared and peppered the British column with musket fire, but Tryon reported that the Fifty-fourth Regiment drove off the rebels "with great alacrity and spirit" and took Grumman's Hill just outside Norwalk at about 4:30 A.M.[23] His men halted to wait for Garth's division to catch up to them.

Gen. Parsons gathered his American forces while the British moved inland. At around 6:00 A.M., about 150 Continentals under Parsons' command and 800 militiamen with two field guns commanded by Gen. Oliver Wolcott moved onto the heights outside Norwalk known as the "Rocks," lobbed a few cannon shots at the British, and advanced towards Grumman's Hill. A steady rain began, and though the Yankees pushed against the British for two hours they lacked the strength to overpower Tryon's force. The American attack faltered and the troops retreated to nearby towns. Garth's division arrived from the landing beach at about 11:00 A.M. and Tryon's united force entered Norwalk.

Just as at Fairfield, the American retreat left Norwalk unprotected. Most citizens had hidden their possessions and sent their women and children to inland villages, but Tryon's men still set the torch to 135 houses, eighty-five barns, fifteen stores, twenty-five shops, five vessels and four mills. This time Tryon issued strict orders to protect the churches but later he weakly claimed "it is very difficult when the houses are close ... to prevent the spreading of flames."[24] Both churches in Norwalk burned. Tryon later reported to Clinton, matter of factly, "many salt pans were destroyed, whale boats carried on board the fleet, and the magazine, stores, and vessels set in flames, with the greatest part of the dwelling houses." Perhaps mindful that he may have carried his theories of desolation warfare too far, he added, "I should be very sorry if the destruction of these two villages [Fairfield and Norwalk] would be thought less reconcilable with humanity than with the love of my country, my duty to the king, and the laws of arms."[25] Clinton later dryly wrote that Norwalk, along with New Haven and Fairfield, "suffered very severely."[26] Before darkness fell, the British retraced their route back to the beach and departed across Long Island Sound for Huntington.

Washington and Clinton periodically received dispatches that described the action in Connecticut, and both generals monitored the situation with apprehension. Washington ordered two more brigades to the area but none of the Continentals reached the coastal towns in time to help. Governor Trumbull begged for more soldiers, but Washington was wary of reducing his forces that protected the Hudson. "It is very probable in the present case," he wrote in response, "that one principal object of the operations on your coast may be to draw us off from the [Hudson] River, to facilitate an attack upon it." The general told Trumbull that he could not send any more troops because of "the smallness of our force" and "I could do little more than lament the depredations of the enemy at a distance."[27]

Gen. Clinton was anxious for the Americans to come to Connecticut's aid and cross the Hudson, and he had moved his army to Mamaroneck on the coast of the sound to be in position to either assist Tryon or strike at the Continental Army if it moved towards the coast. But as every day passed it became clear that Washington would not respond with anything more than a few brigades, and Clinton wanted to pounce on the entire Continental Army. Clinton's understanding of the situation at the time is difficult to identify. After the war, he said that he realized that Tryon's destructive methods only further alienated the American population, failed to draw Washington into battle, and were counterproductive — realizations that probably benefited from hindsight. Commodore Collier recalled that in mid–July 1779 he and Clinton received "well authenticated" intelligence that "the chastisement that the rebels received in Connecticut, was attended with very favorable consequences for the King's cause; that murmurs, both against Washington and the Congress, rose *very high*; [and] many of the principle people of [Connecticut] ... seemed determined to throw off all subjection and allegiance to the Congress."[28] Collier said that he and Clinton met at Throg's Neck, where they agreed to continue the raids by next hitting the port of New London. Either way, in mid–July Clinton must have begun to realize that his attempt to lure the Americans into battle by raiding Connecticut was failing.

By then, Washington was already planning a way to strike back at the British, but not in the way that Sir Henry Clinton expected.

XI

"You'll Hear from Me This Evening"

The West Bank of the Hudson River, Early July 1779

After he finally received Gen. Washington's recall order to join the Continental Army marching to the Hudson, Anthony Wayne made a hurried trip from Philadelphia to the commander-in-chief's new headquarters at New Windsor, New York, where he learned the details of the situation: the British were fortifying the posts at King's Ferry and, though they had not moved any further up the Hudson, Washington still believed that West Point remained their objective. In order to block any British move towards the post, the brigades of the Continental Army held positions in a broad arc from Smith's Clove to West Point and to the east side of the Hudson. The Corps of Light Infantry was on the west bank of the Hudson in between King's Ferry and West Point at a place known as Sandy Beach, near Fort Montgomery. Engineers and work parties continued to improve West Point's fortifications, but Washington was already looking for ways to offensively blunt the British advance. He ordered Wayne to officially assume command of the Light Infantry from Col. Butler, the temporary commander, at Sandy Beach and begin a mission with three parts: to "oppose any movement of t he enemy against the forts," to "gain an accurate knowledge of the scene of action," and to develop "a favorable opportunity for striking an advantageous stroke."[1]

Wayne arrived at Sandy Beach on July 2 and saw his command for the first time. There was little outward indication that the Corps of Light

Infantry was the Continental Army's most elite unit. The soldiers wore uniforms that differed in color depending on the soldiers' parent regiments (the Continental Army had only recently chosen the familiar blue as their standard uniform color and the new coats would not be available until later in the year). Troops from Pennsylvania, Virginia and Delaware wore brown coats with red facings; Marylanders wore blue coats faced with red. Most of their uniforms were over a year old and worn from hard service. Some of the men lacked shoes. The Light Infantry had few copies of Gen. Steuben's "Blue Book," rations were in short supply, and there was not enough fodder for the horses. Wayne soon told the Commissary General Department that his light corps was "much neglected in almost every article of provision. They have had but two days' fresh provisions since they arrived [at Sandy Beach] and not more than three days' allowance of rum in twelve days."[2] He also requested uniforms, provisions, rum, and copies of the "Blue Book" directly from Gen. Washington, writing, "I flatter myself that we shall have it in our Power to introduce Uniformity among the Light Corps ... [and] infuse a Laudable Pride and Emulation into the Whole which in a soldier is a substitute for almost every other Virtue."[3] But army stores were limited, and Washington responded that he could supply only one hat or cap, a blanket, a shirt, and one pair of shoes per man, and would send copies of the "Blue Book" as soon as possible.

The British stronghold at Stony Point was the closest enemy position to Sandy Beach and substantial information on the site was already available. Maj. Henry Lee's battalion of light cavalry and infantry had scouted the position since mid–June and provided detailed reports on the strength of its defenses. Based on his experience with the Culper Ring and other spy operations Washington suggested that Lee pay local Loyalists, who would have contact with the British, for information. In early July he raised the stakes and directed Lee to send a scout to Stony Point under a flag of truce, but in the guise of a military escort for a local woman who could enter the works to visit some of the Loyalist troops. If the British did not blindfold the scout, he would get a close look at the defenses. Lee passed the mission to his subordinate, Capt. Allan McLane.

Thirty-three years old, McLane was a prosperous property owner in Philadelphia before he volunteered for service as a lieutenant in the Delaware militia at the beginning of the war. He gained command of a company of mounted infantry scouts that saw action at every major battle from Long Island to Germantown. In between battles McLane harassed British columns, captured enemy patrols, and operated his own spy ring.

In 1778 one of his agents provided information that helped Washington foil a British attempt to capture Gen. Lafayette. McLane enjoyed the limelight and did not mind taking risks to achieve notoriety. A fellow officer later wrote of him, "I know of no individual, of his rank in the army, who engaged in such a variety of perilous adventures, or who, so invariably brought them to a happy issue."[4] In June 1779 Washington assigned McLane's company to Lee's command, an order that wounded the independent-minded McLane's sense of honor.[5] He was doubtless happy for the daring assignment to scout inside Stony Point, a mission that would surely gain him the attention of the commander-in-chief.

Years later, McLane related to a fellow officer how on July 2 he dressed as a militia officer, "a simple countryman" with a white flag, and accompanied a Mrs. Smith when she went to Stony Point to deliver some goods to her two sons in the King's American Regiment.[6] As Washington and Lee had hoped, the British failed to blindfold McLane, and a young Redcoat officer chatted with him as Mrs. Smith made her delivery. "Well Captain," asked the Redcoat, "what do you think of our fortress—is it strong enough to keep Mister Washington out?" McLane played up the part of the rube, replied that he was only a woodsman who knew nothing of such matters, and assured the officer that Washington would not be so foolish as to attack the post. The officer asserted that Stony Point, "the Gibraltar of America, and defended by British valour, must be deemed impregnable."[7] It is possible that McLane's account contains some postwar exaggeration, but there is no doubt that he had ample opportunity to observe the defenses in detail; he made mental notes on the regiments that manned the works, the extent of the abatis, cannon emplacements, the parapet around the top of Stony Point, and the *Vulture* and *Cornwallis* at anchor on both flanks. McLane sent formal reports to Maj. Lee, after he returned to American lines, which went on to Washington and Wayne.

The same day of McLane's exploit, Gen. Wayne and Col. Butler rode down from Sandy Beach and scouted Stony Point from a distance. The next day, July 3, Wayne reported to Washington that Stony Point was "formidable," with extensive fortifications and cleared ground west of the post that exposed any soldiers who attacked with standard linear tactics to murderous musket and cannon fire from the works. Wayne also saw that an attack with innovative tactics could succeed, writing, "I do not think a *Storm* praticable—but perhaps a *Surprise* may be effected—could we fall on some stratagem to draw them out."[8] Capt. McLane and his men quietly maintained positions outside the works and observed British activities.

On July 6 Washington joined Wayne to personally reconnoiter the position again, protected by McLane's soldiers. Combined with McLane's information, the two generals saw that Stony Point was indeed well defended but had weaknesses. The marsh west of the hill was fordable at any time but high tide, and assaulting columns could maneuver around the edges of outer abatis where it met the water. Several of the cannon in the Upper Works, high on the crest of Stony Point, were sited to fire at distant objects and probably could not hit American troops once they were inside the works. Wayne and Washington realized that the British were well prepared to defeat against a daylight frontal assault. They also realized that Stony Point was vulnerable to a determined attack on its flanks, especially at night.

Washington returned to his headquarters at New Windsor on July 7, read the first reports of the British raids in Connecticut, and considered his options for striking back. "While the enemy are making excursions to distress the country it has a very disagreeable aspect to remain in a state of inactivity on our part," he wrote to Wayne two days later.[9] Since he was wary of moving substantial forces to Connecticut, another option was to attack Clinton's army in Westchester County. The Continental Army had just over 12,000 soldiers fit for duty and Washington estimated that Gen. Clinton had 11,000 troops, which did not give the Americans enough of a numerical edge for a large attack.[10] "I am exceedingly mortified," Washington wrote Congress two days after he learned of the Connecticut raids, "that the circumstances of the Army in respect to numbers, oblige me to a mere defensive plan, and will not suffer me to pursue such measures as the public good may seem to require, and the public expectation to demand."[11]

In addition to the manpower shortages, Washington called the Continental Army's ammunition supply "far from being sufficient," in June.[12] The army was also critically short of supplies and provisions because the Congressional Treasury remained short of capital. Washington told Congress that "little aid can be afforded from the army in its present situation.... How this can be remedied and the army supplied, I know not."[13] Under these conditions it is unlikely that the Continentals could have logistically sustained a series of maneuvers or a conventional, pitched battle against Clinton's forces.

Washington decided that instead of attacking British forces head-on in Westchester County, he could retake the stronghold of Stony Point with the Corps of Light Infantry and accomplish multiple objectives: it would reverse the British push up the Hudson, restore an important American supply link with New England, and show the country that the Continental Army would not remain idle as Britain advanced into New York and burned Connecticut towns. It could also force Clinton to pull all his forces back to Manhattan and save Connecticut from further raids. Washington's concept was what is called an "economy of force" operation in modern military doctrine, which is to "employ all combat power available in the most effective way possible."[14] An economy of force operation employs forces judiciously at carefully selected points and gets a commander "the most bang for the buck," as the saying goes. In the case of 1779, Washington defended the Hudson with the entire Continental Army, but he would hit the British at a key site with only a fraction of his force. Washington told Wayne "the reputation of the army and the good of the service" demanded an attack on Stony Point, and he ordered further reconnaissance to identify the state of the garrison and the best approaches to the position.[15] When Wayne responded that he had scouted the area again and confirmed that he could attack Stony Point on its southern flank, Washington had all the information he needed to go forward.

On July 10 Washington sent Wayne a long, detailed letter discussing what he called his "ideas for the enterprise." He envisioned that a column of light infantrymen should advance "with the utmost secrecy" at night on Stony Point from the south side, preferably when it was exceptionally dark or raining. The column should consist of two groups: a vanguard "of prudent and determined men, well commanded" to drive in British outposts, silence the sentries, and remove the abatis, and that followed by a main body to push through the gaps carved by the vanguard. Supporting columns should advance near the center and north side of the works. Having already led the surprise attack on Trenton, Washington knew the measures needed for success. He ordered Wayne to continue the reconnaissance of Stony Point until the time of attack, suggesting "single men in the night will be more likely to ascertain facts than the best glasses [telescopes] in the day."

For the different attack columns, he directed, "the Officers commanding them are to know precisely what Batteries or particular parts of the line they are respectively to possess that confusion and the consequences of indecision may be avoided." Only 100–200 picked men should compose the main assault column, he said, because "secrecy is so much more essential to these kind of enterprises than numbers…. If a surprise takes place, they are fully competent to the business, if it does not, numbers will avail little." He cautioned Wayne to keep knowledge of the operation limited to his key officers and not to notify the men until the attack was imminent, "as it is in the power of a single deserter to betray the design." To allow the light infantrymen to identify each other in the darkness, Washington suggested they wear a white feather or cockade in their caps, as they had at Trenton. As a final measure to ensure that no accidental musket discharge could give away the assault as the men closed on Stony Point, Washington specified that the Light Infantry was to "advance (the whole of them) with fixed Bayonets and Muskets unloaded." The commander-in-chief did not set a date for the attack but directed Wayne to develop the final plan and to notify him when it was ready. He closed by promising to send Wayne reinforcements of light infantry from nearby regiments.[16]

The prospect of such a daring assault undoubtedly spoke to Wayne's thirst for glory, but as a veteran combat leader he also knew that a night bayonet attack would mean close, brutal, chaotic fighting. Instead of the usual battle situation where the soldiers fired their muskets at an enemy line that was fifty or more yards away, Wayne's men would have to close to within a few feet of each enemy soldier to stab him with their bayonets while defending themselves from enemy musket shots and bayonet thrusts. The fighting would quickly devolve into hand-to-hand combat where it would be extremely hard for officers to control their soldiers in the darkness.

It is psychologically difficult for a human being, even a trained and battle-hardened soldier, to sink cold steel into the flesh of another human, and bayonet attacks succeeded only if the soldiers who conducted them conjured up primal ferocity. Confusion and fear often overpowered military discipline and rational thought during bayonet fighting. Wayne's contemporary, Major-General William Heath, wrote after the war: "Nocturnal enterprises, in which the bayonet is principally made use of, are generally uncommonly bloody."[17] At the battle of Princeton in January 1777, the Seventeenth Foot, the regiment that now held Stony Point, broke through American lines with a bayonet charge and reportedly bayoneted and bludgeoned the wounded Continentals on the field. In September 1777, Gen. Charles Grey (who had commanded the attack on Wayne's division at Paoli) led the British Second Battalion of Light Infantry in a night attack that caught the Third Regiment of Continental Dragoons sleeping at a farm near Baylor, Pennsylvania, and his soldiers bayoneted the dazed cavalrymen and ignored pleas for mercy.

Gen. Wayne's corps included some of the Continental Army's toughest soldiers, hardened from three years of combat, and Gen. Steuben's Blue Book and training program had given them added discipline and confidence so they could use their bayonets just as well as the British. Many were survivors of the night at Paoli in 1777. They may have relished the opportunity to turn the use of the bayonet on the enemy. They would not have long to wait. The day after he sent Wayne his instructions, Washington ordered the Connecticut Line to send eight more companies to the Light Infantry, and the new troops reported to Wayne at Sandy Beach on July 14, a welcome reinforcement of 305 soldiers who were every bit as veteran and colorful as the men that already formed the Light Corps.[18]

Lt. Col. Return Jonathan Meigs arrived in command of the Third Regiment of Light Infantry consisting of two battalions of Connecticut troops. Meigs had been a captain in the Connecticut militia when the Lexington Alarm occurred in April 1775 and he immediately took his company to join the American army at Boston. His regiment fought in the invasion of Canada, where Meigs kept a journal written in ink made from gunpowder and water mixed in his palm. The British captured him in the assault on Quebec, along with Christian Febiger, who was also destined for the light infantry, and paroled Meigs in January 1777. In May of the same year he was home in West Haven, Connecticut, when he learned that the British kept a large supply of stores at Sag Harbor. Meigs assembled a force of 170 men, two armed sloops, and thirteen whaleboats, sailed to Sag Harbor at night, destroyed the British depot and captured ninety men.

The Meigs family lore explained that he received his unique first name, Return, because his father, Jonathan Meigs, had courted a local girl and asked for her hand in marriage one evening. The lady at first demurred, and Jonathan left the house in a huff. The young woman reconsidered and called down the road, "Return, Jonathan Meigs!"[19] The wedding soon followed, as did their first son, whom they named Return. At thirty-nine years of age, Meigs was one of Wayne's older officers.

Twenty-six-year-old Lt. Col. Isaac Sherman commanded the First Battalion in Meigs's regiment. Sherman had enlisted at Cambridge, Massachusetts, the day after the battle of Lexington, and he recalled "conceiving the cause to be just, I did not hesitate ... and effected the object of raising a company of men without much difficulty."[20] He received a captain's commission, served at Boston and Long Island, and suffered through Washington's retreat through New Jersey in the winter of 1776. Sherman wrote that his men "marched near twenty miles in one day, and for want of shoes, the blood was from their feet was distinguishable nearly the whole of the

A Continental Army lieutenant talks to a group of soldiers. The lieutenant carries a spontoon, the edged weapons that the officers of the light infantry used in the attack of Stony Point. This picture shows the uniform patterns adopted in 1779 but is a somewhat idealized rendering — the soldiers are in pristine uniforms at a level of completeness rarely attained in the Continental Army, and the three enlisted men are in the uniforms of three different states. The Continentals of 1779 wore uniforms that were worn and faded from at least a year's service (Library of Congress).

distance."²¹ The commander of Meigs's Second Battalion, Lt. Col. Henry Champion, also joined the army immediately after the Lexington Alarm; he saw his first action at Bunker Hill. In 1777 he helped General Kosciuszko lay out the defenses of West Point. He was serving in Gen. Parson's Connecticut Brigade in the Hudson Highlands when he received orders to reinforce the Light Infantry.

Maj. William Hull, also twenty-six, arrived in command of the Fourth Regiment of Light Infantry. He was part of the third generation of Hulls born in America, graduated with honors from Yale in 1772, then worked briefly as a schoolmaster and studied to be a clergyman before settling on the law as a career. Like Benjamin Tallmadge, he was a close friend of Nathan Hale's. Hull had only recently passed the bar in Litchfield, Connecticut, when the war began and Litchfield residents elected him captain of the company they raised. He saw action at Boston, Trenton, Princeton, and Monmouth. During the Saratoga campaign in September 1777, Hull led three hundred soldiers who fought themselves to the point of exhaustion and suffered nearly 50 percent casualties in three hours of charging, countercharging, and hand-to-hand combat at the battle of Freeman's Farm. He was in command of a detachment of the Eighth Massachusetts at West Point when he received Washington's order for his battalion to join the Light Infantry at Sandy Beach. The addition of two companies of North Carolina infantry under Maj. Hardy Murfree gave Hull an undersized regiment of about 400 men.

William Hull, by James Sharples, Sr., from life, c. 1795–1801. A veteran of Saratoga, Hull led his battalion of Massachusetts troops in a bayonet charge across the crest of Stony Point. This portrait was originally thought to depict his commander at Stony Point, Anthony Wayne (Independence National Historical Park).

With 1,150 men now assigned, the Corps of Light Infantry had the strength to assault Stony Point. On July 14 Wayne suggested to Washington that the attack take place the next night, probably because there would be no moon. The commander-in-chief concurred and the final pieces quickly fell into place. Washington sent twenty-four artillerymen commanded by two captains to join Wayne's force so that, once the attack succeeded, they could use the captured British cannon to shell Verplanck's Point. Capt. McLane once again played the bumpkin militiaman and entered the Stony Point defenses on the 14th, this time with a local widow named Calhoun, who brought chickens and greens for the British troops. That night he camped outside the British lines. Washington urged Wayne to meet with Maj. Henry Lee once more for a final reconnaissance report and warned him: "Your interview must be managed with caution or it may possibly raise suspicion."[22] Col. Christian Febiger drafted a will for his wife on the fourteenth, "as there is a probability of my going on a very hazardous expedition, in which there is some danger of my taking a place among the deceased heroes of America."[23]

July 15 was the final day before the attack. Washington sent secret orders to Brigadier-General Peter Muhlenberg, commanding a nearby brigade of troops, to move towards Stony Point at midnight and be ready to reinforce Wayne's attack, cautioning him to "make your movements as secret as possible and march perfectly light."[24] To prevent anyone from alerting the British, Wayne sent an infantry company under Capt. James Chrystie to patrol the roads that led to Stony Point and arrest any male in the vicinity. He closed his order to Chrystie: "You'll hear from me this evening."[25]

Though the soldiers may have guessed of an impending mission judging by the activity around them, the morning of July 15 was much like any other for Wayne's junior officers and enlisted men. Sometime before noon, the general ordered the entire Corps of Light Infantry to form at the camp at Sandy Beach, "fresh shaved and well powdered," with full field equipment and one day's rations, ostensibly for a full inspection.[26] Capt. John Burnham of the Massachusetts Light Infantry recalled how that day the men were "ordered to clean up and put their army in the best order." It was the first time the entire Corps was present on the same field. Wayne, his officers, and sergeants conducted the inspection as scheduled. But instead of releasing the men back to their tents upon completion, Wayne ordered the ranks into marching order, probably to the great surprise of most of the troops: as Capt. Burnham remembered, "We were paraded and ordered to march, no man knowing whither."[27] At Gen. Wayne's order the soldiers shouldered their muskets and in a long column, marched south out of the Sandy Beach camp, towards King's Ferry and Stony Point.

XII

Stand to Arms

West of Stony Point, July 15, 1779

In single file on narrow tracks that wound through the New York woods, the Corps of Light Infantry moved south from their camp at Sandy Beach and then west four miles to the town of Queensboro, where they halted for rest. They resumed the march to the south, passed Torn Mountain, and threaded through the trails southwest past the western ends of Bear and Donderberg mountains. The hills prevented the British on the height of Stony Point from seeing the American movement. But since the area was "thickly settled," as Pvt. Vincent Vass of the Virginia light infantry recalled, Capt. James Chrystie's company, which Wayne had sent out earlier in the day, kept civilians in their homes and guarded the mountain passes to prevent observation by enemy scouts.[1] Conscious of the need for absolute secrecy, Wayne kept his men quiet; Col. Christian Febiger wrote to his wife: "We marched very silently."[2] As darkness fell at about 8:00 P.M., the column stopped at a farm owned by the Springsteel family, a mile and half west of Stony Point. A strong, unseasonably cold wind howled down the Hudson River Valley from the north, and the trees around Springsteel's farm shook as the Yankee troops dropped their knapsacks and stretched out in the grass for another rest.

Continental scouts stayed active to ensure that Wayne had accurate information right up to the time of the attack. Capt. Allan McLane had entered the fort again with the widow Calhoun the previous evening, and Maj. Thomas Posey, Washington's neighbor from Virginia who commanded a battalion in Febiger's regiment, spent all day observing Stony

Point with McLane and Henry Lee. When the woods became dark, Wayne took Col. Butler to meet with Posey, Lee, and McLane for their final reconnaissance report. The five officers met somewhere east of Springsteel's farm, and in the gloom the scouts gave Wayne and Butler some more detail on Stony Point's defenses. There is no record of the meeting but they probably informed Wayne about a significant change: the Royal Navy sloop *Vulture* and the gunboat *Cornwallis* had moved across the Hudson close to Verplanck's Point, probably to find secure anchorage in the high winds. The approaches to Stony Point were now out of range of the naval guns. The Light Infantry would still have to fight their way through the land defenses; but without the ships' cannon the British flanks were even more vulnerable than Wayne and Washington had planned.

Wayne and Butler returned to Springsteel's farm. Since Stony Point remained a formidable objective Wayne took a few minutes to pen a fatalistic letter to his friend Col. Sharp Delaney. "This will not reach your eye until the writer is no more," he wrote, referring to himself in the third person. He sent Delaney some personal papers so, he continued, "my friend may be enabled to defend the character and support the honor of the man who loved him — who fell in defense of his country and the rights of mankind." Wayne railed against "the neglect of Congress" towards the army but said of his commander-in-chief, "If ever a great and good man was surrounded with a choice of difficulties, it is Gen'l Washington." He asked Delaney to ensure the proper education of his son and daughter, and of his wife he wrote, "I fear that [she] will not survive this Stroke — do go comfort her." Dramatic to the end, Wayne closed with, "I am called to sup, but where to breakfast — either within the enemie's lines in triumph, or in another world." He dated his letter "written on the eve of storming Stony Point" and added "near the hour & scene of carnage."[3]

At about 11:00 P.M. Wayne called his men to attention and gathered them around him. It was a moonless night and the soldiers strained their eyes to discern their commander's dark form as Wayne informed his soldiers that their mission was to seize the British fortress at Stony Point. He held a copy of his orders for the attack, but probably speaking from memory (since the night was pitch-black), Wayne explained their three-pronged assault. Wayne, with Col. Febiger's regiment, Col. Meigs' regiment, and Maj. Hull's battalion, 700 men in total, would march in column formation toward Stony Point's southern flank. Col. Butler's regiment, with about 300 men, would hook around to the northern flank. Maj. Murfreee would take his two companies of North Carolina troops to a hill just west of Stony

Point, in between Febiger's and Meigs' columns. At Wayne's order, Febiger's column would work their way around the edge of the outer abatis where it met the river, push through the inner abatis, and swarm into the fortress. Butler's soldiers would assault the northern flank of the hill at the same time. Once the attacks began, Murfree's North Carolina men were to begin a "perpetual and gauling" musket fire at the works to fool the British into thinking that they faced a traditional frontal assault.[4] If successful, the two attacks on the flanks would hit Stony Point like a combination punch and penetrate the British defenses at their weakest points. Wayne planned for the two assaulting columns to converge near the top of Stony Point, and then the Light Infantry would shout the watchword — "The fort's our own!"— to signal success.

The most innovative aspect of Wayne's plan was that the two attack groups would move in columns of platoons only ten men in width. With this formation, instead of the broad lines usually used in linear combat, the Americans could move quickly through the woods and hit Stony Point with maximum momentum. With narrow fronts the columns would pierce the British defenses like the point of a spear puncturing a suit of armor. As Washington suggested, Wayne ordered that the soldiers attack with their muskets unloaded and bayonets fixed to prevent disclosure by a premature musket shot, saying "the strictest Silence must be observed and the closest attention paid to the commands of the Officers.... If any Soldier presumes to take his Musket from his shoulder or Attempt to fire ... he shall be instantly put to Death by the Officer next him, for the misconduct of one man is not to put the whole Troops in danger."[5]

Each man affixed a piece of white paper in his hat as an identification mark in the darkness. As an added incentive to keep the men working towards the top of Stony Point, Wayne promised them that the first man into the inner works of the fortress would win $500 and immediate promotion, the next man would win $400, and so on to the fifth man, who would win $100. Wayne closed his speech, saying that he had the "fullest Confidence in the bravery and fortitude of the Corps.... [T]he Credit of the States they respectively belong to, and their own Reputation will be such powerful motives for each man to distinguish himself that the General [Wayne] cannot have the least doubt of a Glorious Victory." But, he added, "should there be any soldier so lost to every feeling of Honor, as to attempt to Retreat one single foot or Skulk in the face of danger, the Officer next to him is immediately to put him to Death — that he may no longer disgrace the Name of a Soldier or the Corps or State he belongs to."[6]

Wayne finished giving his orders at about 11:30 P.M. and the columns filed out of Springsteel's farm toward Stony Point. Butler's column headed northeast to arrive on the north flank, Maj. Murfree marched his North Carolina troops directly east to arrive at Stony Point's center, and Febiger led his column southeast. With no moon, the night was eerily black and each group moved slowly to make the least amount of noise. Pvt. Vincent Vass recalled that they marched towards Stony Point "as private as possible."[7] About thirty minutes later Febiger's group emerged near the south edge of the marsh outside Stony Point. A strong wind still blew and shook the trees around the group. In the darkness Wayne could make out that the Hudson was at high tide and that water in the marsh was higher than he had expected. He waited for the tide to go out and took advantage of the pause by sending Col. Febiger back along the ranks to remind the men "about the dependence on their bayonets only." When the tide went out at about twenty minutes past midnight, Gen. Wayne ordered his men forward.[8]

* * *

Stony Point, 9:00 P.M.

The defenses at Stony Point included six picquets, posts of several men each, positioned beyond the lower abatis to give advance warning of an attack. The soldiers in the picquets further spread themselves out into individual sentry positions. On the night of July 15, at about the same time that the Americans rested at Springsteel's farm, these British sentries peered into the dark woods around them and shielded themselves from the howling wind. Corporal Simon Davies of the Seventeenth Regiment of Foot was in charge of a picquet with nine soldiers on Stony Point's southern flank, close to the bank of the Hudson. Being so near the water, Davies often timed his shift changes by the watch bells on the sloop *Vulture*. But that night Davies heard no bells from the ship and assumed their sound was drowned out by the strong wind.

Tensions were high within the British works. In recent days a number of deserters from Continental units reported that Wayne and the Light Infantry were near Fort Montgomery, that Washington and Wayne had reconnoitered Stony Point, and, most alarming, that "Gen. Wayne urges the attack of Stony Point." Another deserter said, "Gen. Wayne wanted to attack Stony Point but Washington would not consent."[9] Lt. William Armstrong of the Seventeenth recalled that the situation became even more tense on the night of July 15 because "two Spies sent out by Lt. Col. Johnson had come in and given intelligence that the Enemy was moving down in force."[10]

Lt. Col. Johnson, the British commander, considered the intelligence to be credible. That night he ordered his soldiers to sleep in their uniforms and equipment "to be in readiness at a Minutes Warning" and cancelled the use of passwords and countersigns to prevent them from being overheard by rebel scouts.[11] Johnson also ordered that if the post was attacked, four companies of the Seventeenth and two companies of the Seventy-first Highlanders would man the Lower Works, along the outer abatis, while four more companies of the Seventeenth and Capt. Morris Robinson's detachment from the Loyal American Regiment would defend the Upper Works.

Johnson's subordinate officers reacted to the warnings in a variety of ways. Either because Johnson did not clearly communicate the gravity of the situation or because they had experienced previous false alarms, Lt. William Armstrong did not think that the threat was immediate. However, Capt. Lawrence Campbell of Fraser's Highlanders recalled that, based on Johnson's information, he was "induced to think an Attack was intended that Night."[12] Campbell had been in one of the battalions of the Seventy-first Regiment that was captured when it unluckily sailed into Boston in June 1776. Now paroled, he had overall command of both companies of Highlander Grenadiers at Stony Point. Lt. William Horndon of the Seventeenth Regiment was in charge of the artillery at the Lower Works, and he took the time to visit all of his gun positions before retiring to his tent for the evening and instructing his sergeant of the guard to call him immediately in case of alarm. Capt. William Darby of the Seventeenth Regiment was officer of the day on July 15 and was sure that no enemy could approach Stony Point unnoticed, even at night. But Darby also visited each picquet position that evening and reminded them that in the event of attack they were to raise the alarm and then withdraw into the Lower Works. Darby took his post on the south side of the abatis and peered tensely into the blackness of the moonless night.

Lt. John Ross of the Highlanders, on duty with thirty men at the "Officer's Picquet," located on a small hill directly west of Stony Point, also looked into the darkness as the cold wind shook the trees around his isolated post. At around midnight one of his sentries fired at something and, Ross recalled, "I sent a Corporal & some Men down, to know what was the cause of it." The corporal returned with the sentry who had fired the shot, who reported that a body of Americans was moving not far from the picquet, "and the rest of the Men were of the same Opinion," reported Ross. He believed that the men may have fired at bushes rustled by the wind, as they had done before, but to be safe, Ross ordered his drummer to beat the roll "To Arms."[13]

The sound of firing and the drum roll from Ross' picquet brought Lt. Col. Johnson rushing out of his headquarters tent on the crest of Stony Point. He met Capt. Robert Clayton of the Seventeenth, commander of the infantry defenses of the Upper Works, and told him to man the parapet and to send one company to defend the northern portion of Stony Point, in between the two abatis. Clayton hurried to carry out the orders, and Johnson went to the outer abatis.

Lt. John Roberts, the officer in charge of the artillery in the Upper Works, was in his tent when he heard the shots. Roberts was accustomed to sentries firing at shadows, but when several shots rang out he threw on his uniform and "ran to turn the Men out."[14] His fellow artillery officer Capt. William Tiffin was in his own tent when a soldier rushed in and told him that there was firing beyond the abatis. Tiffin ran to turn his artillerymen out but found their tents empty—the men had already manned their guns. He took position at a gun on the north side of the Upper Works and spoke briefly with Lt. Roberts at a battery of eighteen- and twenty-four-pounder guns on the south side of Stony Point's crest. By the time he got there, Capt. Clayton had already manned the parapet with four companies of the Seventeenth and Capt. Robinson's detachment from the Loyal American Regiment.

Along the Lower Works, just inside the abatis, Highlander lieutenants William Nairne and Patrick Cummings heard the shots and ran out of their shared tent. Cummings went to identify the cause of the firing and Nairne hurried to his company's alert position where his men were already forming. Capt. Lawrence Campbell, the Highlander officer who had expected the attack that night, was pleased that the Grenadiers formed their ranks quickly, and he told Lt. Nairne to have his troops kneel behind the abatis. To his left, Campbell could discern the men of the Seventeenth Regiment under Capt. Francis Tew forming on the southern half of the Lower Works.

As with Campbell's soldiers, the alarm from Lt. Ross' picquet sent the men of the Seventeenth Regiment to the Lower Works. Lt. William Simpson recalled that a servant rushed into his tent as the drum rolled, "upon which I immediately repair'd to my Alarm Post at the outward

Abbatis."[15] The commander of the artillery at the Lower Works, Lt. William Horndon, took position at the brass twelve-pounder cannon at Fleche Number One. Cpl. John Newton, in charge of a squad with the mission to protect the howitzer battery on the southern slope of Stony Point, immediately informed Capt. Darby about the firing and then took his squad to their station at the howitzer. The artillerymen who manned the gun also arrived, but in the extreme darkness they fumbled at preparing their cannon. Newton peered into the night for the Americans, "not thinking proper to fire, till I saw some Object to fire at." As the gunners stumbled about their howitzer, Newton heard noise from the water on the south side of Stony Point, then saw the dim shapes of men moving near the outer abatis, which he "supposed to be the Enemy advancing."[16]

At his advance sentry post on Stony Point's southern flank, Cpl. Simon Davies also heard the firing from Lt. Ross' picquet, which was to his right, and put his men on alert. A few minutes passed with no further firing and he allowed his soldiers to relax a bit and sit on their knapsacks, but, he recalled, "I had scarcely sat down, when I heard another Sentry from the Officer's Picquet challenge twice, then fire, upon which I ordered the Men to stand to their Arms." Then Davies heard firing from his own soldiers. He went to investigate and later stated that, "about half way thither, I met them both retiring as fast as they could, and upon my asking the reason of their retiring, they said that there was a large Body of the Enemy advancing."[17] Davies knelt down, listened intently, and heard a group of men coming through the trees and officers telling soldiers to keep silent and not fire. Cpl. Davies quickly gathered his sentries and retreated to the Sergeant's Picquet, about a quarter of a mile outside Fleche Number Three, but found it already abandoned.

Cpl. John Ash of the Seventeenth manned a picquet with six soldiers located on the north end of Stony Point, near King's Ferry. When Ash heard firing from Lt. Ross' position and perceived that Stony Point was under alarm, he gathered his men and retreated to the Lower Works, in accordance with his standing orders. Both Ash and Cpl. Davies, from the southern picquet, led their men towards the abatis at about the same time, where they encountered columns of American soldiers wading through the water, furiously chopping their way through the barricade, and swarming inside the defenses of Stony Point.

XIII

The Push of the Bayonet

Stony Point, 12:30 A.M., July 16, 1779

The main American attack column, with Gen. Wayne and Col. Christian Febiger, moved through the woods towards Stony Point's southern flank and pushed British Corporal Simon Davies and his sentries back towards the fortress. To the west of Stony Point, it was Maj. Murfree's North Carolina soldiers, taking position to open their diversionary fire, who had alarmed the Highlander Lt. Ross and his men. A Connecticut officer in Wayne's column recalled that the Americans advanced without "taking any notice" of the Redcoat sentries, skirted the southern end of the outer abatis and waded into the thigh-deep waters of the Hudson in Haverstraw Bay, "directly under one of the enemy's works."[1]

Wayne's column moved in three subgroups. Twenty soldiers armed with axes and hatchets led the way, ordered to chop a gap through the abatis for the column to pass through. Commanded by Lt. George Knox of the Ninth Pennsylvania Regiment, the eighteenth-century military term for the group was a "Forlorn Hope" because it had so little chance of surviving the action. Twenty paces behind Knox's men, Lt. Col. de Fleury, the French volunteer, led a vanguard of 130 soldiers who were to push through the gap made by the Forlorn Hope and establish a foothold inside the fort. Approximately 550 soldiers—comprising Col. Febiger's Virginia and Pennsylvania troops, Col. Return Meigs' Connecticut soldiers, and Maj. William Hull's Massachusetts battalion—formed the main body that would expand de Fleury's foothold and swarm up the slopes of Stony Point. Gen. Wayne marched with Febiger, and as their men waded into the water

Knox's Forlorn Hope was ahead of them already hacking at the logs of the inner abatis.

Up to this time the British had heard only scattered and confusing noises that indicated the movement of men through the woods. The sound of Knox's chopping confirmed an American attack and its location, and

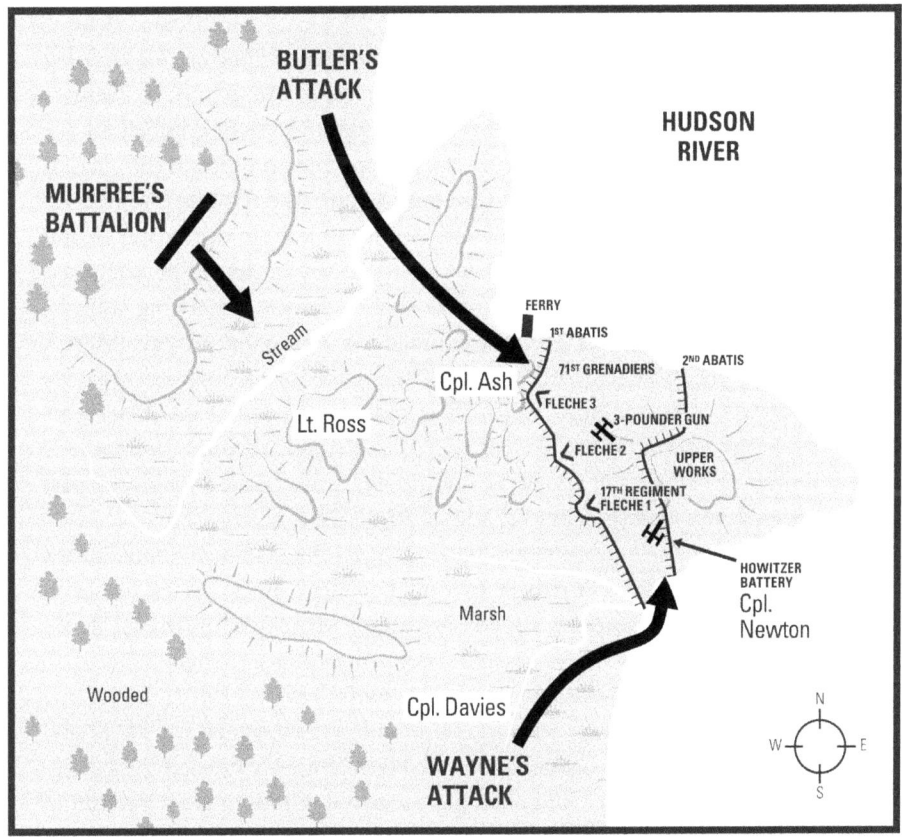

Gen. Washington and Gen. Wayne planned to seize Stony Point with tactics that capitalized on the skills of the American Corps of Light Infantry and exploited weaknesses in the British defenses. Though Stony Point was defended by tough, veteran soldiers in multiple belts of fortifications, the Americans stormed this position known as "Little Gibraltar" just after midnight on July 16 armed only with cold steel. Their opponents were alert, and waiting for them (map adapted by the author and Brandi Phipps from the 1784 British army map *A Plan of the Surprise of Stoney Point by a Detachment of the American Army commanded by Brigr. Genl. Wayne, on the 15th July 1779*, in the holdings of The Society of the Cincinnati, Washington, D.C.).

the Redcoats unleashed the fortress' firepower. The anonymous Connecticut officer in Wayne's group wrote that at 12:30 A.M. "the enemy fired on us generally from all their works.... The fire was very brisk from cannon and grape shot ... as well as from small arms with ball and buck shot, through which our troops advanced with the greatest regularity and firmness without firing a gun or once breaking their order, except to climb the abattis."[2]

Maj. Hull wrote that for reasons unknown Knox's Forlorn Hope failed to completely cut a path through the obstacles, so the men in de Fleury's vanguard helped clear the way. Even Maj. Thomas Posey grabbed an axe from an exhausted soldier in the Forlorn Hope and chopped at the barrier. It must have been a terrifying few minutes for the Americans. Muzzle flashes from British guns were the only source of light in the darkness, and musket balls whistled in at the Yankees, splashed in the water, shattered the stakes of the abatis, or hit bodies with sickening smacking sounds. Whereas the light infantrymen maintained the silence that Wayne ordered, they clearly heard British officers and sergeants shouting orders to organize the defense of Stony Point. With their muskets unloaded the Americans had no way to defend themselves except to struggle through the obstacle and press their bayonet attack. Posey and de Fleury pushed their men past the logs, re-formed their ranks, and continued the advance.[3]

While Wayne's column struggled through the abatis on Stony Point's southern flank, Maj. Murfree's men opened their diversionary fire from the west and Col. Butler's supporting attack struck the northern flank. Butler's column moved with same three subgroups as Wayne's. Lt. Col. Samuel Hay, Wayne's old friend, led the main body of 200 Pennsylvania troops. Maj. "Crazy Jack" Stewart commanded the vanguard of 100 Marylanders, and Lt. James Gibbon from the Sixth Pennsylvania led the twenty soldiers in the Forlorn Hope. Twenty years old, Gibbon was a veteran of three years in the Continental Army and had been taken prisoner in the New York campaign in 1776. Maj. Stewart originally named another lieutenant for the Forlorn Hope, but Gibbon and Lt. James McCullough both claimed the honor of leading the unit, probably based on their seniority in rank. Gibbon won the command after the three officers drew lots. Now leading the Forlorn Hope in action at the base of Stony Point, Gibbon's men chopped a gap through the abatis large enough for ten men, the width of Butler's column, to pass through.[4]

Opposing Butler's assault in the British lines, Lt. William Nairne of the Seventy-first Grenadiers waited behind the abatis where his fellow

Highlander Capt. Lawrence Campbell had placed them a few minutes earlier. To Nairne's left, volleys from the Seventeenth Regiment crashed and lit up the night. The three-pounder cannon mounted behind the line opened fire, and in its muzzle flash Nairne saw the Yankees of Butler's column rushing through the gap in the abatis. The Scotsmen leveled their muskets and let loose a volley from nearly 100 guns. Lt. William Horndon, at Fleche Number One in between the Seventeenth Regiment and the Grenadiers, heard "a great firing of Musquetry from the right to left" and opened fire with his twelve-pounder cannon. In the flash from the gun Horndon saw "a Body of [Americans] coming thro' the Water," but the narrow firing port in the earthen wall of the fleche prevented Horndon from traversing the gun far enough to the left to bear on the attackers.[5] British soldiers from the picquets, still retreating through the woods, emerged from the darkness in front of Horndon and jumped into his fleche for cover. Horndon had his infantrymen open musket fire on the attackers in the marsh, and sent two soldiers to find more cannon ammunition.

After they passed the abatis, the men in Wayne's southern attack column began scaling the slope of Stony Point through "a most tremendous and incessant fire of musketry," as Wayne reported.[6] Col. Febiger, marching with him, wrote that Stony Point's defenders "received us pretty warmly."[7] The side of the hill was "almost perpendicular" according to Maj. William Hull, and "very rugged and steep" in the words of a British defender.[8] The ascent would have been difficult under any circumstances and it was almost impossible on a moonless night with British musket balls cutting the air. The light infantrymen were soaked from the waist down, hefted ten-pound muskets topped by sharpened eighteen-inch bayonets, and carried haversacks, bayonet scabbards, and cartridge boxes slung over their shoulders on cross-belts. In flat-soled Continental Army shoes and with their equipment swinging wildly from their belts, the Yankees scrambled and muscled their way over the rocks and up the hillside, often sliding backward in the dirt, still following Wayne's order to not utter a word.

Fortunately the Redcoats could hardly see the Yankees in the darkness and much of their fire went over the attackers' heads. But British musket balls found their marks. Captain Ezra Seldon fell with a ball in his hip. One shot passed through the crown of William Hull's hat, another struck his boot. A musket ball hit a Connecticut sergeant in the eye and exited the opposite cheek. Pvt. Vincent Vass was wounded twice; "a musket ball scaled the bone of my hip — a buck shot entered my thigh," he wrote.[9] Soon after he crossed through the abatis, a ball cut a two-inch gash across

Wayne's scalp. Scalp wounds bleed profusely and the general fell to the ground as blood gushed down his head, but he continued to direct his troops into the fort. Col. Febiger took command of the advance.

Once they scaled the steepest part of the hill, Col. Febiger's troops emerged on a more level slope, where they reformed ranks and pressed the attack towards the Upper Works. The ground was less rugged but Febiger's men still had to advance uphill against determined British defenders. American platoons and squads split off from the tight column to eliminate pockets of British resistance. Maj. Hull wrote that his soldiers "made free use of the bayonet" and Lt. John Wilmot said that some Redcoats fought "partly dressed" and that some were killed even before they could get out of their tents—statements that speak to the speed and viciousness of the assault.[10] Col. Febiger ordered Lt. John McDowell from the Eighth Virginia Regiment to veer to the north with some men to force their way through the sally port of the Upper Works. Another

A soldier of Maj. Thomas Posey's battalion storms the height of Stony Point on July 16, 1779, wearing the distinctive hunting shirt favored by Virginia riflemen. General Wayne's decision for his soldiers to attack with their muskets unloaded and bayonets fixed ensured an assault that was swift and brutal (painting by Don Troiani, www.historicalimagebank.com).

group of Febiger's men charged the British howitzer battery, which Cpl. John Newton defended with his squad of twelve Redcoats. Newton's soldiers countercharged, the fighting became hand to hand, and he received two American bayonet wounds and was eventually knocked unconscious when a Continental clubbed him with the butt of a musket. Newton awoke as a prisoner of the Americans.

On the northern side of Stony Point, Col. Butler's column pushed through the fire from the Highlander Grenadiers and swept up the hill where it was not especially steep but still rugged. The British three-pounder cannon blasted grapeshot and a ball wounded Lt. Col. Hay in his thigh. By the time the attack was over, the crew of this British gun fired sixty-nine times, and seventeen of Lt. Gibbon's twenty men in the Forlorn Hope were dead or wounded. But Gibbon still led the column, and Maj. Stewart ordered him to angle south towards the top of Stony Point. The rest of Butler's men followed, bayoneting Redcoats and taking prisoners all the way. Highlander Lt. John Ross of the Seventy-first Grenadiers, whose sentries had first heard the Americans approach, was near the three-pounder cannon after he fell back from his picquet; he recalled, "I had just got within the works when I receiv'd the push of a bayonet from a man who knocked me down the hill with the butt end of his firelock. Imagining that this was one of our own men, who had done it thro' a mistake, I damned him for a scoundrel."[11] It was actually an American from Butler's attack that knocked Ross down, and Lt. Patrick Cummings of the Seventeenth Regiment ran the Yankee through with his sword, and then Cummings himself fell, bayoneted by another Continental soldier.

When the firing began Lt. Col. Johnson had rushed from his tent near the crest of Stony Point and moved down the slope, where he directed the fire from the three-pounder gun and organized the defense along the abatis. Outside the fort, Maj. Murfree's North Carolinians kept up what Maj. Hull called "an incessant fire" that successfully confused the British about the location of the main American attack.[12] Lt. William Simpson's company of the Seventeenth Regiment, at the southern portion of the abatis, perceived Americans in the darkness and fired volleys for about ten minutes until the lieutenant heard a group of men behind him that he assumed were British. He said, "I ... found my mistake by being wounded and taken prisoner." Soon after his capture Simpson heard Lt. Col. Johnson also mistake the Americans for British, ordering them to "face the damned Rebels."

The Continentals, almost equally disoriented and now apparently breaking Wayne's order for silence, shouted at Johnson, "Damn ye, who are you?" and charged the colonel with their bayonets but Johnson escaped. The fighting raged all over the slope of Stony Point and Lt. Simpson observed that the Americans were "in a great confusion and under a smart fire."[13] The chaos of night fighting was illustrated when a Continental soldier knocked Simpson down with his musket, inexplicably, since Simpson was already a prisoner, and then, just as inexplicably, the Americans moved on and left him alone. Yankee Pvt. Robert Devin, waiting outside Stony Point in reserve with Muhlenberg's Brigade, later said, "The confusion and noise in the fort cannot be described."[14]

At the Upper Works, Capt. William Tiffin of the Royal Artillery was probably one of the most confused British officers. Tiffin had arrived at Stony Point less than a day earlier and at the time of the attack, he did not know the different directions the various batteries were supposed to fire or if the cannon had enough ammunition. He received no orders from Lt. Col. Johnson. Capt. Robert Clayton, commander of the four companies of the Seventeenth and Capt. Robinson's Loyalists who manned the Upper Works, had his men line the parapet while he stationed himself with a battery of two guns on the north side of the Table. The winds were high on top of the hill and, despite the commotion below him at the Lower Works, Clayton neither saw nor heard any Americans. Artilleryman Lt. John Roberts came upon Clayton and asked, "For God's sake, why are not the artillery here made use of, as the enemy are in the hollow, and crossing the water."[15] But the field guns were intended for daytime use and no gunpowder was stored with them. Roberts ran to tell his men to hurry with the ammunition. He found Capt. Tiffin, and the two officers agreed that fire from the howitzer on Stony Point's south slope (the site of Cpl. John Newton and his squad) could shatter the American attack. Roberts went down the hill to supervise firing the gun, but about twenty yards from the key artillery piece he realized that Newton, his squad, and the cannon were already in rebel hands.

At about the same time, Col. Febiger's column, with Lt. Col. de Fleury, Lt. Knox's Forlorn Hope, and troops under Capt. Clough Shelton all in the lead, scrambled up the southern slope and scaled the parapet of the Upper Works. Febiger came up close behind Shelton. Maj. Thomas Posey was wounded in the leg but still went over the wall at the head of his Virginians, turned around and shouted the Light Infantry's watchword, "The fort's our own!"[16] Pvt. Peter Francisco, the towering Portuguese-Virginian, went down after a ball cut a nine-inch gash in his abdomen.[17] The Connecticut soldiers under Col. Return Meigs and Maj. Hull's Massachusetts men poured over the wall after Posey. "All of this was done under a heavy fire of artillery and musketry, and as strong a resistance as could be made by the British bayonet," remembered Hull.[18] He pushed his column east across the Upper Works while Febiger angled to the south.

Frederick Robinson, the sixteen-year-old Loyalist ensign in the Seventeenth Regiment, was one of the troops that defended the Upper Works and recalled that he could see the Yankee light infantry "by the flashes of the Artillery and small arms only."[19] A British sergeant next to him fired his musket and the muzzle flash illuminated the figure of an American who had been charging towards him, falling dead only a few feet from the terrified young officer. Lt. William Armstrong of the Seventeenth Regiment could not see any Americans in the darkness either, but he ordered his troops to fire when the sounds of fighting became too close to ignore. Armstrong ceased their fire when he heard who he thought was Lt. Col. Johnson to his front, then a soldier told him that rebels had entered the Upper Works behind them. Armstrong recalled, "Just as he had delivered this information two men, who from having large pieces of white paper in their hats, I suppos'd them to be rebels, came up close to me; these I ordered the company to bayonet." Armstrong also directed his men to turn around and fire to their rear, and "just as I had utter'd these words I received a contusion in the head from a ball, which rendered me insensible, and in that situation I was taken prisoner."[20] Capt. Robert Clayton, commander of the Upper Works, was in the middle of the mêlée and despite the firing that crashed all around him he saw no men he could identify as Yankees all the way up until the time that the American light infantry surrounded him and made him their prisoner.

The Americans fanned out all over Stony Point, breaking the Redcoats into scattered small groups. Some British surrendered once they were surrounded, but there was little unit cohesion in the night battle, and other groups fought on. Maj. William Hull was familiar with the high adrenaline that occurred during close combat, having commanded a furious bayonet charge two years earlier at the battle of Freeman's Farm, and he wrote that the Light Infantry was "compelled to continue the dreadful slaughter owing to the fierce and obstinate resistance of the enemy."[21] Back at the abatis near Fleche Number Three, where Col. Butler's column had attacked, Highlander Lt. William Nairne fought on until the Americans bayoneted their way down on his flank and demanded his surrender. Three other Scots officers—Lt. John Ross, Capt. Francis Tew and Lt. Cummings, who had saved Ross's life a few minutes earlier—held their position near the three-pounder cannon even after they heard firing and shouting behind them from the Upper Works, "as we did not know whether they were rebels or our own men," according to Ross.[22]

Stony Point's commander, Lt. Col. Johnson, continued to try to organize a defense and ordered Tew to withdraw to the Upper Works. Less than twenty men were fit to follow Tew. Although his small party worked their way to the Upper Works, American soldiers killed the first two of his men who came through the sally port, and Tew gave up the effort. Along with Lt. Ross and his men, Tew took his small command south along Stony Point's slope but ran into another group of soldiers—possibly their own countrymen who mistook them for Americans—who demanded their surrender. Ross recalled "Capt. Tew made use of some hasty expression ... but ... was immediately fired on and killed."[23] Ross made his way into the Upper Works and found Lt. Col. Johnson. Probably due to exhaustion and disorientation, Ross, curiously, asked Johnson if he could go to his tent. He heard Americans ordering British soldiers to surrender and then was taken prisoner himself.

Inside the Upper Works on Stony Point's crest, the battle was ending. Maj. Posey pushed his Virginians across to the north side of the Table and seized a battery of two twenty-four pounders—"at which post I made numbers of the enemy prisoners," he wrote.[24] Maj. Hull drove his column east until the troops faced across the Hudson, towards Verplanck's Point. One Light Infantry officer wrote that as the British resistance waned there was "a little small arms firing and considerable bayoneting."[25] Pvt. Vincent Vass continued fighting despite his two wounds and later wrote that as the Yankees cornered Redcoats "the British cryed out quarter, quarter, brave Americans."[26] Young Ensign Frederick Robinson with the Seventeenth Regiment recalled, "Our party was driven back, and in an instant all was confusion, everyone striving the best for himself. I was seized by an American Officer, who exclaimed, 'I've got a very young Prisoner,' then snatched off my hat, and left me. A soldier took my sword, but like his officer, did not think me worth attending to."[27]

Col. Febiger turned his column to the south and captured a British officer whom he ordered to take him to the fort's commander. How he expected his captive to find Lt. Col. Johnson in the darkness and confusion is not known, but Febiger luckily had the right man, as he wrote to his wife: "I had the pleasure of taking Col. Johnson, who commanded, myself, and ordered him to his tent."[28] About ten minutes later Col. Butler's soldiers, still with Lt. Gibbon and "Crazy Jack" Stewart at their head, scaled the parapet from the north, entered the Upper Works, and pushed the remaining Redcoats back along the Table. Thomas Posey helped Stewart climb through an embrasure and the officers shook hands inside the fort. Gibbon was exhausted, muddy up to the neck, and his uniform was "torn almost to rags." A captain named Jordan, from Maj. Stewart's battalion, told him, "You little devil, you have left us nothing to do."[29] Lt. Col. de Fleury went to the flagstaff and lowered the British Union Jack. Pvt. James Noble, the Virginia soldier who had once been left for dead at Germantown, was wounded again. But he possibly hauled down the regimental colors of the Seventeenth, as he remembered, "[Lt. Col. de Fleury] ordered the British flag to be took down" and that Noble had "the honor and satisfaction of taking it down himself."[30] With the Upper Works in their hands, all the American troops shouted their watchword—"The fort's our own!" A Connecticut officer checked his watch, and saw that it was exactly 1:00 A.M.[31]

Small groups of British soldiers were still scattered all over Stony Point but they soon realized that their post was lost. Lt. William Simpson of the Seventeenth Regiment, who had been taken prisoner once and then left alone, walked to the Upper Works and surrendered. Lt. William Horndon at Fleche Number One kept his men firing until he heard the Americans cheering. He sent three soldiers to search for an escape route but the men found all their avenues blocked by Continentals. Horndon told his men — which included Cpl. Simon Davies, who had first heard Gen. Wayne's column approach near the marsh — "My lads I believe we are Prisoners," and then waited for the Americans.[32] When no Yankees appeared after an hour, Horndon sent Cpl. William West to find an officer to accept their surrender. The corporal recalled that when he walked towards the Upper Works a group of Continentals charged him with their bayonets, "and one of them ran his Bayonet thro' my coat, but a Rebel Officer coming up protected me, and asked me what I was come for."[33] West took the officer to the fleche, and Horndon surrendered his men after the American promised that they would be treated well. During the battle Cpl. John Ash, who had heard Col. Butler's column approach from his picquet on the north side of Stony Point, became trapped near the outer abatis while the Grenadiers fired at the Americans. He recalled that, "the Shots from the 71st Grenadrs. came so thick amongst us, as to Wound one of my Men, upon which I thought it proper to retire a little further back under Cover."[34] Ash moved his men to the edge of the marsh, out of range of his countrymen's muskets, where they remained all night until daylight, when they finally surrendered.

Col. Febiger had ordered Lt. Knox and a Capt. Lawson out with patrols to prevent British troops from escaping, but in the darkness, neither officer found any Redcoats. Lt. Col. Isaac Sherman, in Meigs' Regiment, saw some British troops milling about the banks of the Hudson, "which led me to conclude that they were gone down to the landing in order to get on board the shipping in the river," as he recalled.[35] Sherman sent Lt. Timothy Taylor of the First Connecticut Regiment and twenty-five men out to prevent their escape, and Taylor returned with thirty prisoners. Taylor may have captured part of the group organized by Capt. Lawrence Campbell, who had commanded the two Grenadier companies at the outer abatis. Halfway through the battle Campbell fell with musket balls, in both legs, that were probably fired by British troops. He tried to walk to the Upper Works to get his wounds dressed, "but was prevented by a Number of unarmed soldiers of the 17th Infantry who were running from the Fort, and upon enquiring the reason of their Confusion, I was informed by them that the upper works had been stormed and every person within them put to the Sword."[36] Despite his wounds Campbell joined a group of soldiers that found a flat-bottomed boat at the King's Ferry landing and rowed across the Hudson to HMS *Vulture*. Lt. John Roberts, who had tried to bring the Royal Artillery howitzer battery into action but found it overrun by the Americans, followed a path down to Haverstraw Bay on Stony Point's south side, stripped off his uniform coat and swam to the ship. Campbell and Roberts were the only two British officers to avoid capture.

While the Americans rounded up the last of the British soldiers and collected their weapons, Gen. Wayne's aide, Capt. Henry Fishbourne, and Henry Archer, a civilian volunteer who had accompanied Wayne, carried their wounded commander up the slope and into the Upper Works, "bleeding, in triumph," as Maj. Hull wrote.[37] When the general arrived, his adrenaline-charged light infantrymen began realizing that they had overwhelmed Stony Point with amazing speed and efficiency. After seeing the high number of British infantrymen and artillery pieces that had defended the fortress, the Americans were probably stunned at their own success. Maj. Hull wrote that when Wayne arrived over the parapet, his 1,000 soldiers shouted three "long and loud cheers" that "boomed in the darkness, reverberated off the rocks and mountains," and "sent back an echo in glad response to the hearts of the victors."[38] At 2:00 A.M. Wayne penned a dispatch to Gen. Washington that said only, "The forts & garrison with Col. Johnson are ours. Our officers & men behaved like men who are determined to be free."[39] Wayne later wrote that he had wished to send his commander a longer report, but "the loss of blood which continued to issue in a torrent from my wound rendered it expedient for me to be Concise."⁴⁰

Cheers also rang from the crew of the *Vulture* and the garrison of Verplanck's Point, who thought that the British had repulsed the American attack. Their cheering probably reminded the Continentals that the battle was not completely finished as long as the British held the eastern end of King's Ferry. The artillerymen that accompanied the Light Infantry were anxious to turn their newly captured guns on their opponents across the river. But the British officer in charge of the gunpowder, possibly Capt. William Tiffen, stated that he took orders only from Lt. Col. Johnson and refused to relinquish the keys to the magazine. William Hull recalled, "He was informed that Colonel Johnson was superseded in command, and that there must be no delay, or the consequences might be unpleasant. The key was produced."⁴¹ The American artillerymen opened fire on the *Vulture* and Verplanck's Point, and the British cheering ceased.

When dawn arrived a few hours later, the creeping light revealed a shocking scene. Muskets, knapsacks, soldier's belongings, and collapsed tents littered the ground. Steam rose from the morning dew on the still-hot barrel of the Seventeenth Regiment's three-pounder cannon and the ground in front of the gun was ripped from the grapeshot rounds. Steam also rose from Fleche Number One where Lt. William Horndon had blindly blasted at attackers with his twelve-pounder cannon. The fourteen other pieces of artillery, overrun before they could be brought into action, sat cold and silent next to ripped-open ammunition cases with rammers, sponges and firing implements strewn near them. The two abatis were smashed and broken where the American columns had pushed through them. Thirteen men from Wayne's Light Corps were dead, some of their bodies twisted into crumpled positions that showed the brutality of hand-to-hand combat, and sixty-four soldiers were wounded (the men of Col. Febiger's regiment and Maj. Hull's detachment, which formed the main attack, accounted for fifty-three casualties).⁴² Sixty-three British and Loyalist American troops also lay dead where they fell, with another sixty-one wounded. Continental artillerymen continued firing at the *Vulture* and *Cornwallis* until the two vessels slipped downstream and out of range. As the sun rose, the slopes of Stony Point reverberated with the thunderous crash of the cannon and the screams of the wounded.

The dawn also allowed the Americans to deal with the immediate aftermath of any battle—caring for the wounded, processing prisoners, and burying the dead. Light Corps surgeon Samuel McKenzie bandaged and operated on the American wounded, and the surgeon of the Seventeenth Regiment, Dr. Richard Auchmuty, attended to the Crown soldiers. McKenzie, thirty-nine, had served with Gen. Wayne since 1776 and was likely a seasoned battlefield doctor. His assistants, like the twenty-six-year-old surgeon's mate from Meigs' Regiment, Theo Wadsworth, probably had little medical training beyond an apprenticeship with a town doctor. With sixty-four men wounded by musket balls, bayonets, and grapeshot, Dr. McKenzie faced grisly work. The Americans who were not wounded gathered the remaining British and Loyalist troops for counting and identification by name, rank, and regiment. The process identified 543 prisoners in all, including six Continental Army deserters in the ranks of the Seventy-first Highlanders. Desertion to the enemy was a treasonous offense under the Articles of War, and Wayne's men separated the six from the other prisoners to face a court-martial. While this process went on throughout the morning, work parties buried the dead where they lay.

As soon as there was enough daylight for travel, Gen. Wayne's aide-de-camp, Capt. Henry Fishbourne, borrowed a horse — probably from Maj. Lee's mounted dragoons since the Light Corps brought none to Stony Point — and rode as fast as he could to deliver Wayne's brief battle report to Gen. Washington at the New Windsor headquarters. Though Wayne's note was only a few sentences, the overwhelming success of the assault was clear. Washington was elated, and just after 9:00 A.M. he transmitted the news to John Jay, president of the Continental Congress, saying, "I have the pleasure to transmit Your Excellency the inclosed Copy of a Letter from Brigadier Genl. Wayne, which this moment came to hand. I congratulate Congress upon our success, and what makes it still more agreeable from the report of Captn Fishbourn who brought me Genl. Wayne's Letter, the post was gained with but very inconsiderable loss on our part. As soon as I receive a particular account of the affair, I shall transmit it."[43] He wasted no time in informing the rest of the Continental Army, and wrote in the orders of the day: "The Commander in Chief is happy to congratulate the Army on the success of our Arms under Brigadier General Wayne, who last night with the corps of Light Infantry surprised and took the enemy's post at Stony Point with the whole Garrison, Cannon and Stores with very inconsiderable loss on our side. The General has not yet received the particulars of the affair, but he has the satisfaction to learn that the officers and men in general gloriously distinguished themselves in the attack. He requests the Brigadier and his whole corps to accept his warmest thanks for the good conduct and signal bravery manifested upon the occasion." Gen. Washington made the password of the day "Wayne" and the countersign "Light Infantry."[44]

The final phase of the battle played out across the Hudson at Verplanck's Point but was plagued by problems. To seize the eastern terminus of King's Ferry, on July 15 Gen. Washington ordered Gen. McDougall to attack Verplanck's Point with two brigades under Brigadier-Generals Nixon and Patterson after the assault at Stony Point was confirmed as successful. Washington had ordered Wayne to send all of his dispatches to McDougall first, to ensure that the latter officer received immediate news on the status of the attack. When Wayne sent his initial report straight to Washington at New Windsor, McDougall did not know that Stony Point had fallen, "which occasioned a loss of several hours," Washington wrote.[45] Washington also assigned Col. Rufus Putnam (who was originally slated to command a regiment on the Light Infantry) to take a detachment from Gen. Nixon's brigade and open fire on Fort Lafayette in support of Wayne's attack. Putnam found Nixon's brigade on the afternoon of the fifteenth and, suspecting that Wayne's attack was about to begin, asked the brigadier why he had not marched toward Ft. Lafayette. Nixon told Putnam, somewhat cryptically, that "he had obtained leave from Genl. McDougall to delay his march."[46] At that point, Putnam wrote that he was "exceedingly perplexed to know how to act" but still intended to carry out his mission, regardless of Nixon's mysterious delay. Putnam said, "As soon as I saw that Wayne had commenced his attack on Stony Point we fired on their out block house and guard at the creek and thus alarmed the garrison on Verplanck's Point, which was the only object contemplated for that night."[47] Col. Webster, the British commander at Fort Lafayette, did not return fire. Putnam kept his soldiers near the British works but, as he wrote, "in the course of the day Nixon's and Patterson's brigades arrived, but without their field pieces, artillery men, or so much as an ax or spade, or any orders what they were to do." A full attack on Verplanck's Point never took place.[48]

With only an ineffective American force outside his works, Col. Webster dispatched a major named Benson to ride to Clinton's headquarters and inform the general that the fortress of Stony Point, Britain's "Little Gibraltar," was in American hands.

XIV

Colors Flying

Southeastern New York, July 16, 1779

At the temporary British army headquarters at Mamaroneck, New York, officers heard the booming of cannon from the Hudson all through the early hours of July 16, but Gen. Clinton was the last commander in the region to learn about the battle of Stony Point. Maj. Benson, the messenger from Verplanck's Point, arrived at Mamaroneck in mid-morning, but Sir Henry was at Throg's Neck on Long Island, conferring with Commodore Collier on the possibility of continuing the raids in Connecticut. Clinton had been fixated on Tryon's raiding and when he returned to his headquarters that afternoon and learned that Stony Point had fallen, he said that his "astonishment could not but be extreme" because he had not "the smallest apprehension that any attempt of the enemy" could occur against Stony Point or Verplanck's Point before he was able to come to their assistance. Clinton said he "looked on the place [Stony Point] as perfectly secure ... especially as it was under the charge of a vigilant, active and spirited officer and a very ample garrison."[1]

Definitely surprised and possibly angry, Clinton still "was not without hopes that Mr. Washington, in the course of the struggle for it, might be drawn into an engagement," he wrote, and was "anxious that no measure should be omitted for the recovery of the post."[2] Early on July 17 he sent troops to Dobb's Ferry on the east bank of the Hudson and pushed some cavalry and light infantry toward Verplanck's Point, two moves that had no effect on the situation except that they chased off the problem-ridden American attack on Ft. Lafayette. Clinton also cancelled plans for further raids in Connecticut, recalled Commodore Collier's squadron from Long Island Sound, and prepared to retake Stony Point with three regiments under Brig. Gen. Stirling. But strong northerly winds prevented Stirling's force from sailing up the Hudson, and Clinton could do nothing more except contemplate how to regain control of the campaign.

While Clinton stewed on July 17, American and British troops alike at Stony Point were recovering from the battle. There was limited medical care available on the battlefield, so Light Corps surgeon William McKenzie sent the American wounded to hospitals in Albany. Doctors of the age had little understanding of postsurgery recovery and the causes of infection were as yet unknown to medical science, so hospital care did not guarantee survival. Light infantryman Pvt. Vincent Vass, wounded in the hip and thigh, recalled that his "messmate Samuel Arnold was wounded in the hip, we went up to Albany Hospital and through mercy I got well — but my poor messmate died — mortification took place."[3] The lack of adequate medical care at Stony Point so alarmed Dr. Auchmuty, captured surgeon of the defeated Seventeenth Regiment, that he asked Gen. Wayne to send the wounded Redcoats across the lines to British hospitals. Wayne agreed but insisted on a prisoner exchange for the same number of Continental officers and troops. The Americans eventually transferred four British officers and thirty-nine soldiers to British care in New York City.[4] The record is unclear if there was an exchange for Continental troops.

In the midst of the recovery Gen. Washington, Gen. Steuben, and Maj. Gen. Nathaniel Green arrived at Stony Point to view the battlefield. By then Washington had Wayne's full battle report, written only that morning, which included a detailed description of the action and the customary naming of officers who distinguished themselves. "Too much praise cannot be given to Lt. Col. Fleury (who struck the enemy's standard with his own hand)," he told Washington, "and to Maj. Stewart ... for their brave and prudent conduct. Colonels Butler, Meigs and Febiger conducted themselves with that coolness, bravery and perseverance, that will ever ensure success." He also cited Lt. Col Hay, "wounded in the thigh, bravely fighting at the head of his battalion," and Maj. Henry Lee, "to whom I am indebted for frequent and very useful intelligence, which contributed much to the success of this enterprise."[5]

Wayne was still recovering from his scalp wound, so the field officers of the Light Corps were the hosts for the visiting senior generals. Washington was usually guarded about his emotions, but Maj. Hull wrote, "I recollect how cordially he took me by the hand, and the satisfaction and joy that glowed in his countenance.... Washington minutely viewed every part of the fortifications. His attention was particularly drawn to those places where the two columns ascended the hill, mounted the parapets, and first entered the works. He expressed his astonishment that we were enabled to surmount the difficulties and attain our object with so inconsiderable a loss. And here he offered his thanks to Almighty God, that he had been our shield and protector amidst the dangers we had been called to encounter."[6]

Washington's aides, Colonels Tench Tilghman and Alexander Hamilton, supervised the inventory of the captured equipment. In addition to the 543 British prisoners, the Americans seized a total of fifteen cannon, 334 muskets, nearly 30,000 cartridges, and stores that included spades, picks, axes, 140 tents, a spyglass described as "elegant," shoes, breeches, gaiters, a tablecloth, three crowbars, and a speaking trumpet.[7] Wayne promised his soldiers that with congressional approval he would sell the captured stores and distribute the profits to them. Washington later forced Congress to comply, writing, "some pecuniary rewards were promised by General Wayne to his corps. This was done with my concurrence ... and in addition to them, as a greater incitement to their exertion, they were also promised the benefit of whatever was taken in the fort. The artillery and stores are converted to the use of the public; but in compliance with my engagements, it will be necessary to have them appraised and the amount paid to the captors, in money. I hope my conduct in this instance will not be disapproved."[8] Congress did not disapprove.

It is possible that Hamilton and Tilghman also supervised sending the British prisoners to their captivity. The enlisted prisoners left Stony Point under a guard from Maj. Lee's dragoons on a long march south to Hardytown, Pennsylvania, where they would remain until exchanged. An escape attempt the first night of the march left nine British prisoners from the Seventeenth Regiment wounded. As was the custom of the time, Lt. Col. Johnson and the officers went into "parole" near Lancaster, Pennsylvania, where the captured officers billeted in private homes with the agreement, on their word of honor, not to escape, take part in, or even discuss the conflict with Americans until exchanged. It is unknown if any of the British officers ever learned that the location of their parole was only about fifty miles from Waynesboro, the family estate of Anthony Wayne.

Washington expected Clinton to attempt to retake the fort with an attack by land and from the river and told Congress, "I found it would require more men to maintain it than we could afford, without incapacitating the army for other operations. In the opinion of the Engineer, corresponding with my own and that of all the general officers present, not less than 1500 men would be requisite for its complete defense ... exposed to the risk of a general action, on terms which it would not be our interest to court.... These considerations made it an unanimous sentiment to evacuate the post, remove the cannon and stores and destroy the works. "[9] On Sunday, July 18, the Light Infantry dismantled the Stony Point fortifications and shipped the captured stores up the river to West Point. The American row galley *Lady Washington* helped haul away the captured cannon until British gunners at Verplanck's Point opened fire and forced the gunboat to run aground. The crew threw their cargo overboard to lighten their load but the craft remained a stuck, stationary target that the British guns quickly holed in several places. The *Lady Washington* sank in shallow water and the crew burned her. Crewman Anthony Glean recalled "the officers and crew barely escaped from the ship."[10]

The Light Infantry evacuated Stony Point once all the stores and cannon were removed, but before their departure Wayne convened a court-martial to determine the fate of the American deserters found in the British ranks. The court found five of the deserters—William Fitzgerald, Isaac Wilson, John Williams, Joseph Case, and John Blackman—guilty of "deserting to the enemy" and sentenced them to death. For reasons unknown, one of the deserters was not tried. Gen. Washington confirmed the sentences and on the afternoon of July 18 the Light Infantrymen hung the deserters near the flagstaff on the crest of Stony Point. With the business concluded, Gen. Wayne marched his soldiers back to Sandy Beach, the place where they had begun their assault three days earlier.[11]

By July 19 the strong northerly winds that had buffeted the Hudson abated, and Gen. Stirling's force to retake Stony Point sailed to Haverstraw Bay, where Clinton soon joined them, still hoping to draw the Americans into a general action. The Continental Army remained in its defensive positions near West Point, and Clinton observed, "It is most probable ... that that wary officer suspected my intentions."[12]

Actually, Washington believed that Clinton intended to attack West Point, and he told Congress "prudence requires that our dispositions should have immediate reference to the security of this post."[13] On July 19 he bolstered West Point's defenses with three of Gen. McDougall's brigades, and the Light Infantry patrolled the west bank of the Hudson from Ft. Montgomery along with some more Virginia troops. Washington's orders, such as when he directed McDougall that "every officer and man may be acquainted with his post in time of action and know where to repair, without confusion or delay, in case of a sudden alarm," showed more urgency than the measured, reassuring updates he sent to Congress. Another of his orders was that "the Artillery is also to be distributed and every minute arrangement made at once, that everything may be in the most perfect readiness at the shortest notice. A full supply of water to be immediately provided."[14] He told supply officers to keep their powder stores "ready to issue at a moment's warning" and to keep two days' provisions ready at all times. Shortages of supplies, Washington stressed, "will not be admired as an excuse and the officers commanding Corps are to consider themselves as responsible to the Commander in Chief for strict obedience to this order."[15] The equipment seized at Stony Point became immediately beneficial when Washington issued this order on July 20: "If the troops wanting Arms have not been supplied they are to be furnished out of those brought from Stony Point and not a moment's time is to be lost in doing of it." But instead of attacking West Point, Clinton merely embarked at Haverstraw Bay and retook the abandoned Stony Point on July 21. As Collier remembered, "The rebels set fire to everything there that would burn, and went off with their usual alertness."[16]

Clinton later wrote that the situation in late July was making his spirits sink.[17] The British manned Stony Point with 1,300 troops, rebuilt the fortifications, and reinforced the garrison at Verplanck's Point to 700 men, but by that time the Continental Army's position at West Point and on both sides of the Hudson gave the American's a short supply line to New England and significantly reduced the strategic value of King's Ferry.[18] After over a month of fighting Clinton had gained little and suffered nearly 1,000 casualties. On July 21, the same day that British troops reoccupied Stony Point, a ship from England arrived in New York City carrying Lt. Gen. Earl Charles Cornwallis and disheartening dispatches from London. British spies had informed the king that France was sending 3,000 troops and five warships to America; General Haldimand, the king's commander in Canada, urgently requested 2,000 soldiers to defend against a possible American and French attack from upper New York; and Commodore Collier's squadron was ordered to relieve the Royal Navy forces at Penobscot Bay, leaving Clinton only three warships at New York. Clinton's offensive was failing, and his only hope for reviving it was to resume the action upon the arrival of the 6,000 troops that Germain had promised earlier in the year. In the meantime Clinton cancelled offensive operations and brought his forces back to the fortified lines around Manhattan. In contrast to his energy at the beginning of the campaign, Clinton returned to his usual state of melancholia. To Gen. Haldimand in Canada, he later called his situation "weak and miserable."[19]

In stark contrast, Anthony Wayne and the Light Infantry enjoyed the thanks of their countrymen as news of the Stony Point victory spread. Mr. Archer, Gen. Wayne's volunteer civilian aide at the battle, received the honor of carrying Washington's full report of the action to the Continental Congress. Archer kept a brutal pace on his ride from New Windsor, riding twenty-one miles one day, then forty-six, and then sixty-three miles, and then he breakfasted about sixteen miles from Philadelphia. When his horse was worn out he commandeered another from some passing dragoons. He "came into the City with Colours flying, Trumpet sounding, and heart elated," he told Wayne, and "drew crowds to the doors and windows and made not a little parade, I assure you Sir these were Baron Steuben's instructions ... tho' I could not help thinking it a little of the appearance of a puppet shew."[20]

A show it may have been, but the Congressional delegates were thrilled to hear the details of the battle and read Washington's praise for Wayne, such as "his own conduct, throughout the whole of this arduous enterprise, merits the warmest approbation of Congress. He improved upon the plan recommended by me and executed it in a manner that does signal honor to his judgment and to his bravery. In a critical moment of the assault he received a flesh wound in the head with a musket-ball; but continued leading on his men with unshaken firmness."[21] Archer told Wayne, "Say the political Speculators, the war would have ended with the taking of Verplank's Point."[22] The "political speculators" were certainly wrong, but their statements were indicators that the taking of Stony Point gave a much needed boost to American spirits at a time when many people were wearying of the war. Pennsylvania congressional delegate Dr. Benjamin Rush wrote to Wayne: "There was but one thing wanting in your late successful attack upon Stony Point to complete your happiness, and that is the wound you received should have affected your hearing, for I fear you will be stunned thro' those organs with your own praises.... Our streets for many days ring with nothing but the name of General Wayne. You are remembered constantly next to our great and good General Washington over our Claret, and Madeira.... Best congratulations to Col. Butler and Major Stewart who shared so largely with you in the danger and glory of your late victory."[23]

Even Maj. Gen. Charles Lee, who received Wayne's censure during his court-martial following the battle of Monmouth, wrote to Wayne: "I do most sincerely declare, that your action in the assault of Stony-point is not only the most brilliant, in my opinion, through the whole course of the war, on either side, but that it is one of the most brilliant I am acquainted with in history."[24]

On July 26 Congress passed a resolution that officially recognized the bravery of Wayne, his soldiers, and especially Lt. Col. de Fleury, Maj. Stewart, and Lts. Gibbon and Knox, the leaders of the two "Forlorn Hopes." Knox, Gibbon, and Mr. Archer received "brevet," or provisional, commissions as captains. There was no regular system of battle decorations at the time so Congress ordered the casting of special medallions commemorating the action — a gold medal for Wayne and silver medals for de Fleury and Stewart. They previously had authorized only two such awards: one to Washington, in recognition of his successful siege of Boston, and one to Gen. Gates for Saratoga, which were two of the most significant American victories of the war up to that point.[25] John Jay conveyed the laudatory congressional resolutions to Wayne with a letter that said, "Your late glorious achievements have merited, and now receive the approbation and thanks of your Country.... This brilliant action adds fresh luster to our arms, should teach the enemy to respect our power.... You have nobly reaped Laurels in the cause of your Country, and in fields of Danger and Death."[26]

In August Congress approved $1,500 for the monetary rewards that Wayne had promised to the first five men who entered Stony Point, and they also purchased the captured stores from the Light Infantry for $158,640. Washington wrote that the money was distributed to the troops "in proportion to the pay of the Officers and Men,"[27] but Wayne also allotted the cash by assigning shares to men, shares which may have been linked to their roles in the attack. Gen. Wayne's shares, for example, entitled him to $1,420.51 (nearly equal to his annual pay as a brigadier-general), but Light Corps surgeon Samuel McKenzie, who was certainly not equal in rank but presumably helped carry his commander into the fort, received the same amount. Four of Maj. Henry Lee's mounted soldiers who must have played important parts in the battle received a total of five shares split between them, a total of $394.58, or $98.64 per man.[28] Capt. Robert Gamble, commander of a company in Febiger's Regiment, received six shares worth $472.00, his lieutenant received four shares, and his company drummer received one and four-tenths of a share. The private soldiers in the Light Infantry, who had fought the hardest, received only a single share each — $78.65 per man, an amount equivalent to about ten months of their annual pay.[29]

John Jay wrote to Wayne that the American actions at Stony Point would compel the British to "imitate our Humanity," a comment that touched on the acclaim the Light Infantry received because they spared the lives of the Crown soldiers after the surrender.[30] The Connecticut Light Infantry officer who was part of Col. Febiger's column at Stony Point observed as follows: "Notwithstanding the depredation the enemy had lately committed in our State, the cruelties our soldiers have suffered from them ... yet I believe not one of the enemy was hurt after he had thrown down his arms and asked for quarter."[31] Modern laws of land warfare require soldiers to make prisoners of any enemy combatants who can no longer present armed resistance, and they are to protect the prisoners from further harm.

In the eighteenth century the only legal document that dictated the conduct of soldiers and commanders was the "Articles of War," a set of general guidelines that European and American armies followed. No section of the articles that the Continental Congress passed in 1776 required soldiers to bestow mercy on opponents in combat, nor did the articles address the treatment of prisoners. Commodore Collier captured the prevailing military custom of the time when he wrote, "The laws of war give a right to the assailants of putting all to death who are found in arms." But at Stony Point, American soldiers acted differently. Collier continued: "The rebels had made the attack with a bravery they never before exhibited and they showed at this moment a generosity and clemency which during the course of the rebellion had no parallel."[32]

That Gen. Wayne's soldiers did not bayonet captured Redcoats was also a matter of smart tactics. Wayne's plan required the Light Infantry to overwhelm the British defenders as quickly as possible. If they had broken up into small groups and taken the time to bayonet Redcoats who presented no threat, the Americans would have become an uncontrolled mob without momentum. Military discipline kept the Americans in their formations and focused on the goal of gaining Stony Point's Upper Works. Though squads and platoons eventually broke away to eliminate pockets of resistance, and the Continentals certainly did not fight with saintly restraint (as one officer said, some British were killed in their tents), most of the light infantrymen stayed under the control of their leaders and contributed to, rather than distracted from, the successful execution of Wayne's plan. As they had at the battle of Monmouth, the American soldiers at

Stony Point put Gen. Steuben's leadership techniques they learned on the training field into practice on the battlefield.

Though Gen. Washington surely enjoyed the nation's appreciation for his soldiers, Stony Point was but one battle in his effort to stop Britain's offensive. It was only mid-summer. The season for campaigning could last until the late autumn or even early winter, and British forces around New York were still powerful. The fight for control of the Hudson was not over.

XV

Veteranship

West Bank of the Hudson, Opposite Manhattan, August 1779

Gen. Washington knew the victory at Stony Point was at least a successful "check ... to the depredations of the enemy," but the strategic effects of the battle were unclear.[1] He knew British forces had moved back to their lines around Manhattan, and he told Congress that he "used every means in my power to gain information of their designs and future operations, but as yet they remain intirely secret." From British officers captured at Stony Point, Washington learned that "Sir Henry Clinton's operations would be offensive and pushed with great vigor. There are sundry other accounts agreeing with these."[2] The "sundry other accounts" to which Washington referred included one from Robert Townsend, a twenty-six-year-old merchant in New York City that Abraham Woodhull recruited into the Culper Ring.

Townsend operated under the alias "Samuel Culper Jr." and reported at the end of July that British troops viewed the loss of Stony Point as "truly alarming," and "General Clinton, I am told, was much alarmed.... It is said, [he] declared that he would make W. [Washington] pay for it."[3] Townshend also recounted British expectations of up to 7,000 reinforcements (5,000 for New York and 2,000 to open an offensive in the Carolinas, he said), but no one knew when, or even if, the fresh troops would arrive. Redcoat deserters also said that Baltimore was Britain's next target in the campaign, and, according to American troops in Connecticut, an apparent raiding force of forty Royal Navy ships sailed east up Long Island Sound again (the force was actually Commodore Collier, sailing his squadron to Penobscot Bay). "Time alone must develop the objects of these different movements" Washington told Congress, but the reports gave him ample reason to expect the British offensive to continue.[4] He considered attacks on West Point, New England, and even Philadelphia as possible British objectives. "Some considerable movement of the enemy is in agitation, but of what nature, and where pointed, I have not been able to discover," he told Joseph Reed, the president of the Pennsylvania Supreme Executive Council.[5]

Washington wanted to stay ahead of the British so he could choose the location and manner of the next action, which was vital for success. At the end of July, Clinton had about 12,000 soldiers in the area around the Hudson, the Continental Army had (by Washington's accounting) 10,300 soldiers. The Continental gunpowder stores were "nearly empty, scarcely equal to the ordinary demands of the service," which forced the commander-in-chief to request a loan of powder from Connecticut and Massachusetts.[6] Like Clinton, Washington also expected the British to resume their offensive once reinforcements from England arrived, and he told Congress "the consequences at least might be very disagreeable."[7] Outnumbered, the Americans could not attack the British and still maintain their defense of West Point, nor could they defend every point that was vulnerable to British attack.

Washington was gaining the upper hand in the campaign and needed to solidify his control on the Hudson and knock Clinton back on the defensive without exposing the undermanned and poorly supplied Continental Army to unnecessary risks. On July 25 he convened a council of war with his senior officers and posed this question: "whether any and what offensive operations can with propriety be undertaken by us against the enemy, at this present juncture." His generals agreed that the further attacks on Stony Point or Verplanck's Point were unlikely to succeed, and that above all they should continue to defend West Point. Washington decided to put West Point "in such a state of defence as it will give it security with its own garrison and leave the rest of the army to operate with confidence elsewhere."[8] The Council also agreed that the Continentals should launch feints against the British, which would keep the enemy off-balance, guessing about American intentions, and help keep the initiative in Washington's hands.

Washington seemed more interested in action than did his senior generals, and what he needed was another economy of force operation. Three days after the council, he ordered Gen. McDougall to scout the roads on the east side of the Hudson for avenues that would be useful for rapid, unobserved strikes at British lines. Contrary to the Council's recommendations, Washington asked Gen. Wayne for his opinion on "another attempt upon Stony Point, by way of surprize."[9] Wayne responded that the Redcoats were sure to be prepared for another surprise assault but that he was confident the Light Infantry could seize the position "with the loss of between four and five hundred men."[10] The planning went no further. In early August Maj. Gen. William Heath, commander of the Continental Left Wing on the east side of the Hudson, proposed a raid on a British outpost at Lloyd's Neck, Long Island; but Washington was lukewarm on the idea since it would net only about thirty enemy troops at most. Heath's idea went no further either.[11] The Continental cavalry scouted for enemy vulnerabilities on both sides of the Hudson, and on August 9 Washington received another proposal for an attack from that active scout and cavalryman Maj. Henry Lee.

At twenty-three, Henry Lee was another of the young, aggressive rising stars of the Continental Army. His family was part of America's planter elite, with a presence that went back to 1600 when his ancestor Richard Lee came to Virginia as a member of King Charles I's Privy Council. A 1773 graduate of Princeton, he was about to go to England to study law when the Revolution began. In June 1776 he gained a commission as a captain commanding the Fifth Troop of the Virginia Light Horse Regiment, which was later transferred into the First Regiment of Continental Light Dragoons and assigned to Washington's main army. Slight of build and of only medium height, Lee applied the gentlemen's code of service to leading his unit. He inspired his men with his belief in the American cause and stressed that they needed to avoid the disgrace of defeat or ever being perceived as mere ordinary soldiers.

Lee fostered unity by ensuring that his men were well cared for and properly uniformed and equipped, sometimes at his own expense. An expert on horses from his gentlemanly upbringing, Lee chose only the best mounts for his unit and had his soldiers carefully tend to them. He also appreciated the need for discipline and occasionally dealt with his men harshly (misconduct in action merited a death sentence, in Lee's opinion). He called his leadership philosophy "veteranship," and it resulted in a cavalry unit with high morale and skill.[12] Lee's men became experts at raids, ambushes and moving quickly. He selected the targets for raids after reconnaissance, made thorough plans, and executed the attacks with cunning, discipline and aggressiveness. Lee's raids were so damaging to the British that in January 1778 Sir William Eskine launched a counterraid to capture him at the Spread Eagle Tavern (the raid where the Americans fooled and wounded Banastre Tarleton), but his dragoons fought off the Redcoat cavalry after twenty-five minutes.

Lee and his men also had a brutal streak. When the Continental Army was at Smith's Clove in July 1779, one of Lee's patrols commanded by Capt. Philip Reed captured three deserters, and Reed shot and decapitated the one deserter who was American-born. The next day Lee had the deserter's head placed on a pole at the Smith Clove camp.[13] Washington strongly disapproved of the execution and ordered the body buried immediately, especially to prevent similar treatment of American prisoners. Lee dryly told him, "Although from what I believe here it has had a very immediate effect for the better on both troops & inhabitants."[14]

Lee's obvious ambition irritated some of his peers but Congress promoted him to major in April 1778 and made his unit a "partisan corps" that operated independently. Washington endorsed the move, commended Lee's men for "exemplary zeal, prudence, and bravery," and added that "Captain Lee's genius particularly adapts him to a command of this nature."[15] Washington and Steuben also favored integrating the lightly armed cavalry "legions" with infantry for protection and flexibility

Henry Lee, by Charles Willson Peale, from life, c. 1782. Young, audacious and an excellent leader, Lee helped scout the British fortifications at Stony Point. A month later he repeated Anthony Wayne's tactics in the assault on Paulus Hook (Independence National Historical Park).

in combat, so in June 1779 Congress added Captain Allan McLane's infantry company to Lee's command and after Stony Point officially designated his unit a "Legion," to Lee's delight. In August 1779 Lee's Legion consisted of about 200 cavalry and infantry from Virginia, Pennsylvania, Delaware, Maryland, New Jersey and Connecticut. From the village of New Bridge, they patrolled Bergen County, New Jersey, on the east bank of the Hudson opposite Manhattan.

A historian later called southern Bergen County (which became Hudson County) "the gate to New Jersey" for military operations.[16] American forces moved into the area in 1776 and built cannon batteries on Bergen's Point and nearby Paulus Hook, a sixty-five-acre spit of land that jutted southeast at the southern end of a peninsula formed by the Hackensack River to the west and the Hudson to the east. It took its name from the Dutch in the seventeenth century, when Paulus was the family name of its first European owners of the area that became southern Bergen County; "hoeck" was the Dutch word for "point." A ferry, began in 1764, ran from Paulus Hook to the foot of Grand Street in New York City.[17] During the Revolution, Mr. Cornelius Van Vorst, commonly known as "Faddy," owned the area. When the British landed around New York Harbor in July

A private of Maj. Henry Lee's Legion in 1779. On August 18, 1779, Lee's soldiers marched all night and crossed a salt marsh in a bayonet attack against the British fort at Paulus Hook (painting by Don Troiani, www.historical-imagebank.com).

1776 the Paulus Hook battery traded shots with the Royal Navy ships *Phoenix* and *Rose*, and Washington often observed British activity from Paulus Hook. But on September 15, when British forces occupied Manhattan, the *Phoenix*, *Roebuck* and *Tartar* bombarded Paulus Hook heavily and the American garrison fled. Crown troops occupied the abandoned post eight days later. By November all of Bergen County was under British control.

Bergen was also home to about 275 Loyalist families, the highest concentration of any county in New Jersey. Using the ferry between Paulus Hook and Manhattan, Bergen farmers helped supply the British garrison in New York City.[18] But as in Westchester County on the opposite side of the Hudson, Bergen suffered from raids by American, British and Loyalist units. Abraham Van Buskirk, a Bergen County physician, apothecary, and former representative to New Jersey's Provincial Congress, was active in the Patriot cause before the war. But when British forces arrived, he raised the Fourth Battalion of Col. Skinner's Loyalist New Jersey Volunteers, a unit of men with mostly Dutch ancestry. After the defenses of Paulus Hook were strengthened, Van Buskirk made the small fort his base for arbitrary and brutal "predatory excursions" throughout Bergen County. Van Buskirk particularly earned the enmity of people on both sides.[19] In 1777 he captured a former Patriot colleague, Judge John Fell, chairman of Bergen County's Patriot Committee of Safety, and sent him to a British officer in Manhattan with a letter introducing him as a "notorious rebel and rascal." "You must be ... a very great rascal, indeed," the British officer told Fell, "if you equal this Colonel Buskirk."[20]

Since late July Allan McLane's company, as part of Lee's Legion, had reconnoitered southeastern Bergen County, never spending more than two nights in the same spot. The lower end of the Hackensack peninsula was rough, uninhabited country and excellent cover for McLane's soldiers to surreptitiously observe Paulus Hook. At one point McLane arranged for a local farmer named Van Riper to carry provisions into the British fort and then inform the Americans of what he saw inside.[21] What McLane learned was enticing. The British improvements to the original fortifications included a circular parapet 150 feet in diameter with a barracks and three blockhouses inside. Six cannon — twelve- and eighteen-pounders— faced out towards the land and sea. An abatis and a ditch, twenty feet wide and deep enough that oyster boats traversed it, ran across the landward side of the parapet. As at Stony Point, high tide flooded a salt marsh in front of the defenses, and only a narrow causeway built by British engineers known as "Howe's Bridge" afforded access to the fort's main sally port. The garrison consisted of Van Buskirk's battalion of about 200 soldiers and British troops from the Invalid Battalion, which was a group of soldiers previously wounded in action and unfit for robust field duty but still capable of holding fixed defenses. Maj. William Sutherland of the Invalid Battalion commanded the post. McLane's scouts saw that the sentries at Paulus Hook had grown lax and that the post's isolation, weak garrison, and poor security made it vulnerable to attack.

Most likely acting on information gained from McLane's scouting, on August 9 Lee suggested that his legion repeat Wayne's successful tactics and storm Paulus Hook at night with unloaded muskets, capture the garrison, and escape back up the peninsula. Lee went to the New Windsor headquarters, and Washington said that he supported the attack concept but his "principal fear" was that British forces could ferry across the Hudson and trap Lee's on the peninsula. To help ensure a safe getaway after the raid Washington directed that, instead of withdrawing by land up the peninsula, Lee move to Douwe's Ferry, located about two miles west of Paulus Hook, and cross the Hackensack to put a water barrier between Lee's unit and any pursuing forces. He ordered the collection of a number of boats so Lee's men could cross the Hackensack quickly, without waiting for the single ferry boat to shuttle back and forth across the river.

Washington told Lee to abort the attack if the element of surprise was lost, and once in the fort to ignore capturing enemy cannon and heavy stores since they would encumber his men and slow the escape, "as a few minutes delay might expose the party, at least to imminent risk." He dissuaded Lee from pursuing any stray groups of British troops or escaped prisoners, stressing that the objectives of the raid were only to "bring off the garrison immediately, and to effect a secure retreat."[22] The general also believed the attack required at least 300 men, so he reinforced Lee's Legion with 100 Virginia soldiers under Maj. Jonathan Clark, two Maryland companies under Capt. Levin Handy, and another 100 Virginians from Col. Muhlenberg's Brigade, bringing Lee's total force to about 400 soldiers. Washington also ordered Gen. Alexander "Lord" Stirling, in command on the east bank of the Hudson, to remain ready to assist Lee's escape. "I need not add that the greatest caution will be necessary not to give a suspicion of our design and to keep it a matter of profound secrecy," he cautioned Stirling.[23] With these changes Washington approved the plan and set the attack for August 19.

On August 18, the Virginia and Maryland reinforcements gathered with Lee's Legion at New Bridge. Lee read the officers his plan, which closely mirrored Wayne's attack on Stony Point. The combined group would leave their camp at night, cross the Hackensack River and head south for Paulus Hook. An advance guard, flanking parties, and rear guard made up of "troops of known fidelity and directed by officers of vigilance" would protect the main column from Loyalist patrols.[24] Allan McLane's soldiers were already out scouting for enemy troops along the banks of the Hudson and keeping their objective under observation. When the column neared Paulus Hook, Lee would consult with the scouts and if he still had the element of surprise the group would split into three columns to advance toward the fort from north to south in a three-pronged attack. Forlorn Hopes armed with axes would precede each column and chop through the abatis. When the columns breached the abatis and swarmed inside the fort, one column would head toward the wharf to cut off an enemy retreat by boat, another would round up prisoners in the post barracks, and another would attempt to take the main blockhouse. Once his soldiers gathered all the prisoners they could, the group would retreat to Douwe's Ferry and escape back across the Hackensack. The watchword for the attack was "Stony Point."[25]

The combined assault force departed their camp at about 4:00 P.M. and headed south, intending to complete the march in three hours and launch their attack at 12:30 A.M. Only one major road led to Paulus Hook but the column's guide somehow took a wrong turn. For three hours the men wandered through "deep, mountainous woods" and lost half of Maj. Clark's Virginians, the trailing portion of their group. "This affected me most sensibly," Lee said with considerable understatement, "as it not only diminished the number of the men destined for the assault, but deprived me of the aid of several officers of distinguished merit."[26]

The legion finally arrived outside Paulus Hook at about 4:00 A.M., almost eight hours behind schedule. The Hudson tide was coming in and flooding the attack route across the salt marsh. Lee found Lt. Michael Rudulph, one of McLane's scouts observing Paulus Hook, who reported that the fort was quiet and the marsh still passable. He probably also informed Lee about a stroke of luck: Paulus Hook was undermanned. Earlier that evening Van Buskirk took most of his battalion out of Paulus Hook to set an ambush at a nearby village named English Neighborhood. Gen. Pattison (who had led the taking of King's Ferry at the end of May), the local British commander, replaced the troops with forty Hessians from the Von Knyphausen Regiment under a Capt. Von Schallern. The Hessians were more alert in their duties than the lax Loyalists but they hardly made up for the loss in manpower of Van Buskirk's 200 men. That night Maj. Sutherland told Von Schallern to turn in, but the Hessian kept his soldiers under arms anyhow.[27]

With dawn approaching and the marsh flooding, the time for Lee's planned final reconnaissance and organization was running out. At this point the prickly gentleman's code of honor complicated combat operations. Either on the march or outside Paulus Hook, the Virginian Maj. Clark informed Lee that since his major's commission dated from earlier in 1778 than Lee's, he considered himself entitled to command the assault

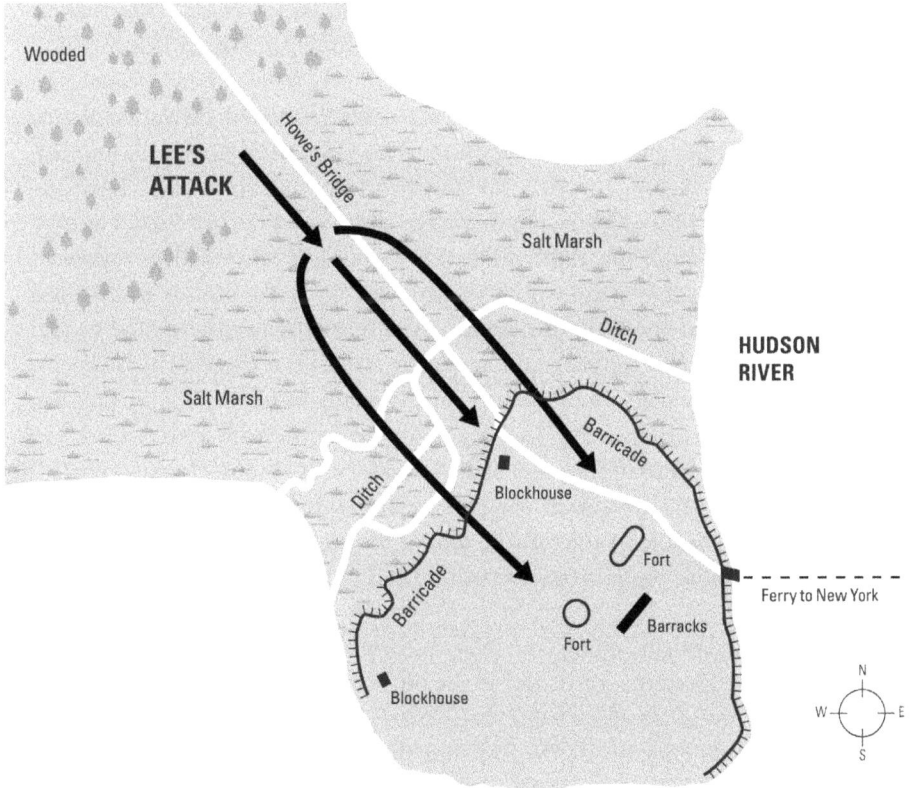

In the early morning of August 19, 1779, Major Henry Lee's men splashed across the salt marshes to raid the British stronghold at Paulus Hook. Gen. Washington hoped the attack would help keep Gen. Clinton's forces on the Hudson off their balance and on the defensive (adapted by the author and Lara Dalinsky from an original British army map, held at the Library of Congress).

as the senior officer. Lee was having none of it, because a night bayonet attack was no time to compare rank seniority and he believed that he was senior to Clark anyhow. "Not a moment being to spare," Lee said, "I paid no attention to the punctilios of honor or rank, but ordered the troops to advance in their then disposition." He quickly divided his men into three attack columns. Maj. Clark's Virginians went to the right (or west, since the group was attacking in southerly direction), Capt. Handy's Marylanders took the left (east), and Capt. Robert Forsythe stayed in the center as a reserve. Forlorn Hopes went ahead of the left and right attack wings. Lee dispatched a messenger to the nearest American position at Prior's Mill to inform the officer holding the escape boats at Douwe's Ferry that his assault had been delayed. Then Lee ordered the columns to attack. "The troops pushed on with that resolution, order, and coolness, which insures success," he wrote.[28]

Despite Lee's recollection that his soldiers moved forward "in the most profound silence" the British sentries along Paulus Hook's parapet heard them splashing through the marsh and opened musket fire. The Forlorn Hope for Maj. Clark's column on the right, led by Lt. Archibald McAllister, cut through the abatis first, Capt. Handy's Marylanders followed soon after, and American troops surged over the walls into the fort's interior. Once over the walls the center column of the Legion turned to the left (towards the Hudson) and captured one of the three British blockhouses. Lee recalled, "So rapid was the movement of the troops, that we gained the fort before the discharge of a single piece of artillery." A Lt. Cockburne, commanding the British artillery at Paulus Hook, reported that a sentry alerted him as soon as the attack began, but the Americans were inside the fort by the time he ran for his guns. Marylander Capt. Levi Handy recalled "we gained their works, and put about fifty of them to the bayonet."[29]

Lt. Cockburne, along with Maj. Sutherland, Capt. Von Schallern and twenty-five Hessians, retreated to the blockhouse at the center of the fort and fired out at the Americans. Lee's men were not restricted from firing their muskets once inside the fort, but their cartridges were soaked from splashing across the salt marsh so they had no way of shooting back at the enemy in the blockhouse. A Hessian account recorded that Lee called for the blockhouse's surrender and offered fair quarter but that Capt. Von Schallern replied, "If you want me, attack me, both sides will then have more honor from the affair."[30] A Tory newspaper in New York City reported: "The Rebels repeatedly challenged the redoubt to surrender, or they would bayonet them, to which they received a fire and 'No,' for answer."³¹ Lee wrote that he intended to set fire to the fort's barracks but "on finding a number of sick soldiers and women with young children in them, humanity forbade the execution of my intention."³²

At his headquarters on Broadway across the Hudson, Gen. Clinton heard the firing. The prearranged signal that the post was under attack was for Maj. Sutherland to fire two cannon and send up three star shells; since there was neither cannon firing nor signals, Clinton assumed that the noise was Van Buskirk's ambush or some other skirmish. He sent a staff officer across the river to verify the activity and was shocked when the man reported the fort under attack. Clinton hastily threw together a force of light infantry, grenadiers, Hessians and artillery and began ferrying them across the Hudson to save Paulus Hook.

The Americans swarmed throughout the fort searching for prisoners, and Lt. McAllister from the Virginia detachment hauled down the post's Union Jack. But the approach of daylight reinforced Washington's instructions to ignore capturing cannon or heavy stores. Lee also had to avoid being trapped by a British relief force, and he ordered his Legion to gather their prisoners and make their withdrawal. Maj. Clarke's Virginians moved back across the causeway first, followed by Capt. Handy's men, herding about 160 prisoners. Capt. Forsythe's men formed the rear guard, and Lee marched with them to be in a position to respond to threats from pursuers. British stragglers that had been cut off from the fort during the attack fired at the Americans as they emerged from Paulus Hook but Lee called their shots "ineffectual" and drove his men on.³³ Lee sent Capt. Forsythe ahead to Prior's Mill with instructions to gather the most able men from the assault force as they marched in and form them on the Bergen Heights to cover the legion's withdrawal.

The withdrawal went almost as poorly as the advance. Capt. Handy recalled, "We had a morass to pass of upwards two miles, the greatest part of which we were obliged to pass by files, and several canals to ford up to our breast in water."³⁴ When the legion reached Prior's Mill, a young officer there informed Lee that, for reasons never identified, the message about the delay in the attack had not reached him. Lee realized that meant the information never reached the troops at Douwe's Ferry either and that they had probably released the escape boats. He found a horse and rode to the front of his column where he found Maj. Clarke reaching the ferry site "and no boats to receive them," just as Lee feared.³⁵ The delay in the attack caused the problem. Capt. Henry Peyton, who was charged with marshalling the boats for Lee's retreat, did not hear the assault occur as scheduled at 12:30 A.M. or for hours afterward. In the belief that the operation had been postponed for another night, he sent the boats to Newark so the activity at the ferry would not disclose the plan.

The situation was unfolding just as Washington had hoped it would not. At about 8:30 A.M. Lt. Col. Cosmo Gordon, leading the British relief force that Clinton assembled, landed at Paulus Hook with a company of light infantry under the command of a Capt. Dundass. Dundass immediately took charge of the post and ordered Major Sutherland, now out of his blockhouse, to march north with Dundass' company to catch Lee's Legion. Another company under a Capt. Maynard landed soon after and headed out to join Sutherland.[36] To make matters worse, the American cartridges were still soaked and useless from the wetting in the salt marsh. "I lost no time in my decision," Lee wrote.[37] He ordered his men to continue their retreat overland and rushed a request to Gen. Stirling for a detachment to meet them at New Bridge to fend off the British pursuers.

Lee captured his predicament perfectly. "Oppressed by every possible misfortune," he wrote, "at the head of troops worn down by a rapid march of thirty miles, through mountains, swamps, and deep morasses, without the least refreshment during the whole march, ammunition destroyed, encumbered with prisoners, and a retreat of fourteen miles to make good, on a route admissible of interception at several points by a march of two, three, or four miles, one body [of British troops] moving in our rear, and another (from the intelligence I had received from the captured officers) in all probability well advanced on our right, a retreat naturally impossible to our left, under all these distressing circumstances, my sole dependence was in the persevering gallantry of the officers, and obstinate courage of the troops. In this I was fully satisfied by the shouts of the soldiery, who gave every proof of unimpaired vigor at the moment the enemy's approach was announced."[38]

The second body of enemy troops that Lee referred to was Van Buskirk's Loyalist Battalion, which had been near English Neighborhood all night but, as Gen. Pattison said, they fought only a "trifling Skirmish" with a few rebels and were returning to Paulus Hook.[39] As they moved, the Loyalists saw the detachment from Lord Stirling's division approach and encountered Lee's column, which was moving north. Van Buskirk attacked and pushed back Lee's men, who were exhausted from nearly twenty hours of marching and fighting, and captured three Americans. But the detachment from Stirling's division arrived and deployed in a protective line. A group of Loyalists emerged from the woods and fired into the tail end of the column but Lee's rear guard pushed them away. Sutherland and Van Buskirk broke off their attacks and moved back to Paulus Hook. Lee reported to Washington, "Thus, Sir, was every attempt to cut off our rear completely baffled. The troops arrived safely at the New Bridge with all the prisoners, about one o'clock P.M. on the nineteenth."[40]

Though its execution was imperfect, Lee's raid was another striking success. The Americans suffered only two men killed and three wounded, compared to British losses of nine killed, two wounded, and 158 prisoners, which included thirty-nine of Van Buskirk's hated men.[41] Washington would have been pleased with the raid had he known about its outcome. Gen. Stirling sent a dispatch on the afternoon of the 19th, mere hours after Lee arrived, about the apparent success of the assault; but for reasons he never explained, Lee took two and half days to send Washington a dispatch with the details of the battle. Washington wrote to Lee on the twenty-third: "As Congress are yet uninformed of the enterprise against Powles [sic] Hook, and I am anxious to have them furnished with the particulars, I have to request your report without delay."[42] The same day he sent the chastisement, Lieutenants Rudulph and McAllister, the leaders of the Forlorn Hopes, arrived at army headquarters with the captured flag from Paulus Hook and Lee's full report, written two days earlier.

Lee's dispatch was a matter-of-fact account of the attack's successes as well as its mishaps, mixed with pride at the results. He told Washington, "During the whole action, not a single musket was fired on our side, — the bayonet was our sole dependence.... American humanity has been again signally manifested. Self preservation strongly dictated, on the retreat, the putting the prisoners to death, and British cruelty fully justified it; notwithstanding which, not a man was wantonly hurt."[43] He praised the bravery and support of several subordinates, including Gen. Stirling, Maj. Clarke, Captains Handy and Forsythe, and Lieutenants Rudulph and McAllister. He even thanked Capt. Peyton, the officer at Douwe's Ferry who moved the escape boats away, which indicates that captain's actions were probably typical of the fog of eighteenth century combat. The only thing Lee regretted was that he was not able to capture the hated Loyalist Lt. Col. Van Buskirk.

Washington sent McAllister to Philadelphia to deliver the report and the captured British flag to Congress, saying of Lee, "The Major displayed a remarkable degree of prudence address enterprise and bravery upon this occasion, which does the highest honor to himself and to all the officers and men under his command. The situation of the Post rendered the attempt critical and the success brilliant."[44] This second bold stroke by the Continental Army that embarrassed British arms thrilled the American public again. In a letter to his stepson, John Park Custis, Washington called it a "brilliant transaction."[45] The Philadelphia newspaper *Pennsylvania Packet*, among others, called Maj. Lee an "enterprising genius" and lauded him for his tactical skill.[46] Congress later rewarded Lieutenants Rudulph and McAllister with brevet promotions to captain, and resolved "that the thanks of Congress be given to Major Lee for the remarkable prudence, address and bravery displayed by him." The Congress also ordered the striking of a gold medal for Lee, bearing his likeness on one side and on the reverse an inscription that included, "Notwithstanding rivers and intrenchments, he with a small band conquered the foe by warlike skill and prowess, and firmly bound by his humanity those who had been conquered in his arms."[47] Henry Lee was the only officer below the rank of general to earn such a gold medal during the war.

Gen. Clinton wrote that he was "not very well pleased at this affront [Paulus Hook], happening so recently after the one at Stony Point," which was an understatement. At his order a court-martial inquiry examined Maj. Sutherland's conduct (Brig. Gen. Garth of the Connecticut raids was on the court), found him negligent, and declared his garrison guilty of "shameful misbehavior." A second court exonerated Sutherland, but Clinton remained particularly disappointed in the officer, writing, "I cautioned him myself against surprise ... told him how to secure himself against affront, and he neglected it."[48] Clinton merely confirmed the second court's exoneration without approving of its findings. In a sad second chapter, another court found Sergeant John Taswell, of Van Buskirk's regiment, who manned one of the sentry posts in a blockhouse on the night of the attack, guilty of "quitting his Post, at the Left Hand Block House at Paulus Hook, in a shameful and scandalous manner." The court sentenced Taswell to hang, but Clinton pardoned the hapless soldier and allowed him to leave the army.[49]

The strategic situation became clearer to Washington at end of the summer. On September 11 Robert Townsend, the new spy in the Culper Ring recruited by Abraham Woodhull and operating with the code name "Samuel Culper Jr.," informed Washington that on August 25 seventy British ships carrying reinforcements and Admiral Marriot Arbuthnot arrived at New York City, but that the troops were all newly raised and "in bad health."[50] The soldiers were actually the reinforcements Clinton had waited for all summer, but Arbuthnot brought only 3,800 soldiers, considerably fewer than the 6,000 Lord Germain promised, and as Townsend reported, most suffered from an incapacitating, virulent fever. The fever spread, and Clinton soon had 6,000 men in the hospital. Townsend also reported that British regiments departed New York to reinforce Canada and Charleston, South Carolina. As autumn approached, the number of weeks available for the Redcoats to resume the offensive dwindled and British activities indicated that they were strengthening their defensive fortifications at New York and preparing to launch an offensive in the southern states. Townsend told Washington, "The general opinion is that there will be no campaign opened from N. York."[51]

Townsend's assessment was correct. The day after the Paulus Hook raid, Clinton assessed the results of the summer. He had begun the campaign in the spring intending to seize control of the Hudson, wreck rebel commerce, return the citizens of New York to the Crown, and destroy the Continental Army in battle. Four months later the shipping industry, commerce, and privateers of Virginia and New England were damaged but still operating. The citizens of New York had not abandoned the rebellion, and Washington's army was in a secure defensive position in the Highlands around the improved fortifications of West Point. Clinton successfully extended British control of the Hudson up to King's Ferry, but without the strength to seize West Point the lower Hudson was a road to nowhere. With the loss of 2,000 soldiers that he sent to Gen. Haldimand in Canada and battle casualties from the Connecticut raids, Stony Point, and Paulus Hook, Clinton's army had 6,000 fewer soldiers than at the beginning of the year.

Admiral Arbuthnot became the king's naval commander in America, but he was a doddering seventy-year-old and a poor replacement to the aggressive Commodore Collier. The situation drove Clinton to write to Lord Germain: "my spirits are worn out by struggling against the Consequences of many adverse incidents." He further said he was "obliged by many cogent reasons to abandon every view of making an effort in this Quarter. The precautions which Mr. Washington has had leisure to take make me hopeless of bringing him to a general action and the season dissuades me strongly from losing time in the attempt."[52] He later wrote about "the waste of the season" and that after Paulus Hook it was "necessary to abandon all thoughts of offensive operations on the side of New York and turn my face to the south."[53] In late September Clinton pulled all of the troops that manned advance outposts back to Manhattan, including those at Stony Point and Verplanck's Point, "whose importance of course ceased the moment I gave up offensive operations on the Hudson," he said.[54]

In the autumn of 1779 the Continental Army remained on both sides of the lower Hudson to keep the British in their lines at New York City. Rains soaked the roads and ended the season for action. "After employing the enemy a whole campaign," Washington wrote to his friend Benjamin Harrison, "costing [the British] near a thousand men in Prisoners by desertion, and otherways, and infinite labour [King's Ferry] is at length in Status-quo that is, simply, a continental Ferry again.... [E]xcepting the plundering expedition to Virginia, and the burning one in Connecticut the enemy have wasted another Campaign."[55]

Washington was aware of the impact of the summer campaign even before he wrote to Harrison. In late August, only days after the Paulus Hook raid, he told John Parke Custis, "Our affairs at present put on a very pleasing aspect ... and bids us I think hope for the certain and final accomplishment of our Independence."[56] It was one of the most positive comments of the year from the commander-in-chief about the state of the war. The campaign for control of the Hudson was over, and the victors were Washington, the Continental Army, and America.

Epilogue: The Ghost of "Mad" Anthony

The campaign of 1779 was the last offensive Crown forces undertook in the northern states, though Clinton continued with lesser efforts around New York. In June 1780 Clinton launched Gen. Knyphausen into New Jersey in an attempt to lure Washington away from New York City, but the operation fizzled after Gen. Nathaniel Greene, supported by Maj. Henry Lee's Legion, blunted the advance at the town of Springfield and pushed Knyphausen back to Staten Island.

The appointment of Maj. Gen. Benedict Arnold as the commander at West Point in August gave Clinton another opportunity to control the Hudson. Arnold had been regularly sending intelligence to the British since May 1779, and after gaining command at West Point in 1780 he offered to turn the post over for the price of £10,000, a king's commission as a major-general, and a knighthood. On September 21 Maj. John Andre, still performing as Clinton's intelligence chief, met with Arnold at the home of Loyalist Joshua Hett Smith in the village of Haverstraw, just south of Stony Point, and discussed the arrangement. After the meeting Andre intended to return to British lines by rowing out to HMS *Vulture*, the same ship that once defended Stony Point, and that was anchored in Haverstraw Bay. But the sloop came under fire from the shore and slipped downstream, stranding him. At Arnold's urging Andre decided to escape overland back to Manhattan, so he donned civilian clothes, took King's Ferry to Verplanck's Point, and headed south. But three American militiamen on the west bank of the Hudson intercepted him on the road. Inexperienced with moving through the woods in disguise, Andre mistook the Yankees for Loyalists and unwisely disclosed that he was a British officer. The militiamen intended to rob him and searched Andre thoroughly and found the plans of West Point hidden in his boot.

Andre presented the men a pass from Gen. Arnold, which the men ignored, then offered them a bribe to release him. Though they considered the bribe, the militiamen turned Andre over to their local commander, Lt. Col. John Jameson. Jameson was unaware of Arnold's involvement, and sent Andre and the documents to West Point, where Gen. Washington was coincidentally scheduled to meet with Arnold the next day. Hours later Maj. Benjamin Tallmadge arrived at Jameson's headquarters. When he learned that Andre had been captured carrying the plans to West Point as well as a pass from Arnold, Tallmadge immediately realized that Arnold was a British agent. Tallmadge managed to have Andre returned to Jameson's headquarters but Jameson would not allow the major to arrest Arnold, as Tallmadge intended. A courier delivered Jameson's message about Andre's capture to Arnold on the morning of September 25 while the spy awaited Washington's arrival and ate breakfast with his wife, Peggy, the Loyalist from Philadelphia. Arnold calmly rose, informed Peggy that he was discovered, and ordered his commander's barge to row him down the Hudson to the *Vulture*. The unfortunate crew of the barge was taken prisoner, and Arnold escaped to New York City. Andre became a prisoner of the Americans, and Benjamin Tallmadge spoke with him and was impressed by his gentlemanly bearing. Andre asked Tallmadge about his fate, and Tallmadge told him that he would suffer the same end as Tallmadge's friend, Nathan Hale. A court-martial held at Washington's order convicted Andre of espionage and he was hanged on October 7. Clinton's attempt to seize control of the Hudson through espionage was another failure.

For the American army, the final benefit of the 1779 campaign played out over the next two years. By keeping most of his army out of action in 1779, Washington was able to continue his program of reforms. Over the course of the year he and Gen. Steuben completed the Blue Book and distributed it throughout the army. He continued to improve the structure and duties of the brigade staffs, improved logistics procedures, and appointed officers to ensure that the Blue Book was correctly implemented and consistently applied as the army's new doctrine. The Continental artillery chief, Maj. Gen. Henry Knox, also improved the skills of his corps. Since his army always suffered from shortages, these measures enabled

Washington to employ its limited manpower and resources with maximum efficiency. As historian Richard K. Wright wrote in his authoritative Continental Army history, "The Continental Army came of age between 1778 and 1780."[1]

In 1780 the French also committed an army under Lt. Gen. Jean, Comte de Rochambeau to America, giving Washington an allied commander with whom he worked well. A combined American-French force commanded by Gen. Lafayette cornered the British army under Lord Cornwallis in Virginia in the late summer of 1781, and Washington was ready to complete the trap with the main Continental Army, which now had the training, doctrine, weapons, supply systems, and sophisticated staff structure that made it a true equal of the British army. On August 21 1781, American and French forces departed their lines around New York City, marched south for Virginia, and joined Lafayette to surround Cornwallis on the York River. Gen. Washington's professional Continental Army, built partially from the gift of time gained by the campaign of 1779, met and defeated Cornwallis at Yorktown.

* * *

Gen. Clinton was still in New York when British forces were besieged at Yorktown. In dispatches, Cornwallis implored Clinton to send a force to relieve his trapped garrison, but Sir Henry showed his usual lack of decisiveness, churned for almost a month, and tardily set sail with a relief force on October 17, the same day Cornwallis asked Washington for a ceasefire in order to hold surrender talks. Clinton learned of the capitulation en route to the Chesapeake and returned to New York. British forces at New York still consisted of 12,000 soldiers, a number too few for Clinton to mount a new offensive in any theater. The war had been losing popularity in Parliament for at least two years and Cornwallis' surrender killed what little support remained. King George III's senior ministers begged their sovereign to make peace. The king resisted, but in February 1782 Lord Germain resigned and the government of Prime Minister Lord North fell. The king acquiesced to the demands for peace, and the new government, led by the Marquis of Rockingham, opened negotiations. In March the new American secretary, Lord Shelburne, replaced Clinton as commander of British Forces in North America with Gen. Sir Guy Carleton. Carleton's orders were to conduct no offensive action and to prepare to evacuate all Crown bases in America. Carleton arrived in May, and Clinton returned to England.

Clinton's failure to assist Cornwallis had a long-lasting impact for him. Many actions led to the defeat at Yorktown — not the least of which was the professionalism of the Continental Army, Washington's successful strategic actions, and American-French cooperation — but King George and others in the British government saddled Clinton with blame for the loss. Back in London, Clinton divided his time between reestablishing a relationship with his children and efforts to protect his marred reputation, which included publishing an account of his successful campaigns in South Carolina and Rhode Island. But the other senior British generals of the war — Howe, Burgoyne, and Cornwallis — were better at public relations than the prickly Clinton. Though King George raised all three of these rivals to the peerage, he denied Clinton's continual efforts to attain a title, and Clinton felt that he was the national scapegoat for losing the war. The king offered him military commands when France and Britain went to war again in 1792, but Clinton considered all of them beneath his station and turned them down. In 1794 he accepted the governorship of Gibraltar, but by that time his health was declining and he suffered from severe pain in his legs from old war wounds. He was still in England on December 20, 1795, when doctors operated on an abscess in his leg. Lt. Gen. Sir Henry Clinton died from surgery complications three days later.

Clinton's aggressive naval commander, Sir George Collier, returned to Britain in late 1779. He later fought the Spanish at Gibraltar, served in Parliament, and reached the rank of vice admiral. A persistent case of gout forced the architect of "Desolation Warfare," Gen. William Tryon, to return to England in 1780. He eventually attained the rank of lieutenant-general and died in London in 1798. The French Navy captured Gen. Garth, Tryon's subordinate during the Connecticut raids. Released when the war ended, he became a full general before retiring. Col. William Webster, the commander of the King's Ferry fortifications, fought under Gen. Cornwallis in the southern campaigns and was killed at the battle of Guilford Court House in March 1781.

The aggressive cavalryman Banastre Tarleton and his legion sailed to South Carolina as part of the new British offensive and took part in the siege of Charleston. In May 1780 he earned a reputation for ruthlessness when his soldiers crushed an American detachment at the village of Waxhaws and killed many troops after their surrender in what became bitterly known as "Tarleton's Quarter." His legion became Cornwallis' primary mobile striking force and a terror to the Americans. But at the battle of Cowpens in March 1781, Continentals commanded by Gen. Daniel Morgan (who had resigned for a time because he did not get command of the Corps of Light Infantry) dealt him a near total defeat and Tarleton barely escaped alive. Tarleton rebuilt his command and successfully raided in Virginia; at Yorktown he commanded the British outpost at Gloucester, across the York River. Captured at Yorktown, after his parole he left active duty in the army but returned in 1790, the same year he was elected to Parliament. He was promoted to full general in 1812, made a baronet in 1815, and knighted in 1820. Tarleton died in 1833.

Tarleton's Continental Army counterpart, Benjamin Tallmadge, continued operating out of Westchester County after the campaign of 1779. In November 1780 he conceived and led a daring raid on Ft. St. George, near Smith's Point on Long Island, where he and eighty men captured over fifty prisoners and destroyed tons of wheat stored for the winter without the loss of a man. And although Benedict Arnold confirmed to the British that Tallmadge was Washington's intelligence chief with a spy ring in New York, thanks to Tallmadge's sound security practices Arnold did not know the identities of the American agents and the Culper Ring continued to operate. Tallmadge remained with the Second Light Dragoons until the end of the war. Immediately after the declaration of peace he obtained a special pass from Washington to ride into New York City just before the British evacuation in order to help protect his operatives—who had posed as Loyalists for years—from American reprisals. When the army disbanded in 1783 Tallmadge went home to Setauket and enjoyed serving as the master of ceremonies in the town's ox roast victory picnic held on the village green. He married Mary Floyd, daughter of William Floyd, one of New York's four signers of the Declaration of Independence, and settled in Litchfield, Connecticut, the same town where he had trained with the Second Light Dragoons during the war. His became wealthy from investments in a company that dealt in land in the Ohio Territory, and he served from 1801 to 1817 in the House of Representatives as a member of the Federalist Party. Tallmadge cofounded the Litchfield Auxiliary Society for the Condition of the Jews, and after retiring established a training school for missionaries who worked with the Native American tribes. Since spying was still considered unsavory business for gentlemen, and to protect the privacy of his operatives, he was extremely tight-lipped about his intelligence activities. He died in 1835.[2]

The importance of Tallmadge's Culper Ring diminished when the South became the primary theater of action, though Washington called on the agents again in the spring of 1782 for information on whether the

British intended any offensive action from New York City. By that time British suspicions about spies drove Abraham Woodhull to quit regular Culper Ring operations, although he continued to sporadically supply Washington information until the end of the war. He served as a judge in Suffolk County from 1799 to 1810. Married in 1781, he had three children, and two of them, Elizabeth and Jesse Woodhull, married into the family of his fellow agent, Caleb Brewster. His first wife died in 1806. Woodhull married again in 1824 and died two years later. He never spoke of his service as a spy.[3]

In 1784 Caleb Brewster married Anne Lewis, the daughter of Jonathan Lewis, who was a partial owner of the wharf in Fairfield where Brewster launched his forays across Long Island Sound. He worked as a blacksmith for a short time, in 1793 joined the U.S. Revenue Cutter Service, the forerunner of the U.S. Coast Guard, as commander of the cutter *Active*, and had eight children. In 1816 he retired from the service and lived at his farm in Black Rock, Connecticut, until his death in 1827.[4]

Only Culper Ring agent Robert Townsend, who may have suffered from depression, met a bitter end. He entered business with his brother Solomon after the war but the relationship was contentious. Robert left the business, moved to Oyster Bay, lived with his two sisters, and died in 1834 at the age of 84.[5]

The British and Loyalist defenders of Stony Point, including the post commander, Lt. Col. Henry Johnson, remained prisoners of war until their exchange in December 1780. Upon his release, Lt. Col. Johnson requested a court-martial to clear his name for the loss of Stony Point and the proceedings began in Manhattan on January 2, 1781. Twenty-two officers and soldiers gave testimonies, and the court declared Johnson "culpable" for a "mistaken disposition" of his troops and censured him for not concentrating his defense in the Upper Works and for allowing the sloop *Vulture* and the gunboat to leave their posts. The court called his conduct "reprehensible" but also said, "Lieut. Colonel Johnson, in common with the officers and soldiers at his Post, behaved with an Alertness, Activity, and Bravery, that do them honor."[6] Although the court's findings gave mixed messages, the negative comments on Johnson's conduct did not prevent him from further service; later the same year he commanded a detachment of the Seventeenth Regiment that fought in the southern campaign until Gen. Cornwallis surrendered them, again, with the forces at Yorktown. Another 100 members of the Seventeenth, who were lucky not to be part of the Yorktown garrison, remained in Charleston, South Carolina, until the

British evacuated the post in January 1783 and then went to Manhattan, Britain's last post on the United States' eastern seaboard. The small detachment finally left the American rebellion behind on October 18, 1783, when the soldiers sailed to Nova Scotia. Johnson remained in the British army after the war, achieved the rank of lieutenant-general, and lived to the age of eighty-seven.[7]

Frederick Robinson, the teenage officer in the Seventeenth Regiment, survived the battle at Stony Point but found being a prisoner of Wayne's Light Infantry almost as dangerous. He recalled, "The hatred of the American soldiery towards my father had nearly proved fatal to my brother and myself at the time we were taken, as they frequently expressed a wish to Butcher us in cold blood."[8] Robinson spent his captivity on parole at the home of a farmer named Hoover near Lancaster, Pennsylvania, along with two other junior officers. "We were as comfortable and as happy as we could be in such circumstances," he wrote. "I enjoyed fishing and shooting, with other amusements, to my heart's content."[9] Exchanged in late 1780 along with his older brother Morris, who commanded the company of the Loyal American Regiment at Stony Point, he transferred to the Thirty-eighth Regiment and stayed with them until the end of the war. His regiment was one of the last to leave Manhattan for England, and as a native of New York he felt deeply for the Loyalists the British could not take with them. "I was the only one of the family that witnessed that most humiliating scene," he wrote.[10]

Back in England Robinson stayed with the Thirty-eighth Regiment, married, and served in the West Indies. "I was as happy in my affectionate wife and children as ever a man was," he said, but his wife died in childbirth in 1806.[11] In 1812 he fought against Napoleon in Spain with Lord Wellington's army and led a brigade in storming the town of St. Sebastian, where he was severely wounded in the face. During the War of 1812 he fought in America again near Lake Champlain in New York, and somehow managed to find his father's home and old nanny, then ninety-two, from before the Revolution. "I then went to the place that formerly belonged to my father," he said, "which I found so little altered that it brought tears to my eyes and many a heavy sigh from my heart."[12] Later he became the governor of Tobago, where his beloved ten-year-old daughter, Augusta, died from fever. Robinson eventually gained the rank of full general and died in 1852 with the honor of being the longest-serving soldier in the British army at the time, with seventy-five years service. It is a Tobago legend that the ghost of Augusta Robinson still haunts the Governor's House.

Ezra Stiles, the careful observer and recorder of the British raid at New Haven, continued as president of Yale College, where he encouraged the study of Hebrew and the physical sciences. He made some of New England's earliest experiments with electricity using equipment donated by Benjamin Franklin. Stiles remained the college president until his death in 1795.

As the Corps of Light Infantry was a provisional unit that existed only during active campaigning, Gen. Washington disbanded the group when the army entered winter quarters in December 1779. But before that, in the months immediately after Stony Point, Col. Return Jonathan Meigs, Maj. Thomas Posey, Lt. Col. Isaac Sherman, and Maj. William Hull complained to Wayne that he had not adequately credited their roles in his reports to Congress. Wayne reacted angrily, but after the exchange of several letters with the offended officers, Wayne either soothed their tempers or sent Congress favorable descriptions of the service that Sherman, Hull, Posey and Maj. Hardy Murfree provided at Stony Point.

In some ways the Corps of Light Infantry seemed to come apart while camped at Sandy Beach. During the month of September the Light Infantry convened a series of courts-martial that tried soldiers and officers on such charges as stealing captured stores from Stony Point, disobedience to orders, drunkenness, card-playing, absence at roll call, and inciting mutiny. Pvt. William Matlock was executed for desertion to the enemy. One court tried and reprimanded Lt. Maynard for disobedience of orders and "want of Respect for a Field Officer" for an incident that involved Lt. Col. de Fleury. A second court tried and acquitted de Fleury for disrespectful behavior toward Maynard, and Congress granted the Frenchman leave to return to France.[13] Col. Richard Butler, who held temporary command of the Light Infantry before Wayne's arrival, entered into an argument with a Light Infantry captain named Ashmead, and when the junior officer asked to see Gen. Wayne to seek redress Butler refused him permission. The captain also accused Butler of inciting mutiny in his company by directing his soldiers to disobey Ashmead's orders. A court-martial at army headquarters found Butler not guilty of encouraging mutiny but called him "blamable" for not allowing Ashmead access to Wayne.[14] These incidents, as well as the accusations that flew between Wayne and his offended subordinates, indicate that the light infantrymen were not necessarily as elite as they thought, and the code of honor that compelled the officers to feats of great leadership at Stony Point drove them apart when they lacked a battle to fight.

Gen. Washington formed the Corps of Light Infantry again for the campaign of 1780, this time with the intent that it should be a true elite force and model for the entire Continental Army. Gen. Lafayette took command of the corps, and Gen. Steuben devoted his personal attention to honing the soldiers' skills to a fine edge, especially in use of the bayonet. With many veterans of Stony Point in the ranks Steuben told Washington, "The corps will be the admiration of our allies as much the terror of our enemies."[15] In contrast to the motley clothing and equipment of Wayne's soldiers, the Light Infantry of 1780 wore the new dark blue uniforms of the Continental Army and hard leather helmets with distinctive black and white plumes. The corps disbanded at the end of 1780 without seeing action, and many soldiers returned when Washington re-formed the group again the next February. That same month Gen. Lafayette took three battalions of light infantry to Virginia to oppose incursions by the turncoat Benedict Arnold, now serving as a brigadier-general in the British army. Washington raised another four hundred light troops to replace those that went south with Lafayette and gave command to his former aide-de-camp, Col. Alexander Hamilton. At Yorktown on October 14, 1781, in an echo of the attack at Stony Point, Hamilton led the light infantrymen in a successful night bayonet attack on Redoubt Number Ten, a key bastion that anchored the British defenses. It was one of the final blows to the British that led to the surrender at Yorktown, and the last action of the war for the Light Infantry.

The experience of the Light Infantry certainly remained vivid for Capt. Henry Champion of Connecticut, who celebrated "Stony Point Day" on July 16 every year until he died in 1836 at the age of eighty-two.[16] Corporal Jonathan Bailey was killed at Stony Point serving in Col. Meigs' Regiment but his wife named their son, born two days after the battle, Jonathan Return Meigs Bailey. He, in turn, named his daughter Meigs Bailey.[17]

After recovering from his Stony Point wound at an Albany military hospital, Pvt. Vincent Vass, who had joined the Light Infantry somewhat reluctantly with his friend Samuel Arnold, stayed on as a doctor's assistant until he received his discharge, probably in early 1780. He attended school for a short time in Virginia but the state drafted him to meet their militia quota. Vass wrote, "I took my discharge along with me in hopes to get off, but it would not do, for they said one old soldier was worth half dozen militia, & off we marched."[18] In August 1780 he fought at the battle of Camden in South Carolina and was eventually discharged again. Vass received $451 as his final pay and prize money from Stony Point, but since the money came in the form of severely depreciated Continental dollars he continually fought to get his payments in gold or silver. He obtained a stipend of $60 per year after he showed a senator the scars from his Stony Point wounds. In 1837, at the age of eighty-three, Vass applied to a local judge for the pension he earned as a Continental soldier and presented his voucher for Stony Point prize money that he had kept since 1779. "I took care to save it for it did not come light to me," he said.[19]

Peter Francisco, the giant six-foot-six Portuguese-Virginian, served throughout the southern campaign. He was wounded again at the battle of Guilford Court House in 1781, was later captured by Banastre Tarleton's cavalry, escaped, and fought at Yorktown. After the war he settled on a farm near Richmond, married and had two children. After his first wife's death in 1790 he married again in 1821 and fathered four more children. His second wife died and Francisco married a third time. Francisco became wealthy, served as sergeant of arms to the Virginia House of Delegates, died in 1831, and was buried with full military honors in Richmond. There is a U.S. postage stamp in his honor, and to this day the states of Virginia, Rhode Island and Massachusetts celebrate "Peter Francisco Day" on March 15.[20]

Some of the Virginia, Maryland and Pennsylvania officers of the Light Infantry also continued fighting in the southern campaign. "Crazy Jack" Stewart became well known for his bravery, was promoted to lieutenant-colonel, and commanded the First Maryland Regiment in the liberation of Charleston in 1782. In March 1783, a few weeks before the army in South Carolina disbanded, Stewart's horse threw him head-first into a ditch, breaking his neck. Crazy Jack Stewart, who survived British cannon salvoes on Stony Point, died three days later at the age of thirty-five.[21] Another Marylander, Lt. Col. Otho Williams, wrote to a friend, "The fate of poor Stewart is lamentable. He had some virtues in great perfections, but the natural vehemence of his passions deprived society of their advantages."[22]

Col. Richard Butler commanded the Fifth Pennsylvania during the campaigns in Virginia, including at Yorktown. After the war he returned to western Pennsylvania as the Indian Agent for the army's Northern Department. He returned to the army with a commission as a major-general when war with the tribes erupted in 1791 but was mortally wounded in November of that year. Two of his brothers fought alongside him, and with his dying breaths he ordered his younger brother Edward to save his older brother Thomas.

Capt. Thomas Boude, whose entire company joined the Corps of Light

Infantry with him, also fought in the southern campaign. After the war he served in the Pennsylvania Assembly, dealt in lumber, and was a Federalist member of Congress from 1801 to 1803. James Gibbon, who earned a brevet promotion to captain for leading the Forlorn Hope that breached the abatis at Stony Point, resigned in 1781 after his regiment reorganized and he saw no hope for promotion. Gibbon moved to Richmond, married, and had two sons. During the War of 1812 he was on Virginia's "Committee of Vigilance," which watched the coastline for feared British landings. Gibbon died in 1835, "greatly respected and esteemed."[23]

Capt. Allan McLane, who reconnoitered Stony Point and Paulus Hook, fought in the southern campaign and later returned to scouting British positions around Manhattan. He resigned from the army in 1781, became the revenue collector for the port of Wilmington, Delaware, and commanded the defenses of Philadelphia during the War of 1812.

William Hull, the Massachusetts major who rushed up Stony Point's southern slope in Col. Christian Febiger's column, served to the end of the war. In 1796 he was a volunteer to General Benjamin Lincoln when the United States faced an uprising in Massachusetts called Shay's Rebellion, the first test of Federal authority. After a term as a Massachusetts state senator, Hull began serving in positions that were probably beyond his capabilities. Appointed governor of the Michigan Territory in 1805, his coercion of Native American tribes to concede lands contributed to their unrest. Hull was still serving in that post in 1812 when he accepted a commission as a major-general in command of an army charged to defend Michigan from an expected British invasion from Canada. Instead, he met defeat when he invaded Canada along the Detroit River. The British forced him to retreat to the key post of Ft. Detroit, and Hull surrendered his entire army without a significant fight. A court-martial found him guilty of cowardice and neglect of duty but President Madison pardoned him in recognition of his Continental Army service. He died in Newton, Massachusetts, in 1825, and his daughter and grandson published his memoirs in an attempt to vindicate his name. Hull's most famous contribution to American lore was that it was he, and possibly other friends of Nathan Hale, who wrote that as the ill-fated spy went to the gallows he said, "I only regret that I have but one life to give for my country," a phrase that actually came from a line in the play *Cato* by Joseph Addison, which Hull remembered was a favorite of Hale's.[24]

Christian Febiger, the Danish colonel who led the main attack on Stony Point, returned to the Second Virginia after the Light Infantry disbanded. In 1780 he was assigned as a military procurement agent in Philadelphia charged to purchase and forward supplies to the Virginia regiments on campaign. Febiger fulfilled the role — probably happily, since his wife lived in Philadelphia — until 1781 when he returned to the Virginia Line in time to be present at Yorktown. He retired to Philadelphia in 1783 as a brevet brigadier-general and his community unanimously elected him as the Pennsylvania state treasurer every year until his death in 1796. A fellow former officer had the following inscribed on his gravestone: "As an officer, he was beloved; as a citizen, he was esteemed and respected; as a friend, he was warm and sincere; and as a husband, tender and affectionate."[25]

By the time Maj. Thomas Posey returned to the Seventh Virginia in the spring of 1780, he found that the regiment had marched south and been surrendered as part of the Charleston garrison. With no troops to command, he returned to Virginia on recruitment duty, a frustrating function because he found few men willing to serve. Posey returned to action as a lieutenant-colonel under Col. Christian Febiger at Yorktown. Gen. Washington ordered the Virginians to South Carolina to help force the British garrison at Charleston to surrender. When the soldiers threatened to mutiny because of the shortages of clothes and supplies, Febiger quashed them by hanging one instigator and flogging seventy-three men.[26] Posey finished the war as part of Gen. Nathaniel Greene's army outside Charleston and resigned his commission in March 1783. A widower since 1778, he married again after the war and moved to Spotsylvania County, Virginia, where he served for a decade as a magistrate and county lieutenant. In 1793 he returned to the army as a brigadier-general to fight Native American tribes on the frontier. Posey eventually settled in Kentucky and became speaker of the state senate and lieutenant governor. He moved to the Indiana Territory in 1810 and was elected to the U.S. Senate representing Louisiana. President Madison appointed him governor of the Indiana Territory. Posey died in 1818 at the age of sixty-eight.

The raid at Paulus Hook was Maj. Henry Lee's most famous action in the northern states. He unfortunately endured a court-martial for incompetence at Paulus Hook, brought about by charges from Maj. Clarke, who was disgruntled over his argument with Lee on the command of the raid. The court acquitted him with honor. Congress promoted him to lieutenant-colonel in November 1779 and the next year Washington ordered Lee's Legion to join Greene's army in the southern campaign. Through 1780 and 1781 Lee's Legion fought a brutal partisan war, raiding British outposts in the Carolinas, often operating with the famous "Swamp Fox," Col. Francis Marion, and against Lt. Col. Banister Tarleton and his British Legion. In February 1781 Lee's Legion killed or wounded all 300 soldiers of a Loyalist force under Col. John Pyles in what became known as "Pyles' Hacking Match." Lee's shining moment came at the battle of Eutaw Springs in September of that year, when Gen. Greene trapped a British force. But Greene's attack nearly fell apart, and it was Lee's Legion and Col. William Washington's cavalry that held the British off and allowed Greene to recover.

In late 1781 Lee resigned from the army not only because his health was shattered but also because he felt that Gen. Greene had slighted his exploits in reports to Congress. After the war he served in Virginia's legislature, in Congress, and for one term as governor of Virginia. In 1792, at Washington's appointment, he commanded the militia that quelled the Whiskey Rebellion in western Pennsylvania. He was in Congress for a second term when Washington died, and he delivered the eulogy at the president's funeral, saying that Washington was "first in war, first in peace, and first in the hearts of his countrymen." But Lee was a poor investor, and by the early nineteenth century he was deeply in debt and suffering bouts of depression. The publication of his memoirs in 1812 helped pay some creditors; but as war loomed with Britain again, Lee made an ill-advised public statement in support of an antiwar publisher in Baltimore. A crowd attacked him and he served a short sentence in jail. He later lived in seclusion on a Georgia plantation, owned by his former commander Nathaniel Greene, where he died in 1818. His spirit for strong leadership and audacity in battle passed to his son, Robert Edward Lee, who commanded the forces of the Confederacy in the Civil War.

The victor of Stony Point, Anthony Wayne, continued to enjoy the acclaim of his country while he billeted in Philadelphia in early 1780. The city's illuminati, along with Washington, Henry Laurens, John Adams, Thomas Jefferson, Alexander Hamilton, and John Jay elected him to the American Philosophical Society, the country's foremost intellectual gathering. When the Continental Army prepared for another campaign in 1780 he again requested to lead the Light Infantry, but Washington convinced him to take command of the First Pennsylvania Brigade. Though there was little more than minor action in the northern states that year, Wayne was promoted to command the entire Pennsylvania Division; in the autumn, he served on the court-martial that sentenced Maj. John Andre to the hangman's noose.

The winter of 1780–81 was the coldest of the war, and Washington's army, quartered at Morristown, New Jersey, still lacked provisions, uniforms, blankets, shoes, and rum. The pay for most soldiers was almost a year in arrears and there were rumors that Congress would not allow troops who had enlisted for three years to leave the army at the end of their service terms. Continental soldiers suffered at Morristown even worse that they had at Valley Forge, and many men, especially those in Wayne's Pennsylvania Division, grew increasingly disgruntled. Wayne appealed directly to Philadelphians to provide for his soldiers, and the citizens raised money for the troops and organized a clothing drive. But their efforts were too little, too late.

On January 1, 1781, the troops of the Pennsylvania Line overpowered their junior officers and took control of their camp in a mutiny, after which they intended to march to Congress and demand their pay and provisions. They reached the town of Princeton, where a committee presented the soldiers' complaints to Wayne. They asked that the men who had enlisted for three years be allowed to depart, that all men receive their back pay, and that they be decently clothed and provisioned. Wayne considered their demands reasonable, and the soldiers continued talks with a congressional committee until January 9, when Congress agreed to the soldiers' terms. At Wayne's suggestion, Congress also granted amnesty to all of the mutineers. Next to Stony Point, the quelling of the mutiny of the Pennsylvania Line was one of Wayne's finer episodes of the war.

Wayne returned to Philadelphia when the mutiny ended, and it was at this time that civilian authorities in New Jersey arrested a somewhat eccentric Pennsylvania soldier known as "the Commodore" or "Jimmy the Drover" for a local civil infraction. The Commodore demanded that Wayne intervene on his behalf, but instead Wayne threatened to have the soldier flogged. Jimmy the Drover reportedly responded, "Anthony is mad! Farewell to you; clear the coast for the Commodore, 'Mad Anthony's' friend." As the story spread through the ranks, soldiers decided that "Mad Anthony" fit their fiery, hard-fighting general, and the sobriquet stuck.[27]

Wayne returned to action in the spring of 1781 when Washington sent the Pennsylvania Line to join the force that chased Cornwallis in Virginia. Many of Wayne's troops remained disgruntled after the January mutiny. When they threatened another uprising in May, Wayne executed four conspirators by firing squad. He continued south confident that the mutiny was quashed but more soldiers refused to march. This time Wayne had a platoon fire into the mutineers, killing six men and wounding one. He ordered a soldier to bayonet the wounded man, the soldier refused, and Wayne pointed his pistol at the man and threatened to kill him if didn't carry out the order. The soldier complied, and Wayne marched his division past the dead men. When Wayne's men joined with Lafayette's force in Virginia he initially did not trust them enough to issue powder and ball, but on July 6, at a crossing site on the James River called Green Spring, 7,000 British soldiers under Cornwallis ambushed Lafayette's force, and Wayne's advance guard absorbed much of their fire. Wayne charged into the volleys with his troops and broke the British advance, allowing Lafayette to organize a fighting withdrawal that saved the Americans.

In August Wayne was wounded by American pickets who fired on him when they mistook him for being British. He was out of action through September and his injuries also brought on a case of gout that would plague him for the rest of his life. Wayne recovered in time to command the Pennsylvania Division at the siege of Yorktown and must have enjoyed seeing the Seventeenth Regiment, his opponents at Stony Point, surrender again. Washington sent the Pennsylvanians to join Gen. Greene's army in Georgia. Lt. Col. Thomas Posey and his detachment of Virginians were part of Wayne's command for a time, and on June 24, 1782, Posey and Wayne defeated a force of Creek Indians near the town of Sharon, Georgia, five miles south of Savannah.

In January 1783, in poor health and knowing that the war was drawing to a close, Wayne requested permission to return to Pennsylvania; but at Greene's request he remained in Georgia to guard against threatened British incursions from Florida. Wayne confirmed that no British attacks were imminent, demobilized his Pennsylvanians and finally headed home by sea in July. Congress promoted him to major-general upon his return. After the war Wayne served in the Pennsylvania Assembly and in Congress. He settled, with only marginal success, a tract of land in Georgia that the state awarded him for his service.

In the United States' Northwest Territory — which would become the states of Ohio, Illinois, and Indiana — British soldiers continued to man outposts in violation of the peace treaty that ended the Revolution. Allied with a confederation of Miami, Shawnee, Leni Lenape and Wyandot tribes, the British and Indians prevented settlement of the west. In 1792 President Washington appointed Wayne the commander of the "Legion of the United States," a collection of regular army soldiers and militia, charged to subdue the tribes. On August 20, 1794, Wayne attacked and defeated the tribes at a site where a tornado had once touched down called Fallen Timbers, near present-day Toledo, Ohio. The victory led to the Treaty of Greenville, signed between the tribal confederacy and the United States, on August 3, 1795. The treaty consolidated American control of the Northwest Territory and opened the region for settlement.

Wayne remained at Detroit with his army to ensure the tribes remained quiet. One year after Fallen Timbers he decided to move his headquarters to Pittsburgh for better communications with the War Office. On the way to Pittsburgh in November 1796 he sailed from Detroit to Presque Isle, present-day Erie, Pennsylvania, where a detachment of soldiers garrisoned a small blockhouse. Wayne was extremely ill with gout and rested at the blockhouse under the care of its commander, Captain Russell Bissell. He initially rallied and prepared to continue the journey, but a high fever returned. After enduring extreme pain, Wayne died just after 2:00 A.M. on December 15, 1796. The soldiers dressed him in his best uniform, according to his wishes, and buried him at the foot of the camp flagstaff. Capt. Bissell marked the grave with a simple stone monument etched with the initials "A.W."

Thirteen years later Wayne's son Isaac and daughter Margaretta decided that their father's proper resting place was the family burial plot at St. David's Church in Radnor Township, Pennsylvania, near the Waynesborough estate. Isaac traveled to Erie in August 1809 intending to retrieve Wayne's skeleton. But upon exhumation, Isaac and the man he commissioned for assistance, J.C. Wallace, discovered that the general's body was only partially decomposed. Before the science of embalming it was impossible to transport the remains in such a state, so Wallace dissected the body and boiled the sections in a large iron kettle to separate the flesh from the bones. Wallace reburied the body's flesh and the surgeon's knives used in the operation in the original grave. Isaac carted the skeleton, cleaned and placed in a new casket, 850 miles across Pennsylvania to Radnor Township and interred the general's remains. Years later the Presque Isle blockhouse burned down and the area eventually became overgrown, erasing the location of Wayne's original burial site.

There is a legend that Isaac Wayne's wagon, which bore his father's remains to Radford Township, bounced so much on the rough frontier roads that parts of the skeleton fell out along the way and that every January 1, Wayne's birthday, the general's ghost rides along the roads of western Pennsylvania, searching for his lost bones.

Notes

Introduction

1. Washington to Brig. Gen. Thomas Nelson, February 8, 1778, *The Writings of George Washington from the Original Manuscript Sources, 1745–1799*, ed. John C. Fitzpatrick (Washington, D.C.: U.S. Government Printing Office, 1944), vol. 13.
2. Washington to the president of Congress, December 13, 1778, *Writings of Washington*, vol. 13.
3. Anonymous Letter, September 11, 1777, *Pennsylvania Magazine of History* 29 (1905), 368, in *Rebels and Redcoats: The American Revolution Through the Eyes of Those Who Fought and Lived It*, ed. George F. Scheer and Hugh F. Rankin (New York: World, 1957), 239.
4. Edward L. Lengel, *General George Washington: A Military Life* (New York: Random House, 2005), 64.

Chapter I

1. *Pennsylvania Packet, or the General Advertiser*, December 24, 1778.
2. Harold Donaldson Eberlein and Cortlandt Van Dyke Hubbard, *Diary of Independence Hall* (Philadelphia: J.B. Lippincott, 1948), 238.
3. Henry Laurens to Rawlins Lowndes, July 15, 1778, in Eberlein and Hubbard, *Diary*, 241.
4. Samuel Holten Diary, December 31, 1778, *Letters of Members of the Continental Congress,* ed. Edmund C. Burnett (Washington, D.C.: Carnegie Institute, 1926), vol. 3, 554.
5. *Pennsylvania Packet*, December 5, 22, 24, 1778.
6. Washington to Benjamin Harrison, December 18, 30, 1778, *Writings of Washington*, vol. 13.
7. Washington to Alexander McDougall, February 9, 1779, *Writings of Washington,* vol. 14.
8. Ibid.
9. Ibid.
10. Washington to the Board of War, April 15, 1779, *Writings of Washington*, vol. 14.
11. Washington to the president of Congress, December 13, 1778, *Writings of Washington*, vol. 13.
12. Washington to Steuben, February 8, 1779, *Writings of Washington*, vol. 14.
13. Washington to Harrison, May 5–7 1779, *Writings of Washington*, vol. 15.

14. Washington to the Committee of Conference, January 13, 1779, *Writings of Washington*, vol. 14.
15. Ibid.
16. Ibid.

Chapter II

1. James Thacher, M.D., *Military Journal During the American Revolutionary War, from 1776 to 1783, Describing the Events and Transactions of This Period, with Numerous Historical Facts and Anecdotes* (Hartford, CT: Silas Andrus & Son, 1854), 161.
2. Charles H. Lesser, ed., *The Sinews of Independence: Monthly Strength Reports of the Continental Army* (Chicago: University of Chicago Press, 1976), 104.
3. Ibid.
4. Thacher, *Military Journal*, 158–159.
5. Ibid., 160.
6. Washington's daily schedule is described in John J. Ferling, *Almost a Miracle: The American Victory in the War for Independence* (New York: Oxford University Press, 2007), 327.
7. Washington to the Committee of Conference, February 2, 1779, *Writings of Washington*, vol. 14.
8. General Orders, February 6, 1779, *Writings of Washington*, vol. 14.
9. Anthony Wayne to Washington, February 10, 1779, Anthony Wayne Papers, Historical Society of Pennsylvania, Philadelphia, PA.
10. John W. Wright, "The Corps of Light Infantry in the Continental Army," *American Historical Review* 31, no. 3 (April 1926): 454.
11. Washington to the president of Congress, August 30, 1777, *Writings of Washington*, vol. 9.
12. Washington to the Committee of Congress with the Army, January 29, 1778, *Writings of Washington*, vol. 10.
13. General Orders, August 8, 1778, *Writings of Washington*, vol. 12.
14. Washington to Scott, August 14, 1778, *Writings of Washington*, vol. 12.
15. Anthony Wayne to Mary Wayne, April 28, 1776 (Anthony Wayne Papers, Detroit Public Library), as cited in Paul David Nelson, *Anthony Wayne: Soldier of the Early Republic* (Bloomington: Indiana University Press, 1985), 20.
16. Washington to the president of Congress, July 1, 1778, *Writings of Washington*, vol. 12.
17. Nelson, *Anthony Wayne*, 39.
18. Alexander Graydon, *Memoirs of His Own Time, with Reminiscences of the Men and Events of the Revolution*, ed. John Stockton Littell (Philadelphia: Lindsay & Blakiston, 1846), 259.
19. Nelson, *Anthony Wayne*, 67.
20. Graydon, *Memoirs of His Own Time*, 259.
21. Samuel Hay to William Irvine, September 29, 1777, in *The Spirit of 'Seventy-Six: The Story of the American Revolution as Told by Participants*, ed. Henry Steele Commager and Richard B. Morris (Indianapolis: Bobbs-Merrill, 1958; repr., New York: Da Capo, 1995), 622–623.
22. General Orders, November 1, 1777, *Writings of Washington*, vol. 9.
23. Wayne to Washington, February 10, 1779, Anthony Wayne Papers, Historical Society of Pennsylvania.
24. Don Higginbotham, *Daniel Morgan, Revolutionary Rifleman* (Chapel Hill: University of North Carolina Press, 1961), 94–95.
25. Washington to Wayne, February 16, 1779, *Writings of Washington*, vol. 14.

Chapter III

1. Abraham Woodhull to Benjamin Tallmadge, April 10, 1779, George Washington Papers, Library of Congress, 1741–1799, Manuscript Division (hereinafter cited as George

Washington Papers). Note that the correspondence between the Culper Ring operatives is listed in the Washington Papers with a mix of their true names and code names. I have cited all the letters used here in their true names for consistency.

2. Benjamin Tallmadge to Washington, April 21, 1779, George Washington Papers.
3. Paul H. Smith, "The American Loyalists: Notes on Their Organization and Numerical Strength," *William and Mary Quarterly* 25, no. 2 (April 1968): 269, Third Series.
4. Edwin G. Burrows and Mike L. Wallace, *Gotham: A History of New York City to 1898* (New York: Oxford University Press, 1999), 251.
5. The London Trade is described in Alexander Rose's *Washington's Spies: The Story of America's First Spy Ring* (New York: Random House, 2006), 71–73.
6. Burrows and Wallace, *Gotham*, 251.
7. Ibid., 252–254.
8. Sung Bok Kim, "The Limits of Politicization in the American Revolution: The Experience of Westchester County, New York," *Journal of American History* 80, no. 3 (December 1993): 871.
9. Washington to Jonathan Trumbull, April 12, 1777, *Writings of Washington*, vol. 7.
10. Kim, "Limits of Politicization," 880.
11. Woodhull to Benjamin Tallmadge, November 23, 1778, George Washington Papers.
12. Washington to Governor Livingston, November 7, 1776, *Writings of George Washington*, vol. 6.
13. Thacher, *Military Journal*, 238.
14. *Minutes of the Committee and of the First Commission for Detecting and Defeating Conspiracies in the State of New York, December 11th 1776 — September 28th 1778*, vol. 1 (New York, 1879), 3, 11.
15. Rose, *Washington's Spies*, 96–97.
16. Ibid., 27–32.
17. Washington to president of Congress, November 14 and December 4, 12, 1776, *Writings of Washington*, vol. 6.
18. Rose, *Washington's Spies*, 42–43.
19. Washington to Sackett, February 4, 1777, George Washington Papers.
20. Rose, *Washington's Spies*, 42–50.
21. Washington to the Comte d'Estaing, September 11, 1778, *Writings of Washington*, vol. 12.
22. Washington to Brewster, August 8, 1778, *Writings of Washington*, vol. 12.
23. Washington to the Comte d'Estaing, September 11, 1778, *Writings of Washington*, vol. 12.
24. Rose, *Washington's Spies*, 75–76, 84–87.
25. Washington to Tallmadge, November 18, 1778, *Writings of Washington*, vol. 13.
26. Woodhull to Tallmadge, November 23, 1778, George Washington Papers.
27. Woodhull to Tallmadge, February 26, 1779, George Washington Papers.
28. Brewster to Tallmadge, February 26, 1779, George Washington Papers.
29. Washington to Tallmadge, March 21, 1779, *Writings of Washington*, vol. 14.
30. Woodhull to Tallmadge, April 10, 1779, George Washington Papers.
31. Tallmadge to Washington, April 21, 1779, George Washington Papers.
32. Washington to Benjamin Harrison, May 5–7, 1779, *Writings of Washington*, vol. 15.
33. Woodhull to Washington, April 29, 1779, George Washington Papers.

Chapter IV

1. Henry Clinton, *The American Rebellion: Sir Henry Clinton's Narrative of His Campaigns, 1775–1782, with an Appendix of Original Documents*, ed. William B. Willcox (New Haven: Yale University Press, 1954), 10.
2. William B. Willcox, *Portrait of a General: Sir Henry Clinton in the War of Independence* (New York: Alfred A. Knopf, 1962), 50, 126.
3. Clinton, *The American Rebellion*, 118.
4. Ibid., 115.

5. Ibid., 116.
6. William Smith, *Historical Memoirs of William Smith, 1778–1783*, ed. W.H.W. Sabine (New York: New York Times Publishing, 1971), 96.
7. "Rivington's Royal Gazette," April 17, 1779, in *Diary of the American Revolution, from Newspapers and Original Documents*, ed. Frank Moore (New York: Scribner and Sons, 1853), vol. 2, 152.
8. Smith, *Historical Memoirs of William Smith*, 97.
9. Germain to Clinton, January 23, 1779, *The American Rebellion*, 398.
10. Extract of letter from Clinton to Germaine, May 14, 1779, in Henry P. Johnston, *The Storming of Stony Point on the Hudson, Midnight, July 15, 1779* (New York, 1900; repr., New York: Da Capo, 1971), 31.
11. Clinton, *The American Rebellion*, 11.
12. Washington to John Augustine Washington, March 31, 1776, George Washington Papers.
13. Roger Kaplan, "The Hidden War: British Intelligence Operations during the American Revolution," *William and Mary Quaterly* 47, no. 1 (January 1990): 119–123, Third Series.
14. Clinton, *The American Rebellion*, 122.
15. Ibid.
16. Sir George Collier, *A Detail of Some Particular Services Performed in America, During the Years 1776, 1777, 1778, and 1779* (New York, 1835), 73–74.
17. Ibid., 74–75.
18. Clinton, *The American Rebellion*, 122.
19. Collier, 75.
20. Major Andre's Intelligence Book, undated entry from late May 1779, Henry Clinton Papers, University of Michigan, Ann Arbor, MI.
21. Clinton to General Haldimand, September 9, 1779, *Storming of Stony Point*, 142.
22. Clinton's recollection of the conversation from notes, as cited in Willcox, *Portrait of a General*, 139.
23. Clinton, *The American Rebellion*, 120.
24. *Sir George Collier*, 78.
25. Clinton, *The American Rebellion*, 124. The advance into Westchester County is described in a letter from Gen. James Pattison to Lord Townsend, June 9, 1779, in Johnston, *Storming of Stony Point*, 113–116.
26. Clinton, *The American Rebellion*, 125.
27. General Pattison to Lord Townsend, June 9, 1779, in Johnston, *Storming of Stony Point*, 116–117. The numbers in the British forces engaged in the attack are taken from units named in Pattison's letter and an estimate of British unit strengths at the time.
28. Clinton, *The American Rebellion*, 125.
29. Armstrong to Alexander McDougall, June 1, 1779, George Washington Papers.
30. Washington to president of Congress, June 6, 1779, *Writings of Washington*, vol. 15.
31. General Pattison, commanding British Artillery, to Lord Townsend, June 9, 1779, in Johnston, *Storming of Stony Point*, 118.
32. Commodore Sir George Collier to the English Admiralty, July 14, 1779, in Johnston, *Storming of Stony Point*, 113.
33. Clinton, *The American Rebellion*, 129.
34. *Sir George Collier*, 89.
35. Smith, *Memoirs of William Smith*, 114.
36. Clinton, *The American Rebellion*, 125.
37. Smith, *Memoirs of William Smith*, 109.

Chapter V

1. Woodhull to Washington, May 12, 1779, and to Tallmadge, June 5, 1779, George Washington Papers.

2. Washington to Elias Boudinot, May 3, 1779, *Writings of Washington*, vol. 14.
3. Elijah Hunter to Washington, May 21, 1779, George Washington Papers.
4. Washington to John Augustine Washington, June 20, 1779, and to Knox, June 4, 1779, *Writings of Washington*, vols. 15 and 16.
5. Charles H. Lesser, ed., *The Sinews of Independence: Monthly Strength Reports of the Continental Army* (Chicago: University of Chicago Press, 1976), 116, 117.
6. Washington to Gates, May 14, 1779, *Writings of Washington*, vol. 15.
7. Hamilton to St. Clair, May 28, 1779, *Writings of Washington*, vol. 16.
8. A. Johnston to Anthony Wayne, May 27, 1779, Wayne Papers, Historical Society of Pennsylvania.
9. Shreve to Washington, May 29, 1779, George Washington Papers.
10. McDougall to Washington, May 29, 1779, George Washington Papers.
11. General Orders, June 1, 1779, *Writings of Washington*, vol. 16.
12. Washington to Woodford, May 31, 1779, *Writings of Washington*, vol. 16.
13. Washington to the president of Congress, June 3, 1779, *Writings of Washington*, vol. 16.
14. Washington to Knox, May 30, 1779, *Writings of Washington*, vol. 16.
15. Washington to Stirling, June 2, 1779, *Writings of Washington*, vol. 16.
16. John W. Wright, "Notes on the Continental Army," *William and Mary Quarterly* 12, no. 2 (April 1932): 84–85, Second Series.
17. Washington to McDougall, May 30–31 and June 2, 1779, *Writings of Washington*, vol. 16.
18. McDougall to Washington, June 5, 1779, George Washington Papers.
19. Malcolm to Washington, June 5, 1779, George Washington Papers.
20. Washington to the president of Congress, June 3, 1779, *Writings of Washington*, vol. 16.
21. Washington to Mercerau, June 2, 1779, *Writings of Washington*, vol. 16.
22. Washington to Neilson, June 2, 1779, *Writings of Washington*, vol. 16.
23. Woodhull to Tallmadge, June 5, 1779, George Washington Papers.
24. Washington to Lee, June 6, 1779, *Writings of Washington*, vol. 16.
25. Febiger to his wife, June 7, 1779, Christian Febiger Papers, 1777–1782, Personal Papers Collection, Library of Virginia, Richmond.
26. General Orders, June 7, 1779, *Writings of Washington*, vol. 16.
27. Febiger to his wife, June 7, 1779, Febiger Papers.
28. Parsons to Washington, June 5, 1779, George Washington Papers.
29. Washington to Malcolm, June 9, 1779, *Writings of Washington*, vol. 16.
30. Washington to the president of Congress, June 11, 1779, *Writings of Washington*, vol. 16.

Chapter VI

1. William Malcolm to Washington, June 5, 1779, George Washington Papers.
2. Washington to William Malcolm, June 5, 1779, *Writings of Washington*, vol. 15.
3. Washington to Anthony Wayne, June 21, 1779, *Writings of Washington*, vol. 15 (the letter of June 21 references the May letter, which never reached Wayne).
4. General Orders, June 12, 1779, *Writings of Washington*, vol. 15. The tasked regiments were these: 1st–11th Virginia; Virginia State Regiment and Gist's Virginia Regiment; 1st–7th Maryland; the Delaware Regiment; 1st, 2nd, 3rd, 5th, 6th, 7th Pennsylvania, and 9th and 10th Pennsylvania.
5. General Orders, June 15, 1779, *Writings of Washington*, vol. 15.
6. As cited in Nelson, *Anthony Wayne*, 87.
7. The discussion of honor and leadership comes from Charles Royster's *A Revolutionary People at War: The Continental Army and American Character, 1775–1783* (Chapel Hill: University of North Carolina Press, 1979), 87–89, 208–209.

8. As cited in Royster, *Revolutionary People at War*, 96.
9. Lt. Col. Otho Williams to D. Edwards, May 22, 1783, Society of the Cincinnati Library.
10. Royster, *Revolutionary People at War*, 95.
11. Henry P. Johnston, "Col. Christian Febiger of the Virginia Line of the Continental Army," *Magazine of American History* 6 (New York: A.S. Barnes, 1881), 188–193.
12. Febiger to his wife, June 17, 1779, Christian Febiger Papers, Library of Virginia, Richmond.
13. Thomas Wyatt, *Memoirs of the Generals, Commodores, and Other Commanders Who Distinguished Themselves in the American Army and Navy During the War of the Revolution and 1812, and Who Were Presented with Medals by Congress for Their Gallant Services* (Philadelphia: Corey and Hart, 1847), 43–46.
14. Washington to the president of Congress, December 13, 1778, *Writings of Washington*, vol. 13.
15. Alexander Harris, *Biographical History of Lancaster County* (Elias Barr: 1872), 74.
16. Muster Roll of Thomas Boude's Company of Light Infantry in the 5th Pennsylvania Regiment, Commanded by Col. Francis Johnston, for the month of July 1779, Record Group 93, Roll 82, National Archives, Washington, D.C.
17. Francis B. Heitman, *Historical Register of Officers of the Continental Army During the War of the Revolution, April 1775 to December 1783* (Washington, D.C.: Genealogical, 1914), 279.
18. McKenzie to St. Clair, July 23, 1776, *The Life and Public Services of Arthur St. Clair, Soldier of the Revolutionary War, President of the Continental Congress, and Governor of the Northwestern Territory, Correspondence and Others Papers, Arranged and Annotated*, ed. William Henry Smith (Cincinnati: Robert Clarke, 1881), 438.
19. "Report of Inspection of the Light Infantry Drawn from the Va., Md., and Pa. Lines, June 1779," *Papers of the Continental Congress* 31, printed in John W. Wright's "The Corps of Light Infantry in the Continental Army" in *American Historical Review*, 455.
20. Harold W. Selesky, *A Demographic Survey of the Continental Army That Wintered at Valley Forge, 1777–1778* (New Haven, 1987), 6, 21, and Tables 41, 44, and 45–3.
21. Noble Pension File, Record Group 15, National Archives, Washington, D.C.
22. Burton Pension File, National Archives.
23. Bray Pension File, National Archives.
24. Humble Pension File, National Archives.
25. Vass Pension File, National Archives.
26. "Letter of Peter Francisco to the General Assembly," November 11, 1820, *William and Mary Quarterly* 13, no. 4 (April 1905): 217. At the National Archives, the August 1779 muster roll of Capt. Nathan Samme's Company, Sixth Virginia Regiment, lists Pvt. Peter Francisco as being detailed to the Light Infantry.
27. Washington to Butler, June 21, 1779, *Writings of Washington*, vol. 15.
28. Washington to Wayne, June 21, 1779, *Writings of Washington*, vol. 15.
29. Nelson, *Anthony Wayne*, 94.

Chapter VII

1. Robert H. Boyle, *The Hudson River: A Natural and Unnatural History* (New York: W.W. Norton, 1969), 32, 48–49, 183; Almet S. Moffat, *Orange County New York: A Narrative History* (Washingtonville, NY: 1928), 8; John W. Barber and Henry Howe, *Historical Collections of the State of New York* (New York: S. Tuttle, 1842), 476; "History of Verplank's Point," *New York Times*, March 8, 1896; Frank Bertangue Green, *The History of Rockland County* (New York: A.S. Barnes, 1886), 3–10, 14–37, 87–93, 108–113, 161–162, 278–280, 370–372.
2. *A Treatise on Gun-Powder, a Treatise on Fire-Arms, and a Treatise on the Service of Artillery in Time of War, Translated from the Italian by Captain Thomson of the Royal Regiment of Artillery* (London, 1789), 366.

3. Pattison to Townsend, June 9, 1779, in Johnston, *Storming of Stony Point*, 114.
4. Washington to John Augustine Washington, June 20, 1779, *Writings of Washington*, vol. 15.
5. "Detail of Picquets and Guards Posted at Stony Point 15th July 1779," in Don Loprieno, *The Enterprise in Contemplation: The Midnight Assault of Stony Point* (Westminster, MD: Heritage, 2004), 309; Testimony of Captain Alexander Mercer, "Proceedings of a General Court Martial Held at New York on the 2nd of January & by Adjournments to the 20th of February 1781, upon the Trial of Lieut. Colonel Johnson of the 17th Reg. of Foot," WO 71/152, National Archives, Kew, Great Britain, 126; Testimony of Lt. John Roberts, Court Martial Proceedings, 77.
6. Testimony of Lt. John Roberts, Court Martial Proceedings, 89.
7. Ibid., 88.
8. Clinton, *The American Rebellion*, 130.
9. Ibid., 127.
10. Ibid., 130.
11. Ibid.
12. Ibid., 131.
13. Spring, *Zeal and Bayonets*, 106, Table 2.
14. "A Return of the Killed, Wounded and Taken in the Assault at Stony Point on the 16th Day of July in the Morning Commanded by Brigadier Genl Wayne," from the papers of Capt. James Chrystie, in Johnston, *Storming of Stony Point*, 212.
15. Clinton, *The American Rebellion*, 132.
16. Stephen M. Baule with Stephen Gilbert, eds., *British Army Officers Who Served in the American Revolution, 1775–1783* (Westminster, MD: Heritage, 2004), 48, 83, 97, 175.
17. Richard J. Koke, "The Britons Who Fought at Stony Point," *New York Historical Society Quarterly* 44, no. 1 (January 1960): 65–66. The figure for Seventy-first soldiers at Stony Point also comes from *The Storming of Stony Point*, as cited above for the Seventeenth Regiment (212).
18. Julia Jarvis, *Three Centuries of Robinsons: The Story of a Family* (Ontario, Canada: T.H. Best, 1967), 66–67, 68, 83, 89, 90; Koke, *Britons Who Fought at Stony Point*, 66.
19. Frederick Morris, "Autobiography of Frederick Morris," *Three Centuries of Robinsons*, 88–91.
20. "Letter of Instructions Left with Lt. Stratten, Engr., Verplanks Point, 26th June, 1779," in Loprieno, *Enterprise*, 311; Testimony of Lt. William Marshall, Court Martial Proceedings, 143–144.
21. "Extracts from Lt. Marshall's Journal kept at Stoney Point," in Loprieno, *Enterprise*, 312.
22. Testimony of Lt. William Marshall, Court Martial Proceedings, 146.

Chapter VIII

1. Heath to Sheldon, June 26, 1779, in *The Burning of Bedford, July 1779, as Reported in Contemporary Documents and Eyewitness Accounts*, ed. Dorothy Humphreys Hinitt and Frances Riker Duncombe (Bedford, NY: Bedford Historical Society, 1974), 5.
2. Washington to Moylan, June 28, 1779, Washington Papers.
3. Tallmadge to Heath, June 27, 1779, in Hinitt and Riker, eds., *Burning of Bedford*, 10.
4. Wright, *Continental Army*, 106–107; Wright, "Notes on the Continental Army," 189–190; Fred Anderson Berg, *Encyclopedia of Continental Army Units: Battalions, Regiments and Independent Corps* (Harrisburg, PA: Stackpole, 1972), 29–31.
5. Rose, *Washington's Spies*, 43.
6. Henry Phelps Johnston, *Yale and Her Honor-Roll in the American Revolution, 1775–1783* (New York: privately printed, 1888), 295.
7. Benjamin Tallmadge, *Memoir of Colonel Benjamin Tallmadge, Prepared by Himself, at the Request of His Children* (New York, 1858), 17.

8. Ibid., 19.
9. Ibid., 26.
10. Ibid., 27.
11. Ibid., 29.
12. Rose, *Washington's Spies*, 126.
13. Woodhull to Tallmadge, June 5, 1779, George Washington Papers.
14. Woodhull to Tallmadge, June 8, 1779, George Washington Papers.
15. Woodhull to Tallmadge, June 29, 1779, George Washington Papers.
16. Robert D. Bass, *The Green Dragoon: The Lives of Banastre Tarleton and Mary Robinson* (New York: Henry Holt, 1957; repr., Columbia, SC: Sandlapper, 1973), 11–22, 32–38, 44–49.
17. Jay Harris, *God's Country: A History of Pound Ridge, New York* (Chester, CT: Pequot, 1971), 35–38.
18. Tallmadge, *Memoir of Colonel Benjamin Tallmadge*, 32.
19. Tarleton to Clinton, July 2, 1779, in Bass, *Green Dragoon*, 55–56.
20. "Extract of a letter from an officer at Salem, July 3, 1779," in Loprieno, *Burning of Bedford*, 19–20.
21. Ezra Lockwood's recollection from "Sketches of Poundridge," as cited in Harris, *God's Country*, 38.
22. Harris, *God's Country*, 38–39.
23. Tarleton to Clinton, July 2, 1779, in Bass, *Green Dragoon*, 56.
24. "Rivington's Royal Gazette," July 7, 1779, *Diary of the American Revolution*, 177.
25. Tarleton to Clinton, July 2, 1779, in Bass, *Green Dragoon*, 56.
26. Ibid.
27. John T. Hayes, *Connecticut's Revolutionary Cavalry: Sheldon's Horse* (Chester, CT: Pequot, 1975), 30.
28. Washington to Tallmadge, June 27, 1779, *Writings of Washington*, vol. 15. British soldiers arrested Higday on July 13, and he admitted that he spied for the Americans but pleaded that he needed the money to buy a cow; he portrayed Washington as the aggressor who promised to make him rich but paid him in counterfeit money. Clinton released him, possibly because he hoped to turn Higday as a "double." But since his arrest was well known Higday was useless to either side, and he returned to his private life on Manhattan Island.

Chapter IX

1. Letter of marque for the privateer *General Washington*, Papers of the Continental Congress, 1774–1789, RG 360, M247, National Archives.
2. Clinton, *American Rebellion*, 129.
3. Thomas Clark, *Naval History of the United States from the Commencement of the Revolutionary War to the Present Time* (Philadelphia: M. Carey, 1814), vol. 2, 37, 169–179.
4. Collier, 92–93.
5. Lloyd A. Brown, *Loyalist Operations at New Haven, Including Capt. Patrick Ferguson's Letter with Map Dated May 27, 1779, and Capt. Nathan Hubbel's Raid on New Haven, April 19, 1781* (Meridian, CT: Timothy, 1938).
6. "Instructions to Maj. Gen. Tryon," in Charles Hervey Townshend, *The British Invasion of New Haven, Connecticut, Together with Some Account of Their Landing and Burning the Towns of Fairfield and Norwalk, July, 1779* (New Haven: Tuttle, Morehouse & Taylor, 1879), 33.
7. "Benedict Arnold, the Fighting Druggist," *British Medical Journal* 1, no. 4027 (March 12, 1938): 580.
8. Ezra Stiles, *The Literary Diary of Ezra Stiles, D.D., LL.D., President of Yale College*, vol. 2, March 14, 1776–December 31, 1781 (New York: Scribner's Sons, 1901), 352.
9. "Extracts from the Autobiography of Thomas Painter, Esq.," in Townshend, *British Invasion*, 63–64.

10. Stiles, *Literary Diary of Ezra Stiles*, 352.
11. "Extracts from the Autobiography of Thomas Painter," in Townshend, *British Invasion*, 64.
12. Paul David Nelson, *William Tryon and the Course of Empire: A Life in British Imperial Service* (Chapel Hill: University of North Carolina Press, 1990), 157.
13. Smith, *Memoirs of William Smith*, 111.
14. Nelson, *William Tryon*,169.
15. Smith, *Memoirs of William Smith*, 109.
16. As cited in Michael Sletcher, *New Haven: From Puritanism to the Age of Terrorism* (Portsmouth, NH: Arcadia, 2004), 38.
17. Johnston, *Yale and Her Honor-Roll in the American Revolution*, 107.
18. "Autobiography of Thomas Painter," in Townshend, *British Invasion*, 64.
19. "Deposition of Naphtali Daggett Regarding Alleged British Atrocities, July 28, 1779, Sworn before David Austin," Papers of the Continental Congress.
20. Stiles, *Literary Diary of Ezra Stiles*, 353.
21. "Deposition of Naphtali Daggett," Papers of the Continental Congress.
22. Ibid., 354.
23. Tryon to Clinton, July 29, 1779, in Clinton, *The American Rebellion*, 412.
24. "Deposition of Naphtali Daggett," Papers of the Continental Congress.
25. Garth to Tryon, July 5, 1779, in Townshend, *British Invasion*, 40.
26. Townshend, *British Invasion*, 7.
27. Tryon to Clinton, July 29, 1779, in Clinton, *The American Rebellion*, 412.
28. Collier, 91.
29. Ibid.
30. Townshend, *British Invasion*, 12.
31. Ibid., 17.
32. "Instructions to Maj. Gen. Tryon," in Townshend, *British Invasion*, 32.
33. George Collier and William Tryon, July 4, 1779, Broadside of Address to Connecticut Citizens, George Washington Papers.
34. Collier, 92.
35. Royal R. Hinman, ed., *Connecticut Journal, July 7th, 1779: A Historical Collection of the Part Sustained by Connecticut During the War of the Revolution, with an Appendix Containing Important Letters, Depositions, &c, Written during the War* (Hartford, CT, 1842), 609.
36. "Deposition of Elias Beers," Papers of the Continental Congress.
37. Peter J. Malia, *Visible Saints: West Haven Connecticut, 1648–1798*, (Monroe, CT: Connecticut, 2009), 136–138; Sletcher, *New Haven*, 39, "Affidavit of Abigail English," and "Affidavit of Lois Cook," Papers of the Continental Congress; Townhsend, *British Invasion*, 27–28, 58–59.
38. As cited in Sletcher, *New Haven*, 40.
39. Ibid.
40. Ibid.
41. Tryon to Clinton, July 29, 1779, quoted in Clinton, *The American Rebellion*, 412.
42. Stiles, *Literary Diary of Ezra Stiles*, 357.
43. "Instructions to Maj. Gen. Tryon," in Townshend, *British Invasion*, 34.

Chapter X

1. Andrew Eliot to John Eliot, in Elizabeth H. Schenck, *The History of Fairfield, Fairfield County, Connecticut, from 1700 AD to 1800*, vol. 3 (New York: published by the author, 1905), 390.
2. Schenck, *History of Fairfield*, 386.
3. "William Wheeler's Journal," in *History of Fairfield*, 388.
4. Tryon to Clinton, July 29, 1779, in Clinton, *The American Rebellion*, 412.

5. Eliot to John Eliot, July 15, 1779, in Schenck, *History of Fairfield*, 391.
6. Ibid.
7. Schenck, *History of Fairfield*, 387.
8. Collier, 95–96.
9. Ibid.
10. Tryon to Clinton, July 29, 1779, in Clinton, *The American Rebellion*, 412.
11. Eliot to John Eliot, July 15, 1779, in Schenck, *History of Fairfield*, 391.
12. Ibid.
13. "William Wheeler's Journal," in Schenck, *History of Fairfield*, 389.
14. Eliot to John Eliot, July 15, 1779, in Schenck, *History of Fairfield*, 391.
15. "Rev. Dr. Timothy Dwight's Travels," in Schenck, *History of Fairfield*, 394.
16. "Return of Buildings Burnt at Fairfield 8th and 9th of July '79," Papers of the Continental Congress.
17. Tryon to Clinton, July 29, 1779, in Clinton, *The American Rebellion*, 414.
18. Schenck, *History of Fairfield*, 394.
19. Deborah Wing Ray and Gloria P. Stewart, *Norwalk: Being an Historical Account of That Connecticut Town* (Canaan, NH: Phoenix, 1979), 53–55, 57–58.
20. Washington to Trumbull, July 7, 1779, *Writings of Washington*, vol. 15.
21. Ibid.
22. Washington to Parsons, July 8, 1779, *Writings of Washington*, vol. 15.
23. Tryon to Clinton, July 29, 1779, in Clinton, *The American Rebellion*, 413.
24. Ibid., 414.
25. Ibid.
26. Clinton, *The American Rebellion*, 130.
27. Washington to Trumbull, July 9 and 12, 1779, *Writings of Washington*, vol. 15.
28. Collier, 97–98.

Chapter XI

1. Washington to Wayne, July 1, 1779, *Writings of Washington*, vol. 15.
2. As cited in Charles Janeway Stille, *Major General Anthony Wayne and the Pennsylvania Line in the Continental Army* (1893, repr., Gansevoort, NY: Corner House, 2000), 184.
3. Wayne to the Issuing Commissary, at Camp, July 9, 1779, in Henry B. Dawson, *The Assault on Stony Point by General Anthony Wayne, July 16, 1779, Prepared for the New York Historical Society and Read at Its Regular Meeting, April 1, 1862, with Some Illustrative Notes* (New York: New York Historical Society, 1863; repr., General Books, 2009), Wayne to Washington, July 9, 1779, 14.
4. Alexander Garden, *Anecdotes of the American Revolution, Illustrative of the Talents and Virtues of the Heroes and Patriots Who Acted the Most Conspicuous Parts Therein* (Charleston, SC: A.E. Miller, 1828), 76–79, Second Series.
5. See McLane's notes on a letter received from Washington, June 9, 1779, Allan McLane Papers, New York Historical Society.
6. Garden, *Anecdotes of the American Revolution*, 79.
7. Ibid., 79–80.
8. Wayne to Washington, July 3, 1779, *Wayne and the Pennsylvania Line*, 186–87.
9. Washington to Wayne, July 9, 1779, *Writings of Washington*, vol. 15.
10. Lesser, *Sinews of Independence*, Return for June 1779, 121; Washington to Gates, June 11, 1779, *Writings of Washington*, vol. 15.
11. Washington to the president of Congress, July 9, 1779, *Writings of Washington*, vol. 15.
12. Washington to Knox, June 4, 1779, *Writings of Washington*, vol. 15.
13. Washington to the president of Congress, May 25, 1779, *Writings of Washington*, vol. 15.

14. *Field Manual 100-5, Operations* (Washington, D.C.: Department of the Army, 1993), 2-5.
15. Washington to Wayne, July 9, 1779, *Writings of Washington*, vol. 15.
16. Washington to Wayne, July 10, 1779, *Writings of Washington*, vol. 15.
17. William Heath, *Memoirs of Major-General Heath, Containing Anecdotes, Details of Skirmishes, Battles, and Other Military Events During the American War* (Boston, 1798; repr., New York: William Abbatt, 1901), 180.
18. General Orders, July 11, 1779, and July 13, 1779, *Writings of Washington*, vol. 15.
19. E.O. Randall, "How Governor Meigs Got His Name," *Ohio History* 16, 417.
20. Sherman Pension File, National Archives.
21. Ibid.
22. Washington to Wayne, July 14, 1779, *Writings of Washington*, vol. 15.
23. Febiger to his wife, July 14, 1779, Febiger Papers.
24. Washington to Muhlenberg, July 15, 1779, *Writings of Washington*, vol. 15.
25. Wayne to Captain Chrystie, July 15, 1779, in Johnston, *Storming of Stony Point*, 161.
26. Johnston, *Storming of Stony Point*, 72.
27. Major John Burnham, Manuscript Narrative of an Officer of the Revolution, 1775–1784, Library of the Society of the Cincinnati, Washington, D.C.

Chapter XII

1. Vincent Vass Pension Deposition, National Archives, Washington, D.C.
2. Febiger to his wife, July 21, 1779, Febiger Papers.
3. Wayne to Delaney, July 15, 1779, Anthony Wayne Papers.
4. "Wayne's Order of Battle," in Johnston, *Storming of Stony Point*, 159.
5. Ibid.
6. Ibid., 160.
7. Vass Pension Deposition.
8. "Col. Febiger's Account of the Attack," in Johnston, *Storming Stony Point*, 184.
9. Maj. Andre's Intelligence Book, entries for July 13, 1779, Henry Clinton Papers.
10. Testimony of Lt. William Armstrong, Court Martial Proceedings, 61.
11. Testimony of Capt. Lawrence Campbell, Court Martial Proceedings, 59.
12. Ibid.
13. Testimony of Lt. John Ross, Court Martial Proceedings, 29. The minutes of the court-martial were verbatim records of the testimony taken by a court report in the third person; in this case, the exact quotation is, "He sent a corporal and some men down...." In this citation, and others from the same source that follow, I have changed the third person back to the first person for clarity.
14. Testimony of Lt. John Roberts, Court Martial Proceedings, 78.
15. Testimony of Lt. Simpson, Court Martial Proceedings, 71.
16. Testimony of Cpl. John Newton, Court Martial Proceedings, 123.
17. Testimony of Cpl. Simon Davies, Court Martial Proceedings, 105.

Chapter XIII

1. "The Attack Described by a Connecticut Officer, August 11, 1779," in Johnston, *Storming of Stony Point*, 176.
2. Ibid.
3. John Thornton Posey, *General Thomas Posey, Son of the American Revolution* (East Lansing: Michigan State University Press, 1992), 56. In an unpublished account of the battle, Col. Febiger stated that it was actually Capt. Hugh Shelton who had given orders to remove the abatis, and Knox's orders were to fight off any enemy that interfered with Shelton.

According to Febiger, Shelton's men had their muskets slung and carried axes but found it impossible to chop through the abatis. Though Febiger speaks with authority, since both Shelton and Knox came from his column, this arrangement is incongruous with Wayne's order and more sources indicate that Knox's forlorn hope acted as Wayne had ordered.

4. Lt. John Gibbon to Capt. Allen McLane, November 21, 1821, in Johnston, *Storming of Stony Point*, 197.
5. Testimony of Lt. William Horndon, Court Martial Proceedings, 45.
6. "General Wayne to Washington on the Success of the Assault, July 17th, 1779," in Johnston, *Storming of Stony Point*, 163.
7. Febiger to his wife, July 21, 1779, Febiger Papers.
8. Mrs. Marcia Campbell, *Revolutionary Services and Civil Life of General William Hull; Prepared from His Manuscripts, by His Daughter Mrs. Marcia Campbell, Together with the History of the Campaign of 1812 and the Surrender of the Post of Detroit* (New York: D. Appleton, 1848), 162; Testimony of Capt. Darby, Court Martial Proceedings, 15.
9. Vass Pension Deposition, National Archives.
10. Campbell, *Revolutionary Services of Hull*, 163; Report of Lt. John Wilmot, Maj. Andre's Intelligence Book, Clinton Papers. Wilmot deserted from the Light Infantry on July 24 and it is possible that his statement was an exaggeration designed to denigrate the Americans to his new hosts, the British.
11. Testimony of Lt. Ross, Court Martial Proceedings, 30.
12. Campbell, *Revolutionary Services of Hull*, 163.
13. Testimony of Lt. William Simpson, Court Martial Proceedings, 71–72.
14. Devin Pension File, National Archives.
15. Testimony of Lt. John Roberts, Court Martial Proceedings, 79.
16. Posey, *General Thomas Posey*, 58.
17. "Letter of Peter Francisco," 217.
18. Campbell, *Revolutionary Services of Hull*, 162.
19. Morris Autobiography, *Three Centuries of Robinsons*, 91.
20. Testimony of Lt. Armstrong, Court Martial Proceedings, 63.
21. Campbell, *Revolutionary Services of Hull*, 163.
22. Testimony of Lt. Ross, Court Martial Proceedings, 30.
23. Ibid., 31.
24. Posey to Washington, August 10, 1779, in Dawson, *Assault on Stony Point*, 121.
25. "Attack Described by a Connecticut Officer," in Johnston, *Storming of Stony Point*, 177.
26. Pension Deposition of Vincent Vass, National Archives.
27. Morris Autobiography, *Three Centuries of Robinsons*, 92.
28. Febiger to his wife, July 16, 1779, Febiger Papers.
29. Gibbon to McLane, November 27, 1821, in Johnston, *Storming of Stony Point*, 198.
30. Noble Pension Affidavit, National Archives.
31. "A Connecticut Officer," in Johnston, *Storming of Stony Point*, 177.
32. Testimony of Cpl. William West, Court Martial Proceedings, 120.
33. Ibid.
34. Testimony of Cpl. John Ash, Court Martial Proceedings, 111.
35. Sherman Pension Affidavit, National Archives.
36. Campbell to Clinton, July 24, 1779, Clinton Papers, Clements Library.
37. Campbell, *Revolutionary Services of Hull*, 163.
38. Ibid.
39. Wayne to Washington, July 16, 1779, in Johnston, *Storming of Stony Point*, 85.
40. Wayne to Thomas Burke, August 1, 1779, Wayne Papers.
41. Campbell, *Revolutionary Services of Hull*, 164.
42. "Return of the Killed and Wounded of the Light Infantry at the Storm of Stony Point, under the Command of Brigadier-General Wayne, July 15, 1779," George Washington Papers.
43. Washington to the president of Congress, July 16, 1779, *Writings of Washington*, vol. 15.

44. General Orders, July 16, 1779, *Writings of Washington*, vol. 15.
45. Washington to the president of Congress, July 21, 1779, *Writings of Washington*, vol. 15.
46. "The Attempt on Verplanck's Point—Colonel Rufus Putnam's Account," in Johnston, *Storming of Stony Point*, 224.
47. Ibid.
48. Ibid., 225.

Chapter XIV

1. Clinton, *The American Rebellion*, 131–132.
2. Ibid., 132.
3. Vass Pension Deposition, National Archives.
4. Loprieno, *Enterprise*, 37–38.
5. "General Wayne to Washington on the Success of the Assault, July 17th, 1779," in Johnston, *Storming of Stony Point*, 163.
6. Campbell, *Revolutionary Services of Hull*, 165.
7. "Account of Appraisement of the Quartermaster's Stores, Taken from the Enemy at Stoney Point the 16th of July 1779" and "Inventory of Baggage Taken from the British Officers," Anthony Wayne Papers.
8. Washington to the president of Congress, July 21, 1779, *Writings of Washington*, vol. 15.
9. Ibid.
10. Glean Pension Affidavit, National Archives.
11. General Orders, July 18, 1779, *Writings of Washington*, vol. 15; Loprieno, *Enterprise*, 37.
12. Clinton, *The American Rebellion*, 132.
13. Washington to the president of Congress, July 21, 1779, *Writings of Washington*, vol. 15.
14. General Orders, July 19, 1779, *Writings of Washington*, vol. 15.
15. General Orders, July 20, 1779, *Writings of Washington*, vol. 15.
16. Collier, 101.
17. Clinton, *The American Rebellion*, 137.
18. Minutes of Council of War, July 25, 1779, *Writings of Washington*, vol. 16.
19. "Sir Henry Clinton to General Haldimand, Canada, Reviewing the Campaign, September 9, 1779," in Johnston, *Storming of Stony Point*, 144.
20. Archer to Wayne, July 1779, in Dawson, *Assault on Stony Point*, 74–75.
21. Washington to the president of Congress, July 21, 1779, *Writings of Washington*, vol. 15.
22. Ibid.
23. Benjamin Rush to Wayne, August 6, 1779, Anthony Wayne Papers.
24. Maj. Gen. Charles Lee to Wayne, August 11, 1779, in Dawson, *Assault on Stony Point*, 78.
25. Loprieno, *Enterprise*, 46.
26. John Jay to Wayne, July 27, 1779, Anthony Wayne Papers.
27. Washington to Wayne, August 15, 1779, *Writings of Washington*, vol. 16.
28. "Accounting Appraisement of the Quartermaster's Stores Taken from Enemy at Stoney Point, the 16th of July 1779," Anthony Wayne Papers.
29. "Orderly Book of Captain Robert Gamble of the Second Virginia Regiment, commanded by Colonel Christian Febiger, August 21–November 16, 1779," *Proceedings of the Virginia Historical Society at the Annual Meeting Held December 21–22, 1891, with Historical Papers Read on the Occasion and Others*, R.A. Bank, ed. (Richmond: Virginia Historical Society, 1892), 228.

30. John Jay to Wayne, July 27, 1779, Anthony Wayne Papers.
31. "A Connecticut Officer, July 24, 1779," in Johnston, *Storming of Stony Point*, 178.
32. *Sir George Collier*, 100.

Chapter XV

1. Washington to the president of Congress, July 21, 1779, *Writings of Washington*, vol. 15.
2. Washington to the president of Congress, August 11, 1779, *Writings of Washington*, vol. 16.
3. Townsend to Tallmadge, July 29, 1779, George Washington Papers.
4. Washington to the president of Congress, July 24, 1779, *Writings of Washington*, vol. 15.
5. Washington to Reed, July 29, 1779, *Writings of Washington*, vol. 16. Washington's thoughts on possible British attacks at West Point, New England and Philadelphia are found in the unfinished "Thoughts on a British Attempt on West Point," dated July 1779, *Writings of Washington*, vol. 16.
6. Minutes of Council of War, July 25, 1779, *Writings of Washington*, vol. 16; Clinton, *The American Rebellion*, 129, n.14; Washington to the president of Congress, July 29, 1779, *Writings of Washington*, vol. 16.
7. Washington to President of Congress, August 11, 1779, *Writings of Washington*, vol. 16.
8. Washington to Benjamin Lincoln, July 30, 1779, *Writings of Washington*, vol. 16.
9. Washington to Wayne, July 30, 1779, *Writings of Washington*, vol. 16.
10. Wayne to Washington, July 31, 1779, Wayne Papers.
11. Washington to Heath, August, 10, 1779, *Writings of Washington*, vol. 16.
12. Charles Rosyter, *Light Horse Harry Lee and the Legacy of the American Revolution* (Baton Rouge: Louisiana State University Press, 1981), 19.
13. Royster, *Revolutionary People at War*, 81.
14. Washington to Lee, July 10, 1779, *Writings of Washington*, vol. 15, and Lee to Washington, July 11, 1779, George Washington Papers.
15. Washington to the president of Congress, April 3, 1778, *Writings of Washington*, vol. 11.
16. Charles H. Winfield, *History of the County of Hudson, New Jersey, from Its Earliest Settlement to the Present Time* (New York: Kennard & Hay, 1874), 137.
17. "Oration by the Hon. Charles H. Winfield," in *Memorial Centennial Celebration of the Battle of Paulus Hook, August 19th, 1879, with a History of the Early Settlement and Present Condition*, George H. Farrier, ed. (Jersey City: M. Mullone, 1879), 24.
18. Ruth M. Keesey, "Loyalism in Bergen County, New Jersey," *William and Mary Quarterly* 18, no. 4 (October 1961): 559–560, Third Series.
19. Winfield, *History of the County of Hudson*, 151.
20. Ibid.
21. Adrian C. Leiby, *The Revolutionary War in the Hackensack Valley: The Jersey Dutch and the Neutral Ground, 1775–1783* (New Brunswick: Rutgers University Press, 1962), 220.
22. Washington to Lee, September 1, 1779, *Writings of Washington*, vol. 16.
23. Washington to Stirling, August 12, 1779, *Writings of Washington*, vol. 16.
24. Lee's Order of Battle for Paulus Hook, Papers of the Continental Congress.
25. Ibid.
26. Lee to Washington, August 21, 1779, Papers of the Continental Congress.
27. "Translated from Die deutschen Hulfstruppen im nord-amerikanishen, Befreiungskriege, 1776 bis 1783, von Max von Elking, Vol. 2," in *Memorial Centennial Celebration of the Battle of Paulus Hook*, 88.
28. Ibid.
29. Levin Handy to George Handy, August 22, 1779, in *The Spirit of 'Seventy-Six*, ed. Commager and Morris, 726–727.

30. "Translated from Die deutschen Hulfstruppen im nord-amerikanishen, Befreiungskriege," in *Memorial Centennial Celebration of the Battle of Paulus Hook*, 88.
31. "*New York Gazette and Mercury*," August 23, 1779, in *The Spirit of 'Seventy-Six*, ed. Commager and Morris, 727.
32. Lee to Washington, August 21, 1779, Papers of the Continental Congress.
33. Ibid.
34. Levin Handy to George Handy, July 22, 1779, in *The Spirit of 'Seventy-Six*, ed. Commager and Morris, 727.
35. Lee to Washington, August 21, 1779, Papers of the Continental Congress.
36. "Oration by the Hon. Charles H. Winfield," in *Memorial Centennial Celebration of the Battle of Paulus Hook*, 51; "*New York Gazette and Mercury*," August 23, 1779, in *The Spirit of 'Seventy-Six*, ed. Commager and Morris, 727.
37. Ibid.
38. Ibid.
39. Pattison to Clinton, August 19, 1779, in *Memorial Centennial Celebration of the Battle of Paulus Hook*, 88.
40. Lee to Washington, August 21, 1779, Papers of the Continental Congress.
41. "Return of Prisoners at Powles Hook on the Morning of 19th of August, 1779," Papers of the Continental Congress.
42. Washington to Lee, August 23, 1779, *Writings of Washington*, vol. 16.
43. Lee to Washington, August 21, 1779, Papers of the Continental Congress.
44. Washington to the president of Congress, August 23, 1779, *Writings of Washington*, vol. 16.
45. Washington to John Park Custis, August 24, 1779, *Writings of Washington*, vol. 16
46. "*Pennsylvania Packet*, August 28, 1779," in *Memorial Centennial Celebration of the Battle of Paulus Hook*, Appendix 16.
47. *Memorial Centennial Celebration of the Battle of Paulus Hook*, Appendix 24.
48. Clinton, *The American Rebellion*, 140, note 7.
49. *Memorial of the Centennial Celebration of the Battle of Paulus Hook*, Appendices 21 and 22.
50. Townsend to Washington, September 18, 1779, George Washington Papers.
51. Townsend to Tallmadge, September 11, 1779, George Washington Papers.
52. Extract of Clinton to Germain, August 21, 1779, in Clinton, *The American Rebellion*, 417.
53. Clinton, *The American Rebellion*, 140.
54. Ibid., 147.
55. Washington to Benjamin Harrison, Oct. 25, 1779, *Writings of Washington*, vol. 17.
56. Washington to John Parke Custis, August 24, 1779, *Writings of Washington*, vol. 16.

Epilogue

1. Wright, *Continental Army*, 152.
2. Rose, *Washington's Spies*, 273, 278.
3. Ibid., 261, 271, 278.
4. Ibid., 278
5. Ibid., 276.
6. Court Martial Proceedings, 196–197.
7. E.A.H. Webb, *A History of the Services of the 17th (The Leicestershire) Regiment, Containing an Account of the Formation of the Regiment in 1688, and Its Subsequent Services, Revised and Continued to March 31st, 1912* (London: Vacher & Sons, 1912), 78–84.
8. Robinson Autobiography, *Two Centuries of Robinsons*, 93.
9. Ibid., 92.
10. Ibid., 94.
11. Ibid., 103.

12. Ibid., 108.
13. "Orderly Book of Captain Robert Gamble," 233–237, 242–245, 247, 258.
14. General Orders, September 21, 1779, *Writings of Washington*, vol. 16.
15. Wright, "Corps of Light Infantry," 457.
16. Loprieno, *Enterprise*, 81.
17. Bailey Pension Application, National Archives.
18. Vass Pension Deposition.
19. Ibid.
20. Peter Cliffe, "Hero's Early Life a Mystery; Francisco Wounded, Fought at Key Battles," *Washington Times*, August 27, 2009, B9.
21. Royster, *Revolutionary People at War*, 96.
22. Otho Williams to "D," May 22, 1783, Society of the Cincinnati.
23. John Dwight Kilbourne, *Virtutis Praemium: The Men Who Founded the State Society of the Cincinnati of Pennsylvania* (Rockport, ME: Picton, 1998), vol. 1, 276–277, 421.
24. Rose, *Washington's Spies*, 31–32.
25. Johnston, "Christian Febiger," *Magazine of American History* 6 (1881).
26. Ibid., 139.
27. As cited in Nelson, *Anthony Wayne*, 125.

Bibliography

Bank, R.A., ed. "Orderly Book of Captain Robert Gamble of the Second Virginia Regiment, Commanded by Colonel Christian Febiger, August 21–November 16, 1779." *Proceedings of the Virginia Historical Society at the Annual Meeting held December 21–22, 1891, with Historical Papers Read on the Occasion and Others.* Richmond: Virginia Historical Society, 1892.

Barber, John W., and Henry Howe. *Historical Collections of the State of New York, Containing a General Collection of the Most Interesting Facts, Traditions, Biographical Sketches, Anecdotes, &c., Relating to Its History and Antiquities, with Geographical Descriptions of Every Township in the State.* New York: S. Tuttle, 1842.

Bass, Robert D. *The Green Dragoon: The Lives of Banastre Tarleton and Mary Robinson.* New York: Henry Holt, 1957. Reprint, Columbia, SC: Sandlapper, 1973.

Baule, Stephen M. *British Army Officers Who Served in the American Revolution, 1775–1783.* With Stephen Gilbert. Westminster, MD: Heritage, 2004.

"Benedict Arnold, the Fighting Druggist." In "Nova et Vetera," *The British Medical Journal* 1, no. 4027 (March 12, 1938).

Berg, Fred Anderson. *Encyclopedia of Continental Army Units.* Harrisburg, PA: Stackpole, 1972.

Bodle, Wayne. *Valley Forge Winter: Civilians and Soldiers in War.* University Park: Penn State University Press, 2002.

Bolton, Robert, Jr. *History of the County of Westchester from Its First Settlement to the Present Time.* New York: Alexander S. Gould, 1848.

Boyle, Robert H. *The Hudson River: A Natural and Unnatural History.* New York: W.W. Norton, 1969.

Brown, Lloyd A. *Loyalist Operations at New Haven, Including Capt. Patrick Ferguson's Letter with Map Dated May 27, 1779, and Capt. Nathan Hubbel's Raid on New Haven, April 19, 1781.* Meriden, CT: Timothy Press, 1938.

Burnett, Edmund C., ed. *Letters of Delegates of Congress.* Vol. 3. Washington, D.C.: Carnegie Institute of Washington, 1926.

Burnham, John. Manuscript Narrative of an Officer of the Revolution, 1775–1784. Library of the Society of the Cincinnati, Washington, D.C.

Burrows, Edwin G., and Mike L. Wallace. *Gotham: A History of New York City to 1898.* New York: Oxford University Press, 1999.

Campbell, Marcia. *Revolutionary Services and Civil Life of General William Hull; Prepared from his Manuscripts, by His Daughter Mrs. Marcia Campbell, Together with the History of the Campaign of 1812 and the Surrender of the Post of Detroit.* New York: D. Appleton, 1848.

Chartand, Rene. *American Loyalist Troops, 1775–84.* Oxford and New York: Oxford, Osprey, 2008.

Clark, Thomas. *Naval History of the United States from the Commencement of the Revolutionary War to the Present Time.* Vol. 3. Philadelphia: M. Carey, 1814.

Clinton, Henry. *The American Rebellion: Sir Henry Clinton's Narrative of His Campaigns, 1775–1782, with an Appendix of Original Documents.* Edited by William B. Willcox. New Haven: Yale University Press, 1954.

_____. Manuscript Papers. William L. Clements Library, University of Michigan, Ann Arbor.

Cliffe, Peter. "Hero's Early Life a Mystery; Francisco Wounded, Fought at Key Battles." *Washington* (D.C.) *Times*, August 27, 2009.

Colledge, J.J. *Ships of the Royal Navy: The Complete Record of all Fighting Ships of the Royal Navy from the Fifteenth Century to the Present.* Annapolis: Naval Institute Press, 1969.

Collier, Sir George. *A Detail of Some Particular Services Performed in America, During the Years 1776, 1777, 1778, and 1779.* New York: Ithiel Town, 1835.

Commager, Henry Steele, and Richard B. Morris, eds. *The Spirit of 'Seventy-Six: The Story of the American Revolution as Told by Its Participants.* Indianapolis: Bobbs-Merrill, 1958. Reprint, New York: Da Capo, 1995.

Cook, Don. *The Long Fuse: How England Lost the American Colonies, 1760–1785.* New York: Atlantic Monthly Press, 1995.

Curtis, Edward L. *The British Army in the American Revolution.* Gansevoort, NY: Corner House Historical, 1998.

Dawson, Henry B. *The Assault on Stony Point by General Anthony Wayne, July 16, 1779, Prepared for the New York Historical Society and Read at Its Regular Meeting, April 1, 1862, with Some Illustrative Notes.* New York: New York Historical Society, 1863. Reprint, General Books, 2009.

Duncombe, Frances Riker, and Dorothy Humphreys Hinitt, eds. *The Burning of Bedford, July 1779: As Reported in Contemporary Documents and Eyewitness Accounts.* Bedford, NY: Bedford Historical Society, 1974.

Eberlein, Harold Donaldson, and Cortlandt Van Dyke Hubbard. *Diary of Independence Hall.* Philadelphia: J.B. Lippincott, 1948.

Farrier, George H., ed. *Memorial of the Centennial Celebration of the Battle of Paulus Hook, August 19th, 1879, with a History of the Early Settlement and Present Condition of Jersey City, NJ.* Jersey City: M. Mullone, 1879.

Febiger, Christian. Manuscript Papers. Personal Papers Collection, Library of Virginia, Richmond.

Ferling, John. *Almost a Miracle: The American Victory in the War of Independence.* New York: Oxford University Press, 2007.

Fischer, David Hackett. *Washington's Crossing.* New York: Oxford University Press, 2004.

Garden, Alexander. *Anecdotes of the American Revolution, Illustrative of the Talents and Virtues of the Heroes and Patriots Who Acted the Most Conspicuous Parts Therein, Second Series.* Charleston, SC: A.E. Miller, 1828.

Gratz, Simon. "Biography of General Richard Butler." *Pennsylvania Magazine of History and Biography* 7, no. 1 (1883).

Graydon, Alexander. *Memoirs of His Own Time, with Reminiscences of the Men and Events of the Revolution.* Edited by John Stockton Littell. Google Books edition. Philadelphia: Lindsay & Blakiston, 1846.

Green, Frank Bertangue. *The History of Rockland County.* Google Books edition. New York: A.S. Barnes, 1886.

Harris, Alexander. *Biographical History of Lancaster County: Being a History of Early Settlers and Eminent Men of the County, and Also Much Other Unpublished Information Chiefly of a Local Character.* Lancaster, PA: Elias Barr and Company, 1872.

Harris, Jay. *God's Country: A History of Pound Ridge, New York.* Chester, CT: Pequot, 1971.

Hayes, John T. *Connecticut's Revolutionary Cavalry, Sheldon's Horse.* Chester, CT: Pequot, 1975.

Heath, William. *Memoirs of Major General William Heath, by Himself.* "New Edition." New York: William Abatt, 1901.
Heitman, Francis Bernard. *Historical Register of Officers of the Continental Army During the War of the Revolution, April, 1775, to December, 1783.* Baltimore: Nichols, Killam & Maffitt, 1893. Reprint, Genealogical, 1967.
Higginbotham, Don. *Daniel Morgan, Revolutionary Rifleman.* Chapel Hill: University of North Carolina Press, 1961.
Hinman, Royal R., comp. "Connecticut Journal, July 7th, 1779." In *A Historical Collection of the Part Sustained by Connecticut During the War of the Revolution, with an Appendix Containing Important Letters, Depositions, &c, Written During the War.* Hartford, CT, 1842.
"History of Verplanck's Point." *New York Times.* March 8, 1986.
Hughes, B.P. *British Smooth Bore Artillery: The Muzzle Loading Artillery of the 18th and 19th Centuries.* London: Arms and Armour, 1969.
Jarvis, Julia. *Three Centuries of Robinsons: The Story of a Family.* Ontario, Canada: T.H. Best, 1967.
Johnston, Henry P. "Col. Christian Febiger of the Virginia Line of the Continental Army," *Magazine of American History* 6 (1881).
_____. *The Storming of Stony Point on the Hudson, Midnight, July 15, 1779.* New York: 1900. Reprint, New York: Da Capo, 1971.
Johnston, Henry Phelps. *Yale and Her Honor-Roll in the American Revolution, 1775–1783.* Google Books edition. New York: privately printed, 1888.
Jones, Thomas. *History of New York During the Revolutionary War, and of the Leading Events in the Other Colonies at that Period.* Edited by Edward Floyd De Lancey. Google Books edition. New York: New York Historical Society, 1879.
Journals of the Continental Congress. Washington, D.C.: Government Printing Office, 1908.
Kaplan, Roger. "The Hidden War: British Intelligence Operations During the American Revolution." *William and Mary Quarterly* 47, no. 1 (January 1990).
Keesey, Ruth M. "Loyalism in Bergen County, New Jersey." *William and Mary Quarterly* 18, no. 4 (October 1961).
Ketchum, Richard M. *Saratoga: Turning Point of America's Revolutionary War.* New York: Henry Holt, 1997.
Kilbourne, John Dwight. *Virutis Praeium: The Men Who Founded the State Society of the Cincinnati of Pennsylvania.* Vol. 1. Rockport, ME: Picton, 1998.
Kim, Song Buk. "The Limits of Politicization in the American Revolution: The Experience of Westchester County, New York." *Journal of American History* 80, no. 3 (December 1993).
Koke, Richard J. "The Britons Who Fought at Stony Point." *New York Historical Society Quarterly* 44, no. 1 (1960).
Lambert, Edward R. *History of the Colony of New Haven, Before and After the Union with Connecticut.* New Haven: Hitchcock and Stafford, 1838.
Leach, Charles. "Hospital Rock." *Hog River Journal* 2, no. 2 (February/March/April 2004).
Lee, Henry. *Memoirs of the War in the Southern Department of the United States.* Vol. 1. Philadelphia: Bradsford and Innskeep, 1812.
Leiby, Adrian C. *The Revolutionary War in the Hackensack Valley: The Jersey Dutch and the Neutral Ground, 1775–1783.* New Brunswick: Rutgers University Press, 1962.
Lengel, Edward L. *General George Washington: A Military Life,* New York: Random House, 2005.
Lesser, Charles H., ed. *The Sinews of Independence: Monthly Strength Reports of the Continental Army.* Chicago: University of Chicago Press, 1976.
Letter, Otho Williams. To "D," May 22, 1783. Library of the Society of the Cincinnati, Washington, D.C.
Loprieno, Don. *The Enterprise in Contemplation: The Midnight Assault of Stony Point.* Westminster, MD: Heritage, 2004.

Lossing, Benjamin J. *Eminent Americans: Brief Biographies of Three Hundred and Thirty Distinguished Persons*. New York: Mason and Brothers, 1857.
Malia, Peter J. *Visible Saints, West Haven Connecticut, 1648–1798*. Monroe, CT: Connecticut Press, 2009.
McLane, Allan. Manuscript Papers. New York Historical Society, New York, NY.
Minutes of the Committee and of the First Commission for Detecting and Defeating Conspiracies in the State of New York, December 11th 1776–September 28th 1778. Vol. 1. New York: 1879.
Moffat, Almet S. *Orange County, New York: A Narrative History*. Washingtonville, NY: A.S. Moffat, 1928.
Moore, Frank. *Diary of the American Revolution, from Newspapers and Original Documents, Volume II*. New York: Scribner and Sons, 1853.
Muster Roll of Thomas Boude's Company of Light Infantry in the Fifth Pennsylvania Regiment, Commanded by Col. Francis Johnston, for the Month of July 1779. Record Group 93, Roll 82, National Archives, Washington D.C.
Nelson, Paul David. *Anthony Wayne: Soldier of the Early Republic*. Bloomington: Indiana University Press, 1985.
_____. *William Tryon and the Course of Empire: A Life in British Imperial Service*. Chapel Hill: University of North Carolina Press, 1990.
Papers of the Continental Congress, 1774–1789, 5 vols. Washington, D.C.: National Archives and Records Service, 1978, Record Group 360, NARA M247.
Pasquale, Christopher D. *An Object of Great Importance: The Hudson River During the American War for Independence*. Baltimore: Publish America, 2007.
Pennsylvania Packet; or, the General Advertiser, July and December 1778.
Polf, William A. *Garrison Town: The British Occupation of New York City, 1776–1783*. Albany: New York State American Revolution Bicentennial Commission, 1976.
Posey, John Thornton. *General Thomas Posey: Son of the American Revolution*. East Lansing: Michigan State University Press, 1992.
Proceedings of a General Court Martial Held at New York on the Second of January and Continued by Adjournment to the Twentieth of February 1781, upon the Trial of Lieutenant Colonel Henry Johnson of the 17th Regiment of Foot. WO 71/152, National Archives, Kew, Richmond, Surrey, England.
Purcell, L. Edward. *Who Was Who in the American Revolution*. New York: Facts on File, 1993.
Purcell, L. Edward, and David F. Burg, eds. *World Almanac of the American Revolution*. New York: Pharos, 1992.
Randall, E.O. "How Governor Meigs Got His Name." *Ohio History* 16, no. 417.
Rankin, Hugh F., and George F. Scheer, eds. *Rebels and Redcoats: The American Revolution Through the Eyes of Those Who Fought and Lived It*. New York: World, 1957.
Ray, Deborah Wing, and Gloria P. Stewart. *Norwalk: Being an Historical Account of That Connecticut Town*. Canaan, NH: Norwalk Historical Society, 1979.
Reid, Stuart. *Soldiers of the Revolutionary War*. Oxford: Osprey, 2002.
Revolutionary War Pension Files, Record Group 15, National Archives, Washington, D.C.
Risch, Erna. *Supplying Washington's Army*. Washington, D.C.: Center of Military History, 1981.
Rose, Alexander. *Washington's Spies: The Story of America's First Spy Ring*. New York: Random House, 2006.
Royster, Charles. *Light Horse Harry Lee and the Legacy of the American Revolution*. Baton Rouge: Louisiana State University Press, 1981.
_____. *A Revolutionary People at War: The Continental Army and American Character, 1775–1783*. Chapel Hill: University of North Carolina Press, 1979.
Scheer, George F., and Hugh F. Rankin. *Rebels and Redcoats: The American Revolution Through the Eyes of Those Who Fought and Lived It*. New York: World, 1957.
Schenck, Elizabeth H. *The History of Fairfield, Fairfield County, Connecticut, from 1700 AD to 1800, Volume II*. New York: published by the author, 1905.

Selesky, Harold W. *A Demographic Survey of the Continental Army That Wintered at Valley Forge, 1777–1778*. New Haven, CT, 1987.

Sklarsky, I.W. *The Revolution's Boldest Venture: The Story of General "Mad" Anthony Wayne's Assault on Stony Point*. Poughkeepsie: Kennikat, 1965.

Sletcher, Michael. *New Haven: From Puritanism to the Age of Terrorism*. Chicago: Arcadia, 2004.

Smith, Paul H. "The American Loyalists: Notes on Their Organization and Numerical Strength." *William and Mary Quarterly* 25, no. 2 (April 1968).

Smith, William. *Historical Memoirs of William Smith, 1778–1783*. Edited by W.H.W. Sabine. New York: New York Times Publishing, 1971.

Smith, William Henry, ed. *The Life and Public Services of Arthur St. Clair, Soldier of the Revolutionary War, President of the Continental Congress, and Governor of the Northwestern Territory: Correspondence and Others Papers, Arranged and Annotated*. Cincinnati: Robert Clarke, 1881.

Spring, Matthew H. *With Zeal and Bayonets Only: The British Army on Campaign in North America, 1775–1783*. Norman: University of Oklahoma Press, 2008.

Starkey, Armstrong. "Paoli to Stony Point: Military Ethics and Weaponry During the American Revolution." *Journal of Military History* 58, no. 1 (January 1994).

Stiles, Ezra. *The Literary Diary of Ezra Stiles, D.D., LL.D., President of Yale College*. Vol. 2, March 14, 1776–December 31, 1781. New York: Scribner's Sons, 1901.

Steuben, Baron von. *Baron von Steuben's Revolutionary War Drill Manual: A Facsimile Reprint of the 1794 Edition*. New York: Dover, 1985.

Still, Bayrd. *Mirror for Gotham: New York as Seen by Contemporaries from Dutch Days to the Present*. New York: New York University Press, 1956.

Stille, Charles Janeway. *Major General Anthony Wayne and the Pennsylvania Line in the Continental Army*. 1893. Reprint, Gansevoort, NY: Corner House, 2000.

Symonds, Craig L. *A Battlefield Atlas of the American Revolution*. Baltimore: Nautical Aviation, 1986.

Tallmadge, Benjamin. *Memoir of Colonel Benjamin Tallmadge, Prepared by Himself, at the Request of His Children*. New York, 1858.

Thacher, James, M.D. *Military Journal During the American Revolutionary War, from 1776 to 1783, Describing the Events and Transactions of this Period, with Numerous Historical Facts and Anecdotes*. Hartford, CT: Silas Andrus & Son, 1854.

Townshend, Charles Hervey. *The British Invasion of New Haven, Connecticut, Together with Some Account of their Landing and Burning the Towns of Fairfield and Norwalk, July, 1779*. New Haven: Tuttle, Morehouse & Taylor, 1879.

A Treatise on Gun-Powder, a Treatise on Fire-Arms, and a Treatise on the Service of Artillery in Time of War, Translated from the Italian by Captain Thomson of the Royal Regiment of Artillery. London: Military Library at Whitehall, 1789.

Ward, Harry M. *The War for Independence and the Transformation of American Society*. Reprint, Routledge: London, 2003.

Washington, George. George Washington Papers at the Library of Congress, 1741–1799. Library of Congress, Manuscript Division.

_____. *The Writings of George Washington from the Original Manuscript Sources, 1745–1799*, vols. 11, 13, 14, 15, 16. Edited by John C. Fitzpatrick. Washington, D.C.: U.S. Government Printing Office, 1944.

Wayne, Anthony. Manuscript Papers. Manuscript Collection #699, Historical Society of Pennsylvania, Philadelphia.

Webb, E.A.H. *A History of the Services of the 17th (The Leicestershire) Regiment, Containing an Account of the Formation of the Regiment in 1688, and Its Subsequent Services, Revised and Continued to March 31st, 1912*. London: Vacher & Sons, 1912.

Weigly, Russell F. *Philadelphia: A 300-Year History*. New York: W.W. Norton, 1982.

Willcox, William B. *Portrait of a General: Sir Henry Clinton in the War for Independence*. New York: Alfred A. Knopf, 1962.

Winfield, Charles H. *History of the County of Hudson, New Jersey, from Its Earliest Settlement to the Present Time*. New York: Kennard & Hay, 1874.

Wright, John W. "The Corps of Light Infantry in the Continental Army. *American Historical Review* 31, no. 3 (April 1926).

_____. "Notes on the Continental Army." *William and Mary Quarterly* 12, no. 2 (April 1932), Second Series.

Wright, Robert K. *The Continental Army*. Washington, D.C.: Center of Military History, 2000.

Wyatt, Thomas. *Memoirs of the Generals, Commodores, and Other Commanders Who Distinguished Themselves in the American Army and Navy During the War of the Revolution and 1812, and Who Were Presented with Medals by Congress for Their Gallant Services*. Philadelphia: Corey and Hart, 1847.

Index

Adams, John 103, 193
Adams, Samuel 103
Albany, New York 30, 51, 157, 189
American Philosophical Society 193
Andre, Maj. (and Capt) John 20, 53, 54, 58–59, 61, 95, 181–182, 193
Andrews, Capt. Jedediah 116
Anthony's Nose 52
Arbuthnot, Adm. Marriot 178–179
Archer, Henry 152, 161–162
Armstrong, Capt. Thomas 59
Armstrong, Lt. William 138–139, 149
Arnold, Maj. Gen. Benedict 21–22, 54, 104, 181–182, 185, 189
Arnold, Pvt. Samuel 75, 157, 189
Ash, Cpl. John 141, 151
Auchmuty, Richard 154, 157

Baily, Cpl. Jonathan 189
Baltimore, Maryland 46, 165, 193
Bartlett, Deacon 116
Bartlett, Sam 116
Baylor, Col. Thomas 90, 130
Baylor, Pennsylvania 130
Beacon Hill 112, 113
Bear Mountain 135
Beecher, Lyman 116
Beers, Elias 115
Beers, Nathan 115
Bemis Heights, battle of 14
Bergen County, New Jersey 101, 169–170
Bergen's Point 169
Bissell, Capt. Russell 196
Black Rock, Connecticut 186
Black Rock Fort (Fairfield) 118, 120
Black Rock Fort (New Haven) 112, 116
Blackman, John 159

Bland, Col. Theodoric 90
Blue Book 17, 27, 62, 126, 131, 182; *see also Regulations for the Order and Discipline of the Troops of the United States, Part I*
Boston, Massachusetts 13, 41, 50, 71, 90, 104, 106, 112, 131, 133, 139, 162
Boston Harbor 83
Botetcourt County, Virginia 72–73
Boude, Capt. Thomas 73, 190
Bradley, Capt. Josiah 111–112
Bradley, Capt. William 110
Brandywine, battle of 14–16
Bray, Pvt. John 75
Breed's Hill (or Bunker Hill) 13, 50, 41, 47, 71, 133
Brewster, Lt. Caleb 44–45, 57, 186; *see also* Culper Ring
Bronx River 37, 95, 101
Brookline, New York 37
Brooks, Capt. Lemuel 121
Buckingham County, Virginia 75
Bulkley, Jonathan 121
Bulkley, Mrs. 121
Burnham, Capt. John 134
Burr, Col. Aaron 108, 110
Burton, Pvt. Marshall 75
Butler, Col. Richard 70–71, 76, 125, 127, 136, 157, 161, 188, 190

Cambridge, Massachusetts 13, 24, 131
HMS *Camilla* 58–59, 102, 107, 117
Campbell, Gen. Archibald 45
Campbell, Capt. Lawrence 139–140, 145, 152
Campbell, Adjutant William 108
Canada 12–14, 18, 22, 24, 30, 33, 51, 53, 131, 160–161, 179, 191

Index

Canvas Town 38
Carleton, Guy 183
Carlisle, Abraham 20
Carlisle Commission 17
Carmel, Connecticut 105
Carson, Elizabeth 71
Case, Joseph 159
Chadd's Ford 32
Champion, Lt. Col. Henry 133, 189
Charleston, South Carolina 13–14, 47, 179, 184, 186, 190, 192
Chesapeake Bay 14, 32, 50, 55, 183
Chester County, Pennsylvania 29, 30
Chrystie, Capt. James 134
City Point (Hopewell), Virginia 75
Clark, Col. George Rogers 18
Clark, Maj. Jonathan 171, 173–174
Clayton, Capt. Robert 140, 148–149
Clinton, Lt. Gen. Henry 1–4, 12–14, 17–18, 23–24, 32, 35, 37, 41, 63–64, 65, 67, 83, 85–87, 95, 101, 103, 107, 113, 117, 121, 123–124, 128–129, 155, 158, 161, 165, 175, 178–179, 181, 183; background 47; plans Connecticut raids 81–82, 104, 107; post-Revolution 184; reaction to Stony Point assault 156–157; 159–160; strategic plans 48–55, 57–62; *see also* Hudson River; Tryon, Brig. Gen. William
Cockburne, Lt. 174
Collier, Commodore George 54–55, 57–60, 82, 102, 107, 111, 113–115; 118–120, 156–157, 160, 163, 166, 179, 184
Committee of Conference 22–24, 27
Concord, Massachusetts 13, 28
Congress, Continental 11–13, 16–19, 20–24, 28, 30–32, 34–35, 39, 43, 50, 62, 66, 67, 70, 72–73, 90, 102, 105, 108, 124, 128, 136, 154, 158–163, 165–166, 168–169, 177–178, 188, 191–195
Connecticut (state, colony) 1–5, 10–11, 20, 36, 39, 44–46, 48, 53, 61–63, 65, 85–86, 88–91, 93, 96, 131, 165–166, 180, 185–186; *see also* Carmel; Danbury; Darby; Derby; East Haven; Eddington; Fairfield; Guilford; Hamden; Hartford; Litchfield; Lyme; Meriden; New Haven; New London; North Haven; Norwalk; Norwich; Redding; Sag Harbor; Stamford
Connecticut troops 133, 142, 144–145, 148, 151–152, 163, 169, 189; *see also* First Connecticut Regiment; Sixth Connecticut Regiment
Cork, Ireland 38, 103
Cornwallis, row-galley 59, 81, 127, 136, 153
Cornwallis, Lt. Gen. Charles 160, 183–184, 194, 195

Corps of Light Infantry 3, 44, 64, 89, 125–126, 155, 185, 187, 193; background 27–29; formation 35, 68–76; post–Stony Point assault 159, 161–163, 167, 188–191; at Stony Point 7–10, 127, 130, 135–154, 157–159; Wayne, Anthony 131–133; *see also* Connecticut troops; Maryland troops; New Pennsylvania troops; Stony Point; Washington, George; Wayne, Anthony
Corsica 73
Crawford, John 96, 101
Culper Ring 36, 45, 61, 66, 102, 126, 165, 178, 185–186; *see also* Brewster, Caleb; Tallmadge, Benjamin; Townsend, Robert; Washington, Commander in Chief George; Woodhull, Abraham
Cummings, Lt. Patrick 140, 147, 149
Cunningham, William 39
Custis, John Parke 178, 180

Daggett, Naphtali 108–111
Danbury, Connecticut 11, 121
Darby, Capt. William 139, 141
Darby, Connecticut 110
Darby Pike 110
Darby's Bridge 110
Davies, Cpl. Simon 138, 141, 142, 151
Dayton, Capt. Ebenezer 103
Deane, Silas 103, 104
Defence, privateer 118
De Kalb, Maj. Gen. Johann 64, 67
De Lancey, Oliver 39
Delaney, Sharp 136
Delaware (state) 191; *see also* Wilmington
Delaware Militia 126; *see also* Delaware troops
Delaware Regiment 68; *see also* Delaware troops
Delaware River 73, 92
Delaware troops 11, 68, 126, 169; *see also* Delaware Militia; Delaware Regiment
Denmark 71
Derby, Connecticut 116
d'Estaing, Vice Admiral 18, 44
Detroit 196
Detroit River 191
Donderberg Mountain 135
Dorchester Heights 13
Douwe's Ferry 171–172, 174–175, 177
Duchess County, New York 85
HMS *Duchess of Gordon* 106
Dundass, Capt. 176

East Haven, Connecticut 113
East River 50
Easttown, Pennsylvania 29–30

Eddington, Connecticut 108
Eighth Massachusetts Regiment 133
Eighth Pennsylvania Regiment 70
Eighth Virginia Regiment 73, 75, 146
Eliot, Rev. Andrew 118–120
Elizabeth River 57
English, Benjamin 115
English Neighborhood, New Jersey 172, 176
Erie, Pennsylvania 196
Eutaw Springs 193

Fairfield, Connecticut 5, 103, 117–123, 186
Fallen Timbers, battle of 195–196
Fanning, Col. Edmund 111, 113
Febiger, Col. Christian 4, 8, 67, 71–73, 131, 134–138, 142, 145–153, 157, 162, 163, 191, 192
Fell, John 170
Fifth North Carolina Regiment 59
Fifth Pennsylvania Regiment 73, 190
Fifth Troop, Virginia Light Horse 167
Fifty-fourth Regiment of Foot 82, 107, 122
First Connecticut Regiment 152
First Maryland Regiment 190
First New York Regiment 62
First Pennsylvania Brigade 193
First Regiment of Continental Light Dragoons 167
First Virginia Regiment 75
Fishbourne, Capt. Henry 152, 154
Fishkill, New York 40, 55, 63, 121
Fitzgerald, William 159
Fleury, Lt. Col. Francois-Louis Tesseidre de 9, 73, 75, 142, 144, 148, 151, 157, 162, 188
Floyd, Mary 185
Floyd, William 185
Flushing, New York 37, 82, 93
Forsythe, Capt. Robert 174–175, 177
Fort Arnold 52
Fort Clinton 52
Fort Constitution 51, 52
Fort Detroit 191
Fort Independence 52
Fort Lafayette 53, 58–59, 62, 79, 85, 155–156; *see also* Verplanck's Point
Fort Mifflin 73
Fort Montgomery 51–52, 62, 65–66, 68, 76, 85, 128, 138, 159
Fort Nelson 57
Fort Putnam 52
Fort St. George 185
Fort Ticonderoga 30–31, 33–34
Fourth Light Dragoons 89, 97
Fourth Pennsylvania Battalion 30–31, 33–34, 73
France, alliance, supplies 17, 22, 25–27, 160

Francisco, Pvt. Peter 75, 148, 190
Franklin, Benjamin 30, 188
Fraser, Maj. Gen. Simon 83, 85
Freeman's Farm, battle of 14, 28, 133, 149
French and Indian War 29, 34, 39, 41, 62

Gage, Lt. Gen. Thomas 13, 28
Gamecock, privateer 121
Garth, Maj. Gen. George 107–109, 110–113, 119–120, 122–123, 178, 184
Gates, Maj. Gen. Horatio 14, 31, 62, 122, 162
General Washington, privateer 102
Georgia 12, 18, 54, 193, 195
Germain, Lord George 48–50, 55, 83, 160, 179, 183
Germantown, battle of 14, 16, 32, 35, 63, 70–75, 126, 151
Gibbon, Lt. James 74, 144, 147, 150–152, 162, 191
Gilbert, Capt. John 115
Glasgow, Scotland 83
Glean, Anthony 159
Glover, Col. John 122
Goodrich, Elizur 108–109
Gordon, Lt. Col. Cosmo 176
Graydon, Alexander 33
Green Spring, Virginia 195
Greene, Maj. Gen. Nathaniel 52, 181, 193
Grey, Gen. Charles 130
HMS *Greyhound* 102, 107
Grumman's Hill 122–123
Guilford, Connecticut 116

Hackensack River 169, 172
Haldimand, Gen. Frederick 160–161, 179
Hale, Capt. Nathan 41–44, 182, 192
Hall, Col. Street 116
Hamden, Connecticut 116
Hamilton, Col. Alexander 26, 63, 158, 189, 193
Hancock, John 103
Handy, Capt. Levin 171, 174–175, 177
Harlem, New York 37
Harrison, Benjamin 23, 46, 180
Hartford, Connecticut 104
Hay, Maj. Samuel 33–34, 71, 144, 147, 157
Heath, Maj. Gen. William 89–90, 130, 167
Hell Gate 46
Hessians 11, 14, 32, 37, 57–58, 79–80, 82, 95, 103, 107, 111, 118–120, 122, 172–175
Higday, George 101
Hillhouse, Capt. James 108, 110
Holbrook, Lt. John 116
Horndon, Lt. William 139, 141, 145, 151, 153
Howe, Lt. Gen. William 13–14, 17, 20–21, 32–33, 37, 39, 43, 50, 83, 90, 106, 184

Hoyt, George 119, 121
Hoyt, Jared 99
Hudson, Henry 77
Hudson River 1–4, 7–12, 20, 37, 39–40, 51–52; 169–170; American defenses 62–67, 125; American intelligence 63; British advance in 1779 59–60; British fortifications 78–81; British plans for 1779 55, 58, 60; collapse of British offensive 160, 179–180; crisis in June 1779 62–67; fortifications 52–53; geography and colonial history 77–78; later British attempts 181–182; strategic importance 51, 57; Washington's concerns 123; *see also* Clinton, Lt. Gen. Henry; Fort Arnold; Fort Clinton; Fort Constitution; Fort Lafayette; Fort Montgomery; Fort Nelson; Fort Putnam; Stony Point; Washington, Commander in Chief George; Woodhull, Abraham
Hull, Maj. William 4, 9, 133, 136, 142, 144–150, 152–153, 157, 188, 191
Huntington, Long Island 121, 123
Hussar, row-galley 102, 116, 120

Independence Hall 21
Indiana Territory 192
Intolerable Acts 30
Invalid Battalion 171
Iroquois Confederacy 11, 23, 27; *see also* Six Nations, Tribes of
Irvine, Col. William 31

James River 195
Jameson, Lt. Col. John 182
Jarvis, Capt. Isaac 118–120
Jay, John 154, 162–163, 193
Jennings, Isaac 120
"Jimmy the Drover," 194
Johnson, Lt. Col. Henry 83, 85–86, 139–140, 147–150, 153, 158, 186, 187; *see also* Seventeenth Regiment of Foot

Kaskaskia 18
Kennedy, John 115
Kenzie's Point 118
Kimberly, Lt. Aziel 105
King Charles I 167
King George II 78
King George III 17, 36–37, 39, 83, 114, 183–184
King James II 82
King Louis XVI 17
King's American Regiment 40
King's Ferry 1, 58–60, 61, 63, 65, 67–68, 77–78, 86, 88, 93, 107, 125, 153, 160, 179, 180–181

King's Highway 55, 78
Kingsbridge 37, 58, 83, 95
Knowlton, Lt. Col. Thomas 41
Knox, Lt. George 8–9, 142, 152, 162
Knox, Maj. Gen. Henry 26, 52, 64, 182
Kosciusko, Gen. Thaddeus 52

Lady Washington, row-galley 159
Lafayette, Maj. Gen. Marquis de 12, 73, 127, 183, 189, 195
Lake Champlain 30, 187
Lancaster, Pennsylvania 158, 187
Landgrave Regiment 82, 118, 120, 122; *see also* Hessians
Laurens, Henry 19, 21–22, 193
Leavenworth, Maj. Eli 89, 96, 101
Leavenworth's Ferry 113
Lee, Maj. Gen. Charles 32, 69, 95, 104, 161
Lee, Maj. Henry 3, 66, 95, 126–127, 134, 136, 154, 157, 162, 167, 171–178, 181, 192–193
Lee, Richard 167
Lee, Robert E. 193
Leni Lenape Tribe 195
Lewis, Anne 186
Lewis, Jonathan 186
Lexington, Massachusetts 13, 28, 131
Light Infantry (British) 27–28, 58, 79, 82, 107, 110, 175–176
Lincoln, Gen. Benjamin 191
Litchfield, Connecticut 133, 185
Lockwood, Maj. Ebenezer 89, 96
Lockwood, Capt. Joseph 88, 99
London, England 13, 17, 37, 48, 55, 160, 184
London Trade 38, 45
Long Island 14, 36, 39, 40–42, 47, 50, 62, 85, 86, 91, 93, 95, 101, 103, 121, 126, 131, 156, 167, 185; *see also* New York (state and colony)
Long Island Sound 1, 50, 87, 92, 102–103, 118, 121, 123, 157, 165, 186; *see also* Long Island
Lord Cathcart's Legion 63
Loyal American Regiment 40, 58, 79, 82, 85, 106, 139–140, 148, 153, 187; *see also* Robinson, Col. Beverly; Robinson, Ens. Frederick; Robinson, Capt. Morris; Stony Point
Lyme, Connecticut 104

Madison, James 191
Mamaroneck, New York 124, 156
Manhattan 14, 28, 36–37, 39, 41–42, 43, 45–46, 50–55, 58, 61, 67, 83, 85, 92, 95, 129, 160, 165, 169, 170, 179, 181, 186–187, 191; *see also* New York City

Marion, Col. Francis 193
Martlaer's Rock 51
Maryland (state) 11, 103; *see also* Baltimore
Maryland Division 64, 68
Maryland troops 7, 13, 62, 64, 66, 68, 70, 74, 126, 144, 169, 171, 174, 190; *see also* First Maryland Regiment; Maryland Division; Second Maryland Regiment
Matlock, Pvt. William 188
Maxwell, Brig. Gen. William 28
Maynard, Capt. 176
McAllister, Lt. Archibald 174–175, 177–178
McCullough, Lt. James 73, 144
McDougall, Maj. Gen. Alexander 40, 52, 62–63, 65–66, 89, 155, 159, 167
McDowell, John Lt. 146
McKenzie, Samuel 74, 154, 162
McLane, Capt. Allan 76, 126–128, 169, 170–172, 191
Meigs, Jonathan 131
Meigs, Lt. Col. Return 131, 133, 136–137, 142, 148, 152, 154, 157, 188, 189
Mercerau, John 66
Meriden, Connecticut 116
Miami Tribe 195
Michigan Territory 191
Middlebrook, New Jersey 24–25, 35, 40, 61–62, 64, 66, 73
Mile Square, New York 93, 95–96
Milford Hill 108
Monmouth Courthouse, New Jersey, battle of 18, 35, 70–73, 75, 95, 133, 162–163
Montgomery, Gen. Richard 51
Morgan, Col. Daniel 35, 184
Morris, Capt. Amos 111–112
Morris, Gouverneur 191
Morristown, New Jersey 31, 194
Moylan, Col. Stephen 89
Muhlenberg, Brig. Gen. Peter 134
Murfree, Maj. Hardy 133, 138, 188

Nairne, Lt. William 140, 144–145, 149
Nelson, Horatio 38
New Amsterdam 51
New Hampshire 11, 74
New Haven, Connecticut 1, 5, 103–120, 122–123, 188
New Jersey (state) 1, 11–12, 14, 18, 25–26, 28, 31–32, 37, 39, 41, 43, 49, 53–55, 60–64, 66, 70, 81, 83, 85, 95, 106, 131, 169–170, 181, 194; *see also* Bergen County; English Neighborhood; Middlebrook; Monmouth Court House; Morristown; Newark; Paulus Hook; Perth Amboy; Princeton, battle of; Trenton
New Jersey militia 66
New Jersey troops 11, 28, 66, 169; *see also* New Jersey militia; Second New Jersey Regiment
New London, Connecticut 45, 93, 103–104, 122, 124
New Windsor, New York 125, 128, 154–155, 161, 177
New York City 2–4, 11–12, 14, 17–18, 35–37, 39, 43–45, 47–49, 51–53, 58, 61–63, 81–82, 101–103, 118, 135, 157, 160, 164–165, 169–170, 174, 178–186
New York (state and colony) 1–3, 7, 10–12, 14, 18, 27, 39–41, 50, 52–55, 57, 60, 63–67, 72, 78, 82–83, 85–86, 88, 99–101, 106, 115, 129, 156, 160, 165, 179, 187; *see also* Albany; Brookline; Duchess County; Fishkill; Flushing; Harlem; Long Island; Mamaroneck; Manhattan; Mile Square; New Windsor; New York City; Peekskill; Pound Ridge; Queensboro; Sandy Beach; Smith's Clove; Throg's Neck; West Point; Westchester County; White Plains
New York troops 11, 30, 62, 65–66, 87; *see also* First New York Regiment
Newark, New Jersey 176
Newport, Rhode Island 11–12, 14, 18, 22–23, 44, 47–48, 73, 82, 102, 107
Newton, Cpl. John 141, 147–148
Newton, Massachusetts 191
Niagara Region 23, 27
Ninth Pennsylvania Regiment 70, 142
Nixon, Brig. Gen. John 155
Noble, Pvt. James 74–75, 151
North Carolina 7, 11, 66, 71, 133, 136–138, 142
North Haven, Connecticut 116
Norwalk, Connecticut 44, 103, 121–123
Norwich, Connecticut 104
Nova Scotia 13–14, 30, 82, 187

Oliver Cromwell, privateer 118
Otis, James 103

Painter, Thomas 105–109
Paoli, Pennsylvania 33–35, 53, 71, 73, 75, 130–131
Pardee, Joseph 112
Parsons, Brig. Gen. Samuel 63, 67, 122–123
Patterson, Brig. Gen. John 155
Pattison, Brig. Gen. James 58–59, 78, 172, 176
Paulus Hook 2, 3, 168–180, 191–192; *see also* Lee, Maj. Henry; New Jersey (state)
Peekskill, New York 39, 52, 63
Pennsylvania (state) 11, 14, 20–21, 27, 29–30, 33, 43, 53, 75, 130, 158, 161, 166, 187,

190–193, 196; *see also* Baylor; Chester County; Erie; Lancaster; Paoli; Philadelphia; Presque Isle; Radnor Township
Pennsylvania Packet, newspaper 19, 21, 178
Pennsylvania troops 13, 30–35, 62, 64, 66, 68, 70–71; 73–75, 126, 142, 144, 169, 190, 193–195; *see also* Eighth Pennsylvania Regiment; Fifth Pennsylvania Regiment; First Pennsylvania Brigade; Fourth Pennsylvania Battalion; Ninth Pennsylvania Regiment; Second Pennsylvania Regiment; Sixth Pennsylvania Regiment; Tenth Pennsylvania Regiment
Penobscot Bay 3, 160, 166
Penrose, Mary 30; *see also* Wayne, Polly
Perth Amboy, New Jersey 11, 32
Peyton, Capt. Henry 175, 177
Philadelphia, Pennsylvania 11–14, 17–22, 24, 28, 30, 35, 37, 46, 49, 53–54, 68, 71, 76, 125–126, 161, 166, 177–178, 182, 191–194
Philadelphia Academy 29
Philadelphia campaign 2, 28, 32–33, 52, 83, 92, 95
HMS *Phoenix* 170
Portsmouth, Virginia 57
Posey, Maj. Thomas 72–73, 135–136, 144, 146, 148–151, 188, 192, 195
Pound Ridge, New York 5, 87–90, 93–101
Presque Isle, Pennsylvania 196
Princeton, New Jersey, battle of 14, 34, 47, 83, 130, 133, 167, 194
Prior's Mill 174–175
privateering 37, 50, 62, 81–82, 93, 116, 118, 102–103, 121, 179
Putnam, Maj. Gen. Israel 89
Putnam, Col. Rufus 155
Pyles, Col. John 193

Quartermaster General Department 17, 25, 95
Quebec, assault on 13, 30, 52, 71, 131
Quebec city 71
Queensboro, New York 135
Quinnipac River 112–113

Radnor Township, Pennsylvania 196
HMS *Rainbow* 54, 57
Ranger, privateer 121
Redding, Connecticut 62–63
Reed, Joseph 166
Reed, Capt. Phillip 168
Regulations for the Order and Discipline of the Troops of the United States, Part I 64; *see also* Blue Book

Revenue Cutter Service 186
Rhode Island 11, 14, 18, 45, 46, 73, 82, 93, 184, 190
Rivington's Royal Gazette newspaper 49, 99
Roberts, Lt. John 81, 140, 148, 152
Robinson, Augusta 187
Robinson, Col. Beverly 85
Robinson, Beverly, Jr. 85
Robinson, Ens. Frederick 85–86, 149–150, 187
Robinson, John 85
Robinson, Capt. Morris 85–86, 187
Rochambeau, Lt. Gen. Jean 183
HMS *Roebuck* 170
Rogers, Cpl. Patrick 63
Rogers, Robert 39, 53
Rogers's Rangers 39, 41
HMS *Rose* 170
Ross, Lt. John 139–142, 147, 149–150
Rudulph, Lt. Michael 172, 177–178

Sabin, Lt. Col. Hezekiah 108, 110
Sackett, Nathaniel 43–444, 92
Sag Harbor, Connecticut 131
St. Clair, Maj. Gen. Arthur 34, 63–64, 66, 74
Sandy Beach, New York 125–127, 131, 133–135, 159, 188
Santa Cruz (St. Croix) 71
Saratoga, battle of and campaign 14, 28, 51, 70, 72, 74, 85, 122, 133, 162
Savannah, Georgia 3, 18, 23, 45, 48–49, 85, 195
Savin Rock 105, 107
Scammell, Adjutant Gen. Alexander 69, 74
Schuyler, Brig. Gen. Phillip 30
HMS *Scorpion* 102, 107
Scott, Brig. Gen. Charles 28–29, 44–45
Second Continental Light Dragoons 44, 65, 89, 91, 92, 98–99, 101, 121, 185
Second Maryland Regiment 70
Second New Jersey Regiment 63
Second Pennsylvania Regiment 74
Second Virginia Regiment 67, 71–72, 191
Seldon, Capt. Ezra 145
Setauket, Long Island 36, 44–45, 91–92, 185
Seventeenth Regiment of Foot 58, 79, 80, 82–86, 106, 130, 138–141, 143, 145–154, 157–158, 152, 186–187, 195
Seventh Virginia Regiment 72–73, 192
Seventy-first Regiment of Foot 82–83, 85, 104, 139, 144, 147, 151, 154
Sharon, Georgia 195
Shawnee Tribe 195
Shay's Rebellion 191

Shelburne, Lord 183
Sheldon, Maj. Elisha 89–91, 96, 98
Shelton, Capt. Clough 148
Sherman, Lt. Col. Isaac 131, 152, 188
Shreve, Col. Israel 131, 152, 188
Simpson, Lt. William 140, 147–148, 151
Six Nations, Tribes of 78; *see also* Iroquois Confederacy
Sixth Connecticut Regiment 89, 91
Sixth Pennsylvania Regiment 33, 71, 74, 144
Sixty-fourth Regiment of Foot 58, 79–80, 82
Sixty-third Regiment of Foot 58, 80, 82, 86
Smith, Joshua Hett 181
Smith, Meriwether 22
Smith, William 49, 60, 78, 107
Smith's Clove, New York 64, 66–68, 70–71, 75–76, 81, 89, 125, 168
Smith's Point 185
Smith's Tavern 66
South Carolina 13, 85, 106, 179, 184, 186, 189–190, 192
Spotsylvania County, Virginia 75, 192
Springsteel Farm 135
Stamford, Connecticut 88, 103
Stansbury, Joseph 54
Staten Island 37, 39, 66, 70, 181
Sterling, Scotland 83
Steuben, Maj. Gen. Frederick 17, 27–28, 62–63, 73–74, 157, 168, 182, 189
Stewart, Maj. John 70, 144, 147, 150–151, 157, 161–162, 190
Stiles, Ezra 105–106, 108–110, 113, 117, 188
Stirling, Maj. Gen. Alexander 64, 66, 157, 171, 176–177
Stony Point 2–5, 7–10, 53, 58–60, 62, 65, 67, 76–87, 106, 126–130, 132–155, 156, 167, 169–170, 172, 178–181, 186–195
Sullivan, Gen. John 30
Surrey, England 106
Sutherland, Maj. William 171, 173–178

Tallmadge, Maj. Benjamin 4, 36, 43–46, 87, 89–93, 95–98, 101, 121, 133, 182, 185
Tarleton, Lt. Col. Banastre 93–101, 168, 184–185, 190, 193
HMS *Tartar* 170
Taswell, Sgt. John 178
Taylor, Lt. Timothy 152
Tenth Pennsylvania Regiment 71, 75
Tenth Virginia Regiment 75
Tew, Capt. Francis 83, 86, 140, 149–150
Thacher, James, Dr. 25–26, 40
Third Continental Dragoons 130
Thirty-third Regiment 58, 79, 82
Throg's Neck, New York 124, 156

Tiffin, Capt. William 140, 148, 153
Tilghman, Col. Tench 158
Tobago 187
Torn Mountain 135
Townsend, Robert 165, 178–179, 186; *see also* Culper Ring
Trenton, New Jersey 8, 14, 34, 47, 129–130, 133
Trois Riveres 31, 74
Trumbull, Jonathan, Gov. 39, 63, 89, 122–123
Tuttle, Elisha 115–116
Tuttle, Joseph 112
Twenty-third Regiment of Foot 58, 79, 82
Tyron, Brig. Gen. William 61, 82, 87, 101–104, 106–107, 118–124, 156, 184

Valley Forge 8, 14, 17, 25, 28, 32–33, 69, 72–73, 75, 92, 95, 194
Van Buskirk, Abraham 170, 172, 176–177
Van Vorst, Cornelius 169
Vass, Pvt. Vincent 75, 135, 138, 145, 150, 157, 189–190
Vaughan, John Maj. Gen. 58–59, 79, 82, 85
Verplanck's Point 53, 60, 67, 78–79, 82, 85, 134, 136, 150, 153, 155–156, 159–160, 166, 180–181; *see also* Fort Lafayette
Vincennes 18
Virginia (state) 12, 16, 21, 25–26, 28, 35, 45, 50, 55, 57, 60–61, 75, 90, 103, 135, 167, 180, 183, 185, 189, 190–195; *see also* Botetcourt County; Buckingham County; City Point; Green Spring; Portsmouth; Spotsylvania County; Yorktown
HMS *Virginia* 102, 107
Virginia Division 64; *see also* Virginia Troops
Virginia troops 7, 8, 11, 13, 62, 64, 66–68, 72–75, 126, 142, 146, 148, 150, 159, 169, 171–175, 179, 190, 191, 195; *see also* Eighth Virginia Regiment; Fifth Troop, Virginia Light Horse; First Virginia Regiment; Second Virginia Regiment; Seventh Virginia Regiment; Tenth Virginia Regiment
Volunteers of Ireland 40, 47
Von Knyphausen Regiment 172; *see also* Hessians
Von Schallern, Capt. 173–174
HMS *Vulture* 59, 81–82, 127, 136, 138, 152–153, 181–182, 186

Wadsworth, Theo 154
Wallace, J.C. 196
Wallace, Ens. Thomas 73

Ward, Gen. Artemus 13, 116
Warren, Joseph 103
Washington, Commander in Chief George 1–4, 8, 10–12, 47, 49–50, 55, 133, 138, 152, 156, 182–184, 188–189, 192–195; campaign plans 12–13, 23–24; campaign reactions 179–181; concerns in 1779 22–23, 62; experiences prior to 1779 13–18; forms cavalry corps 89–92; forms Light Infantry 28–29, 68–76; intelligence operations 36, 40–46, 53, 101–102, 185–186; at Middlebrook 25–27; at Philadelphia 19–24; plans Paulus Hook raid 165–167, 171; plans Stony Point assault 125–131, 134, 136–137; responds to British offensive 61–67, 81, 89, 121–124; responds to Paulus Hook raid 177–179; responds to Stony Point assault 154–155, 157–162; selects Wayne to command Light Infantry 33–35; on Stony Pont 78; on supplies 22; views on Hudson River 51–52; *see also* Corps of Light Infantry; Culper Ring; Hudson River; Middlebrook, New Jersey; New Jersey (state); Paulus Hook; Stony Point; Tallmadge, Maj. Benjamin; Wayne, Anthony; Woodhull, Abraham
Washington, John Augustine vi
Washington, Col. William 193
Wayne, Ann 29
Wayne, Brig. Gen. Anthony 3–4, 7–10, 27, 53, 63, 68–71, 73–76, 167, 171–172, 187–189; appointed to Light Infantry 35; background 29–34; plans Stony Point assault 125–132; post–Revolution 193–196; at Stony Point 134–138, 142–148, 151–155, 157–163; *see also* Corps of Light Infantry; Stony Point
Wayne, Hannah 29
Wayne, Isaac 29, 196
Wayne, Margaretta 196
Wayne, Polly 34, 76
Waynesborough 29, 196

Webster, Noah 104
Webster, Col. William 184
Welch Fusiliers 107, 111
Welles, George 108
West, Cpl. William 151
West Bridge 110
West Haven, Connecticut 5, 105, 108, 131
West Indies 18, 21, 37, 48, 71, 83, 187
West Point, New York 1, 51–52, 54–55, 61–67, 76, 89, 122, 125, 133, 159–160, 166, 179, 181–182; *see also* Hudson River; New York (state and colony)
West River 110
Westchester County, New York 39–40, 44, 58, 63, 65, 81, 87, 88–90, 92, 95, 101, 128, 170, 185
Wethersfield, Connecticut 91–92
Whiskey Rebellion 193
White Plains, New York 40, 62–63, 90–91
Whiting, Col. 119, 121
Williams, John 159
Williams, Lt. Col. Otho 190
Williston, Noah 105, 108
Williston, Payson 108
Wilmington, Delaware 191
Wilmot, Lt. John 146
Wilson, Isaac 159
Windham, Connecticut 104
Wolcott, Gen. Oliver 123
Woodhull, Abraham 36, 40, 44–46, 57, 61, 66, 92–93, 101, 122, 165, 178, 186; *see also* Culper Ring
Woodhull, Elizabeth 186
Woodhull, Jessie 186
Wyandot Tribe 195

Yale College 42, 91, 103–105, 108–111. 117, 133, 188; *see also* Hale, Capt. Nathan; Hull, Maj. William; New Haven, Connecticut; Tallmadge, Maj. Benjamin
Yorktown, Virginia 183–186, 189–190, 192, 195; *see also* Virginia (state)

www.ingramcontent.com/pod-product-compliance
Ingram Content Group UK Ltd.
Pitfield, Milton Keynes, MK11 3LW, UK
UKHW041948140426
5217IPUK00014B/701